Ethics and Experience

Ethics and Experience
Life Beyond Moral Theory

Timothy Chappell

McGill-Queen's University Press
Montreal & Kingston • Ithaca

ISBN: 978-0-7735-3641-8   (bound)
ISBN: 978-0-7735-3642-5   (pbk.)

Legal deposit third quarter 2009
Bibliothèque nationale du Québec

Published simultaneously outside North America
by Acumen Publishing Limited

Library and Archives Canada Cataloguing in Publication

Chappell, T. D. J. (Timothy D. J.)
    Ethics and experience : life beyond moral theory / Tim Chappell.

Includes bibliographical references and index.
ISBN 978-0-7735-3641-8 (bound).--ISBN 978-0-7735-3642-5 (pbk.)

    1. Ethics. 2. Conduct of life. I. Title.

BJ1012.C43 2009   170   C2009-901960-4

Typeset in Minion Pro.
Printed in the UK by Cromwell Press Group, Trowbridge, Wiltshire.

For Claudia

Contents

Acknowledgements

Over the past twenty years and more, more people than I can now list have helped me develop my thinking about ethics (such as it is). Without of course claiming companions in guilt, I am aware of particular debts to Liz Ashford, Sarah Broadie, Christopher Coope, John Cottingham, Roger Crisp, Garrett Cullity, Nicholas Denyer, Edward Harcourt, Martin Hollis, Brad Hooker, Rosalind Hursthouse, Jeffrey John, Fergus Kerr, John Lucas, Adam Morton, Tim Mulgan, Tim O'Hagan, Onora O'Neill, Dory Scaltsas, Nick Sparks and Sam Wells. There are many others too.

Since 2006 I have had the privilege to be a member of the philosophy department at the Open University, where, much to my gratitude, my colleagues have constantly proved that collegiality is not just an ideal but can be a reality.

Tristan Palmer commissioned this book, and Kate Williams was indispensable to its production. My thanks to them both.

1

The turn to reason:
how human beings got ethical

The History of every major Galactic Civilization tends to pass through
three distinct and recognizable phases, those of Survival, Inquiry and
Sophistication, otherwise known as the How, Why, and Where phases
… the first phase is characterized by the question "How can we eat?", the
second by the question "Why do we eat?" and the third by the question,
"Where shall we have lunch?"
(Douglas Adams, *The Hitchhiker's Guide to the Galaxy*, 1979: 159)

Our argument is not about just any chance question; it is about the question *how life should be lived.*   (Plato, *Republic* 352d7–8)

Long ago, human beings discovered that they could resolve specific
technical questions – "How can I catch food?", "How can I keep warm
in my cave at night?", "How can I avoid becoming food?" – by applying
reason. They found they could answer these questions by thinking them
through carefully, by generating and criticizing possible solutions, by
trying out those solutions in practice and then refining them, and by
remaining on the lookout for better solutions even when a given problem already had a passable solution.

We may call this discovery the *turn to reason*. It was a revolutionary
move when it happened. The method of solving problems by applying
reason to them quickly became a very successful competitor with older
approaches such as brute force, or guesswork, or doing the first thing
that comes into your head, or consulting the Juju, or copying others, or

mindless repetition of past practice no matter how unsuccessful. (Not that reason has ever entirely replaced these enduringly popular alternatives.)

Creatures like us, in a world like ours, face many different kinds of problems. Alongside specific technical problems such as "How can I catch food?", we also face some extremely general questions. Among the most general of all are those questions our answers to which shape our overall worldview:

- What is real?
- How can we know anything?
- What is life about?
- Why are we here?
- What is our place in the universe?

Over many centuries, the turn to reason spread in one way, as it was applied in more and more cultures by more and more people. It also spread in another way, as it was applied to more and more different sorts of questions, including, eventually, questions like the worldview-shaping questions just listed.

Among the first people to apply the turn to reason to these very general questions were the ancient Greeks of the sixth and fifth centuries BC. The distinctive achievement of the fifth-century Athenian Socrates (469–399 BC), whose words his pupil Plato (c.427–347 BC) claims to be reporting in the second epigraph above, was to apply the turn to reason to the most general question of all: how should life be lived?

Like the best tunes, the best inventions (including inventions of ideas) seem inevitable once they have happened. It becomes difficult to imagine life without them. The turn to reason, and the idea of applying the turn to reason to Socrates' question "How should life be lived?", are two of the best inventions of all time. It is hard for us who live in the world that these ideas have shaped to imagine life without them. We should not let that blind us to the fact that both inventions are anything but inevitable.

It was not *bound* to happen that human beings should hit on the use of reason as a problem-solving technique. In many other species, and for hundreds of millennia even in our own species, it *did not* happen. Nor was it bound to happen that human beings should even formulate

Socrates' question, let alone have the good idea of using reason to address it. There have been plenty of human societies where the turn to reason has barely happened at all. (On a bad day, you may wonder whether it has happened in ours.) There have also been plenty of human societies where reason is applied to some problems, but not to the sorts of problems that are raised by the question "How should life be lived?". There still are.

The application of the turn to reason to very general questions such as "What is real?" and "How can we know anything?" was the invention of philosophy. For that is what philosophy is:

Philosophy is the use of reason to answer worldview-shaping questions.

And the application of the turn to reason to the most general worldview-shaping question of all, the Socratic question, was the invention of the part of philosophy that we call ethics. For that is what ethics is:

Ethics is the use of reason to answer the worldview-shaping question "How should life be lived?"

This definition of ethics (or "moral philosophy" – I use the terms interchangeably) will be central to the argument of this book, so it is worth pausing over. My definition draws our attention straight away to four vital issues:

- *The demarcation question.* What makes something specifically an *ethical* concern? How do ethical concerns differ from other sorts of concern?
- *The why-be-moral question.* Ethics makes demands on us that it can be difficult or even dangerous to obey. When it does, what reason is there to obey these demands?
- *The question of reason.* Is it right to even try to apply reason to the question "How should life be lived?"? If it is, what *sort* of reason?
- *The question of objectivity.* Any assertion that "This is how life should be lived" prompts an obvious question: says who? What is the authority for any answer to the Socratic question, and how can we tell?

3

In Chapters 2–4, I take the first three of these initial questions one by one. The fourth question, about objectivity, requires more attention. It will be our focus in Chapters 5–7. Then, in Chapters 8–10, we shall focus on some important moral theories that philosophers of various sorts have offered to answer the question "How should life be lived?". In Chapter 11, in closing, we shall ask whether a systematic moral theory is the right kind of structure to answer that question, or whether we need something no less based on reason, but rather less systematic, instead.

2

Demarcation:
what does "ethical" mean?

Not to arrange one's life with regard to some end is a mark of great foolishness. (Aristotle, *Eudemian Ethics* 1214b8)

2.1 What ethics is not

Chapter 1 defined ethics as the use of reason to answer the question "How should life be lived?". That definition reminds us immediately of some things that ethics is *not*. For one thing, the definition shows that ethics is not just about what we *do*. The question "How should life be lived?" is certainly about our actions, our behaviour, our choices. But it is about many other things too: not just what we should choose, but also how we should choose it; not just how we should act, but also how we should think and feel and respond, what kind of persons we should be, and so on.

Other things that "ethical" does *not* mean include "legal" and "political". There are ethical rules, and there are legal rules, and there are political rules; but they are different sorts of rules serving different sorts of purposes.

Nor is the ethical the same as the personal or the emotional. When I say "It's wrong to steal or kill" I am not just saying "I don't personally like people stealing or killing". You could say "It's wrong to steal, *and* I don't personally like people stealing", without saying the same thing twice.

5

Nor, again, does "ethical" mean "religious". Of course one possible (and historically important) answer to the question "How should life be lived?" is "To the glory of God". But some people do not give this (or any other) religious answer to the question. Whether they are right or wrong about that, those people are still doing ethics. And even those who do give a religious answer to the question "How should life be lived?" still have an ethical task on their hands. They need to explain in more detail what a life looks like if it is lived to the glory of God, and how living that way generates specific directions about how, for instance, to do your job or treat other people.

So the ethical is not the legal, the political, the personal, the emotional or the religious. What *is* the ethical? What demarcates ethical concerns from other concerns?

2.2 Ethics and the whole of life

In line with Chapter 1's definition of ethics as the use of reason to determine how life should be lived, we should say this: what demarcates something as an ethical issue is that it is an issue about *how we live our lives overall*. This can be put in a tree-diagram (Figure 1). Legal, political, emotional, religious, or personal issues are issues about this or that *aspect* of our lives. Ethical issues are issues about *the whole* of our lives. How the whole of a life should look, and how the various aspects of that life should fit into the whole: those are the *ethical* issues.

We can put it as a point about roles. Each of us occupies a variety of different roles in our lives: as a parent, husband, employee, citizen,

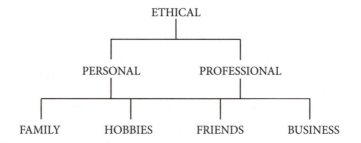

Figure 1

member of a political party or a football supporters' club, and so on. For each of these roles, there is a set of questions about how I am to perform well *within that role*. Above and beyond those roles, there is another set of questions about how I am to perform well *in the whole of my life*, and about how performing well within those different roles fits into performing well in the whole of a life.

It is the questions in this second set that are the questions of ethics. Ethics is not just about what I should do *as a parent*, or *as an academic*, or *as a Green Party member* and so on. Ethics is about what I should do *as a human being*. And it is about how my commitments under that most general description of me relate to my commitments under other, less general, descriptions.

This helps to show what the various sorts of enquiries that go under the name of "professional ethics" are all about. By my definition, thinking about the ethics of health care, or business ethics, or the ethics of the military life, means asking how good performance in these roles fits into a good life overall.

Of course, some of the most interesting questions in professional ethics are about cases where the roles *do not* fit. Consider "whistle-blowers": people who draw public attention to questionable practices within their own company or organization. Is a whistle-blower performing well in the role of an employee? No, what a whistle-blower does breaks company confidentiality, undermines corporate morale and brings his organization into disrepute. Does that mean that a whistle-blower cannot act well? No, the whistle-blower can act well by seeing beyond the need to perform well *in his role as an employee*, to the need to perform well *in his role as a human being*. If all he cared about was how to be a good employee, and he did not care also about how to be a good *person*, then he might be thinking *professionally*; but he could not be thinking *ethically*.

2.3 Pervasiveness and overridingness

If ethics is about performing well in the whole of my life, not just in this or that department of my life, two important points follow. First, we can explain why ethical responsibility is *pervasive* in a way that other responsibilities are not. I have professional obligations while I am at work; but once I leave the office, I shed them pretty well completely. (I may still have duties of company confidentiality and the like during my off-duty hours. But I can usually shed those too if I change my job.) Similarly, I have an obligation to observe the rules and etiquette of tennis or rugby or golf just as long as I am still playing. As soon as the game is over, those obligations are over too. I can walk away from these sorts of responsibilities and obligations because I can walk away from the roles as an employee or a sports player that give rise to them. But I cannot walk away from my *ethical* responsibilities and obligations. I get time off the duties of work, but I do not get time off the duties of morality.

We can see why when we remember that the basic question of ethics is the question "How should life be lived?": that is, "How am I to perform well in the whole of my life?". This implies that you cannot walk away from the duties and responsibilities that go with ethics because you cannot walk away from the role that goes with ethics. For the role that goes with ethics is simply *being you*.

Secondly, and for the same reason, we can explain why ethical responsibility is *overriding* in a way that other responsibilities are not. It can be perfectly reasonable to reject a duty that I have as a sportsman or businessman to perform an ethical duty. ("Sorry I couldn't make our appointment to play squash: I had to help a man who was bleeding to death on the side of the road when I passed.") It does not sound so reasonable to reject an ethical duty in favour of a business or sporting duty. ("Sorry, you'll just have to bleed to death: I'm due on the squash court in five minutes.") Where ethical imperatives clash with other imperatives, it seems pretty clear that they "trump" them: override them or cancel them out. As before, my proposal that ethics is about the question "How am I to perform well in the whole of my life?" shows why. If that proposal is right, then ethical imperatives override other sorts of imperatives for two reasons. One reason is because it matters more to be a good person, overall, than to be a good squash player or a good executive. The other reason is because these other roles only make sense in so far as we see the goal of being a good squash player or executive as part of a larger goal: being a good human being.

To say that ethical responsibility is overriding is not to say that other responsibilities do not matter *at all*. Maybe there are even places where something that we would be inclined to call an ethical responsibility is overridden by some other sort of responsibility. Suppose I cannot do my job without a little bit of rudeness to persistent friends who keep ringing me up at work. No doubt it would be a good thing ethically speaking for me to converse amiably with my persistent friends rather than give them the brush-off and, after all, it is not very ethical to be rude to your friends. (It is not very ethical to be rude to anyone.) But (I might say) these friends should not be ringing me at the office at all, and their offence if I am a bit brusque with them will not last very long … and after all, I have a job to do. It is easy to see how responsibilities like this one (the ethical responsibility not to be rude to friends) can be overridden by other sorts of responsibilities (like the professional responsibility to concentrate on my job in office hours); even if it is hard to imagine a professional responsibility that could override the ethical responsibility to save lives in emergencies.

How big does an ethical responsibility have to be to override any other sort of responsibility? That is a delicate question, to which philosophers have devoted a great deal of energy and ingenuity. The point to get hold of right now is simply this: we can make sense of the idea that ethical responsibilities are overriding without understanding this as meaning that ethical responsibilities trump all other responsibilities *every single time they conflict.*

2.4 "And what if I don't?"

The question of demarcation – the question of what makes anything distinctively *ethical* – leads us to a question about the difference between ethical rules and other sorts of rules. We know what happens when you seriously infringe a legal rule: you get prosecuted. We know what happens when you seriously infringe a professional rule: you get fired. And we know what happens when you seriously infringe a club rule: you get thrown out of the club. What happens when you break an *ethical* rule? Anything? There does not seem to be a clear ethical equivalent of prosecution or expulsion from a club or company. (*Blame*, for instance, is not at all like either.)

So there do not seem to be any distinctively ethical punishments for distinctively ethical misdeeds. What is more, *no* sort of punishment seems to go regularly and reliably with ethical misdeeds. Of course people who act unethically *sometimes* get their comeuppance (in one sense or another). But bad things happen to good people too. Some bad things even happen to good people *because* they are good people.

Many religious believers think that God is at work in the world as a "cosmic policeman", meting out their just deserts, over their lives, to those who act well and to those who act badly. I think the evidence is overwhelming that there is no cosmic policeman of this sort (which is not to say that there is no God). Even if the cosmic-policeman picture of God is right, those who hold it should admit at once that God "moves in mysterious ways". No one can be sure *when* God the cosmic policeman is punishing people for breaking ethical rules, in the simple and clear way that anyone can be sure when an ordinary non-cosmic policeman is arresting or charging those who break legal rules.

So there is a big and difficult question about whether ethical rules have any sort of sanction to back them up, in the way that legal rules or company rules or club rules all have sanctions, and, if they have, what this sanction is. In the absence of any such sanction, a well-known sceptical question becomes pressing: so why should I be moral? We shall take this question further in Chapter 3.

3

Motivation:
why be moral?

"The challenge", said Glaucon, "is that even those whose way of life is just, only live that way against their will – because they are not strong enough to be unjust ...

"Justice is plainly not a good to any *individual*; for whenever someone thinks they are going to be in a position to act unjustly, they *do* act unjustly. Every man holds that, as far as his individual interest goes, injustice is far more profitable than justice ... For anyone who came by this sort of power [to act unjustly and get away with it], and then proved unwilling to act unjustly or get their hands on other people's goods, would be considered most pitifully stupid by those who perceived his behaviour. Nonetheless they would praise him in front of one another: each person's fear that someone might treat *him* unjustly would cause him to hide what he really thinks of the just man."

(Plato, *Republic* 359b5–360d9,
my translation, following Chappell 1996: 121–3)

Thou shalt not get found out.
(The Eleventh Commandment [traditional])

3.1 Demandingness in different moral theories

In Chapter 1, I defined ethics as the use of reason to answer the question "How should life be lived?". Presumably the most basic answer is "Life

ETHICS AND EXPERIENCE

should be lived *well*". But this is not the interesting bit. The interesting – and difficult – bit is saying what *counts* as living well. When we try to do this, we soon run into the difficulty noted at the end of Chapter 2. Surely there are some ethical demands that, if we face up to them honestly, are so stringent that they will stop us living well – and possibly stop us living at all. Such demands give bite to a question that we should be asking anyway: why should we do what morality tells us to do?

Stringent ethical demands do not arise, as is sometimes thought, only in some moral theories. They arise on pretty well every plausible approach to ethics. We can demonstrate this by giving a preview of the four main moral theories that I shall consider in Chapters 8–10:

- *Virtue ethics*: An action is right if and only if (iff) it is what a virtuous agent would characteristically do in the circumstances. Virtuous agents characteristically act in accordance with the virtues (courage, self-control, justice, wisdom, faith, hope and love), and not in accordance with the vices (pride, avarice, lust, envy, gluttony, wrath and sloth).
- *Utilitarianism*: An action is right iff it promotes the greatest happiness of the greatest number.
- *Kantianism*: An action is right iff it is in accordance with a universalizable principle, and not contrary to any universalizable principle. That is, we should never do anything that we cannot rationally will could be done by anyone, and we should treat other people as ends in themselves, not merely as means to ends.
- *Contractarianism*: An action is right iff it is required by the code that all rational persons would agree to in a free negotiation. That is, we should never do anything to others unless they could reasonably agree to our doing it to them. Conversely, we should not let others do to us what we cannot reasonably agree to their doing to us.

All of these moral theories can and sometimes will make very stringent demands indeed on those who try to follow them. The demands of *virtue ethics* are particularly obvious with the virtues of justice and courage. If we live in an oppressive and unjust state, justice apparently demands that we should do what we can to oppose our unjust rulers. But defying unjust rulers in the name of justice can and often does cost people everything, including their lives. Or if we find ourselves in a battle, then courage may demand that we charge an enemy machine-gun nest, or rescue a wounded comrade under fire, or dismantle a land-mine – or quite possibly, risk being shot for refusing to fight.

The *utilitarian* rule that we must always act so as to promote the greatest happiness of the greatest number seems at least equally demanding. Apparently I would make more people happier this Christmas by giving my children no presents and donating the money to famine relief to save the lives of starving children in Africa instead. Why, come to that, am I sitting here writing philosophy, when I could bring about much more happiness by volunteering for a famine-relief project, or even just by going and donating some blood? Surely I *would* cause more happiness to more people by doing these alternative actions. It takes an improbably high estimation of the powers of moral philosophy to deny it! But then utilitarianism says that I *should* do (one or more of) these things rather than write philosophy. These too are very strong demands. They go way beyond what we might think morality demanded of us if we were just following everyday common sense.

Utilitarian demands have another notable feature. (This feature may be shared by some other moral theories, but is most obvious in utilitarianism.) This is that utilitarian demands do not just go *beyond* the apparent requirements of common-sense morality. Sometimes they actually go *against* common-sense morality. For instance, if I would contribute more to the overall good by murdering my grandmother than by doing anything else, then utilitarianism demands that I murder her.

Kantianism demands that we behave in a "universalizable" way – a way of acting that anyone else could adopt – and that we always treat other people as ends in themselves, and never merely as means. These are very demanding ethical rules too, considering the pressures that we are under to make a special case of ourselves, and considering how very richly some people can seem to *deserve* to be treated as mere means. What is more, Kant argues that his two basic rules imply a number of further rules, among them the rule that we should never lie, no matter what: a rule that arguably is even more demanding than the Bible's commandment not to "bear false witness", which sounds like it only forbids us to lie in court or other high-stakes contexts.

Finally, the *contractarian* rule about reasonable agreement implies all sorts of very strong ethical demands. It appears to imply, for instance, that the settlement of America, Australia and New Zealand by Europeans was morally wrong, since in each case the Europeans did one or more of three very un-contractarian things: either they simply took the indigenous peoples' land from them; or they made agreements to share the land on terms that the indigenous peoples involved could not reasonably have accepted if they had fully understood them; or else they made agreements that the indigenous peoples might reasonably have accepted, and then just ignored them.

So all four of these moral theories imply very strong moral demands. This give additional force to the why-be-moral question: the question how doing what ethics demands could help us to live well, or indeed to live at all.

Notice that it is not just what ethics says we *must* do that seems to conflict with our prospects for living well. It is also what ethics says we *must not* do. Suppose you have an opportunity to pull off an undetectable fraud. You will make millions, and there is absolutely no chance that you will get caught. You could use the millions to help yourself live well in all sorts of wonderful ways: sail the oceans in a private liner, put on a concert for African famine relief, buy yourself a castle in the Scottish Highlands, and so on. Given that the fraud is undetectable, there is only one serious obstacle in the way of your doing it. This is your commitment to some moral theory like those listed above, all of which, as typically understood, imply very directly and very clearly that you must not commit the fraud. Here too, apparently, doing what ethics demands is not the same as living well; it is the opposite.

3.2 Can we harmonize being good and living well?

How should we react to this apparent conflict between moral demands and prudential demands (the demands of living well)? Here are five possible responses:

- *Forget about living morally*: If there is a conflict between the moral and the prudential, then forget about trying to do the right thing; just have a ball and enjoy yourself.
- *Forget about living well*: What the apparent moral–prudential conflict shows is that I was wrong in the way I began in Chapter 1 of this book. Ethics *is not* really about the question "How should life be

lived?". For the natural answer to that question is "It should be lived well", that is, by having a good time. And living well is not necessarily the same thing as living morally. But our duty is to live morally even when this means that we will not live well.

- *A compromise is possible:* The apparent moral–prudential conflict is real, but it does not always come up. It is good to do what morality demands. It is also good to "live well". Most of the time we can manage both. Occasionally, in tragic circumstances or when we are in the power of evil people (when we live in a corrupt dictatorship, for instance), living well and living ethically do come starkly into conflict, because there are forces at work around us that will try to make us act immorally. But most of the time the good life and the moral life are not in conflict at all.

- *Pull living well up into living morally:* What the apparent moral–prudential conflict shows is that we need to redefine our understanding of "living well". We are not *really* living well if we are not living morally. Only the brave and just and otherwise moral person, who (for instance) will not engage even in undetectable fraud, and who will die in battle for his comrades rather than act like a coward, can truly be said to be living well. So in the end, the moral–prudential conflict is *only* apparent. There is not really a gap between living morally and living well, because ultimately living well *is* living morally.

- *Pull living morally down into living well:* What the apparent moral–prudential conflict shows is that we need to redefine our understanding of "living morally". We are not *really* living morally if we are not living well. If we end up so inhibited by moral rules that we are unable to have a good life or a good time, then we should get rid of those rules. We should only follow the rules that *do* enable us to live well, for only those are *really* the rules of morality. If following *those* rules means enjoying the benefits of fraud and injustice and cowardice and so on, then so be it. So in the end, the moral–prudential conflict is *only* apparent. There is not really a gap between living morally and living well, because ultimately living morally *is* living well.

The first response ("forget about living morally") is possible (it is sometimes called immoralism), but it seems indefensible. Our concern to do the right thing is not something that we can, rationally speaking, just *ignore*. Hardly any serious philosophers have taken this immoralist line. Some who seem to, such as the nineteenth-century German philosopher Friedrich Nietzsche, do not really, when you examine them more closely: Nietzsche may reject *certain conceptions* of ethical life, but on what he takes to be a true conception he is as concerned with the struggle to live in an ethically adequate way as anyone. Like some other philosophers who at first sight seem to make the first response, such as Plato's characters Polus and Callicles, Nietzsche is really better understood as making the fifth response (see below).

The second response ("forget about living well") is most famously defended by Immanuel Kant, who argues forcefully that living morally has nothing whatever to do with living well. Morality, for Kant, is about doing what is reasonable (in a special Kantian sense of "reasonable" that we shall come to in Ch. 10), whereas living well is about doing what gives you pleasure or satisfies your desires.

Under Kant's influence many other philosophers, such as the Victorian utilitarian Henry Sidgwick, have seen a complete dualism in "practical reason" (in our thinking about what we have reason to do). According to Sidgwick (1874), our reasons for living well (our prudential reasons) and our reasons for doing what is moral (our moral reasons) are two different complete systems of practical reasons (reasons to act), and they are barely in touch with each other at all. Following Kant and Sidgwick, twentieth-century ethicists such as H. H. Prichard found it natural to think that any system of ethics that tried to base our moral reasons on our prudential reasons was simply guilty of a misunderstanding. Hence Prichard's famous question "Does moral philosophy rest on a mistake?", to which his answer was "Yes, if it is about trying to explain our moral reasons by basing them on our prudential reasons" (1949: 1–20; cf. McDowell 1998: 90).

The third response ("a compromise is possible") sees living well and living morally as different things, as the first does. But it points out that they do not always need to conflict.

The third response is quite consistent with the second. Indeed, most of the greatest proponents of the second response to the conflict are also proponents of the third. This is certainly true of Kant, for instance. He thinks that, while living well and living ethically are fundamentally distinct, and it is living ethically that should motivate us, not living well, still God's providence will ensure that those who live ethically will live well in the long run. Rather similarly, Linda Zagzebski (2006) argues that living a "flourishing" life is one objective, and living an ethically admirable life is another, and neither objective reduces to the other. Whether the two objectives prove compatible in my life is a matter of luck, just as, if I had the two objectives to be a champion golfer and to keep my marriage together, it could be a matter of luck whether I managed both.

We can take this third line without trying to define the moral life in terms of the good life, or the good life in terms of the moral life. That is part of the third response's appeal to Kant, Sidgwick, Prichard and the many others who think it is impossible to define either in terms of the other.

By contrast, the fourth and fifth responses that I have listed are precisely about inter-defining the good life and the moral life. As I put it above, the fourth response pulls our notion of living well up into our notion of living morally, whereas the fifth response pulls our notion of living morally down into our notion of living well. For either the fourth or the fifth response, there can be no conflict between the demands of morality and the demands of the good life. But for opposite reasons: in the case of the fourth response, because the demands of the good life *just are* the demands of morality; in the case of the fifth response, because the demands of morality *just are* the demands of the good life.

Classic versions of the fourth response (which you might call the *moralistic* response) are given by Plato and Aristotle. The fifth response (which we can call the *eudaimonistic* response, from the Greek *eudaimonia*, happiness or well-being) is also articulated in Plato. Plato puts it in the mouths of the crude and brutish egoists Callicles and Polus, whom Socrates argues against in Plato's *Gorgias*. According to Callicles and Polus, there are no rules that are worth living by that can seriously threaten our pursuit of good living and pleasure. The rules of conventional morality are all hot air: no one brave and independent-minded will ever follow those rules, unless he allows himself to be conned into it by weaker and more cowardly spirits. Something similar is the view of the egoist Thrasymachus, whose position Glaucon is re-presenting in the first epigraph to this chapter. The rules of ethics, according to Thrasymachus, are a systematic con, imposed on populations by their rulers as a way of controlling them.

In a subtler form, Nietzsche also suggests something very like the fifth response. Nietzsche is no crude egoist like Polus or Callicles or

Thrasymachus. But he does warn us that there is always the *danger* that moral rules will become enslaving and life-denying, not ways of achieving human liberation, unless we test every supposed rule by asking whether keeping it contributes to living well. If it does not, then we should ask whether we really want to recognize such a rule at all. (There are hints, and more than hints, of this thought of Nietzsche's in two other great ethicists about whom Nietzsche had, to put it mildly, mixed feelings: John Stuart Mill, and Jesus.)

So there are five possible responses to the apparent clash between the moral and the prudential, between "doing the right thing" and "living well". How should we choose between them?

I think there is something right in all of them except the first. What the second response is right about is this. Despite what some high-minded philosophers have argued – for example Socrates, who notoriously claims at *Gorgias* 470e that a just man on the rack is happier than an unjust millionaire – we can see very easily what it means to say that there is a difference between living well and living ethically. Sadly enough, human history has produced enough starved and wretched martyrs, and enough fat and contented criminals, to make it obvious that there are forms of living well that we will sacrifice if we insist on "doing the right thing". In unfavourable circumstances, living well and living morally can easily come apart; but that is not to say that our moral reasons and our prudential reasons are completely unrelated. On the contrary – this is one lesson we might draw from the third response – it ought to be a key part of our political programme to make sure that our moral and prudential reasons are normally closely correlated with each other. We need to ensure that it is not too hard for the citizens to live well *and* live morally, without conflict. (Kant and Mill agree.)

Moreover – and here I am agreeing with the fourth and fifth responses – it is crucial to keep testing against each other our conceptions of what it is to live well and what it is to live morally. We should keep asking whether recognizing the demands of ethics *makes for a happy life*. Conversely, we should also keep asking whether the different ways in which we might pursue happiness *are morally defensible*. On the eudaimonistic side, it is a good idea to keep asking what *use* are the various ethical rules and ideals that we recognize. On the moralistic side, we must take seriously the thought that there is a *kind* of happiness or living well that the good man has, even when he is being tortured, and which the wicked tyrant cannot have, however materially well-off he may be. When a human life involves deep injustice, cruelty or cowardice, or a complete lack of self-control or good sense, there is something deeply wrong with that life, no matter what glittering prizes the person living that life may have scooped. Certainly we should see that as a reason to baulk at calling it a *good* life – or at the idea of living that way.

What we call living morally can, in adverse circumstances, come adrift from what we call living well. That's what "adverse circumstances" are: situations where living well and being good are difficult to keep together. A key question for ethics is to see whether, and how, living well and being good might become convergent. And that is a key question for this book, too.

An important part of any good answer to this question is bound to involve us in thinking about what we have *reason* to do: whether, for instance, we have more reason to live like the bloated tyrant, or like the wretched martyr. This brings us back to another question raised at the end of Chapter 1: the question of the place of reason and reasoning in the good life for human beings. I turn to this in Chapter 4.

4

Deliberation:
the question of reason

.

> Do not all charms fly
> At the mere touch of cold philosophy?
> … Philosophy will clip an Angel's wings,
> Conquer all mysteries by rule and line,
> Empty the haunted air, and gnomèd mine –
> Unweave a rainbow, as it erewhile made
> The tender-person'd Lamia melt into a shade.
>
> (John Keats, "Lamia", II)

> To give a reason of anything is to breed a doubt of it.
>
> (William Hazlitt, *On the Difference
> Between Writing and Speaking*, 1824)

4.1 How rational is it rational to be?

In Chapter 1 I defined ethics as the use of reason to try to give an answer
to the question "How should life be lived?". I said that this definition
usefully steers us towards at least four important questions about ethics.
The third of these questions is the main topic of this chapter: whether it
is *right* to try to use reason to determine how life should be lived. After
all, as we saw in Chapter 1, the turn to reason was originally devised for
dealing with problems such as "How can I warm my cave?", or "How
can we irrigate these fields?". The problem set by the question "How

should life be lived?" is a very different sort of problem from those specific technical problems. So it will undoubtedly need a very different sort of solution, and a very different application of the turn to reason.

Of course, this question whether we *should* use reason to decide how to live raises a very basic doubt about the whole enterprise of ethics. But we should not just ignore the possibility that the whole project of ethics might fail, or that certain forms of the project of ethics might fail while others succeed. In Chapter 11, I shall argue that this is exactly what happens. One form of the project of ethics, systematic moral theory, does indeed fail, although certain other forms of ethical enquiry do not.

The project of ethics succeeds only if, when we are faced with the question how life should be lived, and try to answer it by rational means, we come up with a satisfactory answer. The question whether ethicists' most characteristic answers to "How should life be lived?" *are* satisfactory, and in particular whether they are or could be more satisfactory than the answers that we might draw out from, say, Shakespeare, Tolstoy or the Bible, or from certain sorts of human response to great art or music, is a question that I want to be constantly before the reader's mind throughout this book. Alongside this question, there should be constantly in view two further questions: what counts as "satisfactory" in this context; and what counts as "rational"?

On the other hand, of course, as Aristotle pointed out long ago in his youthful work the *Protrepticus* (as we might translate it, "The Call to Philosophize"), there seems to be a paradox lurking in the very question. We might say that to dispute whether we should use reason to decide how to live is *already* to use reason. Like it or not, we are committed to the use of reason in addressing that question. And philosophy is the use of reason to address questions like this one. So, Aristotle argues, we are committed to doing philosophy even if we decide not to do philosophy.

Apparently the same would follow if someone declared, as John Keats did in a famous letter to Benjamin Bailey, "for a life of sensation rather than of thoughts" (22 November 1817). We might argue that Keats's declaration is itself a thought, and is defensible, if defensible at all, only by argument and reason. *Reasoning* your way to the conclusion that reason should only have a small place in your way of living is no better than making the (obviously self-defeating) resolution to live spontaneously. Which gives us more reason to think that, as Socrates famously puts it, "the unexamined life is not worth living" (*Apology* 38a5).

These victories for what we might call "a high view of reason" are too quick to be convincing. After all, people do, in practice, manage to live spontaneously. People also manage to live unexamined lives, lives that do not involve them in doing anything that can be called "philosophy" without stretching the term a lot. And despite what Socrates says, some of these unexamined lives seem very worthwhile. As Keats's older contemporary Wordsworth puts it (a little patronisingly, perhaps):

> Dear Child! Dear Girl! that walkest with me here,
> If thou appear'st untouched by solemn thought,
> Thy nature is not therefore less divine:
> Thou liest in Abraham's bosom all the year;
> And worshipp'st at the Temple's inner shrine,
> God being with thee when we know it not.
> (William Wordsworth, "Evening on Calais Beach")

Even on the most ambitiously rationalist account of reason, reason cannot be used to determine *everything*. A lot of stuff in anybody's life – who your parents are, what interests you at school, who you fall in love with, which jobs you find rewarding or not – is stuff that *just happens*, irrespective of reason.

So the right retort to Aristotle's over-neat argument in the *Protrepticus* is that reason does not have the automatic jurisdiction over everything that Aristotle, Plato and some later philosophers such as Kant have wanted to give it. On the contrary, reason itself demands that we set limits to the operation of reason. The really interesting question is where these limits lie.

4.2 Moderate scepticism about the role of reason: Hursthouse, Stocker, Mr Collins

Various philosophers have drawn these limits more or less tightly. Some have been only moderately sceptical about the role of reason in deciding how to live. For example, many philosophers have been worried about the way that some people – or at any rate some philosophers – use reason in ethics as part of their attempt to determine how life should be lived. Some people's ethical reasoning can be "algorithmic" or "mechanical". They can treat a moral theory, or a set of rules, as a "decision machine": input described situation, output recommended action. There is surely something wrong with this. It is not good enough to apply simple ethical rules, inflexibly and robotically and insensitively, in the same way in every situation you meet. For life is complicated, and circumstances can be morally ambiguous.

So, for instance, Rosalind Hursthouse notes that some ethicists of the "deontological" (rule-based) school suppose

> that they have (or will be able to formulate in time) a complete and consistent set of rules in which second-order ranking rules settle any conflicts among first-order rules, which have been formed with [precision, and with] many necessary exception clauses built into them. Such a system would determine what was required in every situation and ... would not rely on intuition or insight to resolve conflicts. It would, in Onora O'Neill's nice description [see O'Neill 1987], "be an algorithm not just for some situations but for life".   (Hursthouse 1999: 53–4)

As Hursthouse immediately goes on to point out, such a rationalistic ideal is implausible even on the deontological assumption that what ethics is primarily about is formulating and living by rules:

> [M]any deontologists insist that recognising what the "morally salient" features of a particular situation are, applying certain rules rather than others and balancing competing considerations correctly, requires exercising not merely judgement, but also the faculties of "moral sensitivity, perception, and imagination" [O'Neill 1987] – moral wisdom or *phronesis*, in short.   (*Ibid.*)

Here we have the kind of scepticism about systematic moral theory as a source of ethical knowledge that is sometimes called ethical particularism. ("Ethical particularism" can also be a name for something more like a systematic moral theory; see e.g. Dancy 2004.) In Chapter 11, I shall defend scepticism about moral theory. This kind of scepticism is a doubt about a *way* of using reason to decide how to live and what to do. It is not a doubt about reason itself as a means of determining how to live.

Compare a second sort of doubt about reason in ethics, expressed in a famous example by Michael Stocker:

> [S]uppose you are in a hospital, recovering from a long illness ... when Smith comes in. You are so effusive with your thanks and praise that he protests that he always tries to do what he thinks is his duty, what he thinks will be best. You at first think he is engaging in a polite form of self-deprecation. But the more you two speak, the more clear it becomes that he was telling the literal truth: that it is not essentially because of you that he came to see you, not because you are friends, but because he thought it his duty, perhaps as a fellow Christian or Communist or whatever, or simply because he knows no one more in need of cheering up and no one easier to cheer up. (Stocker 1997: 74)

No doubt there is something wrong with Smith's use of reason in ethics in this story. And no doubt what is wrong with Smith is an interesting malady. Ethicists call it "over-moralization", and there will be more to say about it in later chapters, especially Chapter 11. However, there might still be uses of reason in ethics that are not guilty of over-moralization of Smith's sort. So this story only establishes a limited scepticism: a scepticism about *some* uses of reason in ethics.

Ethics may involve the application of reason to the problem of how to live, but the reason in question cannot be simply a matter of computation. A human being is not (to borrow Karl Marx's pungent description of Jeremy Bentham) a desiccated calculating machine, a robot or a Vulcan like *Star Trek*'s Mr Spock: perfectly logical, and just like human beings except that he is entirely without emotions. (Does that make sense? *Could* someone be "just like" you or me, only with no emotions? If he lacked emotions, would he not be totally *unlike* you or me?)

A third case that brings this point out vividly is Mr Collins's proposal of marriage to Elizabeth Bennet in Jane Austen's *Pride and Prejudice*. When Mr Collins's first proposal is dismissed by Elizabeth, his response is this:

> You must give me leave to flatter myself, my dear cousin, that your refusal of my addresses is merely words of course ... It does not

appear to me that my hand is unworthy of your acceptance, or that the establishment I can offer would be any other than highly desirable. My situation in life, my connections with the family of De Bourgh, and my relationship to your own, are circumstances highly in its favour; and you should take it into farther considera-tion that in spite of your manifold attractions, it is by no means certain that another offer of marriage may ever be made you. Your portion is unhappily so small that it will in all likelihood undo the effects of your loveliness and amiable qualifications. As I must therefore conclude that you are not serious in your rejec-tion of me, I shall choose to attribute it to your wish of increasing my love by suspense, according to the usual practice of elegant females.   (Jane Austen, *Pride and Prejudice*, ch. 19)

Mr Collins's refusal to take Elizabeth's first answer seriously is based squarely on his reasoning. He presents her with a rational balance sheet of the pros and cons facing her, leading to the triumphant conclusion in the bottom line: "So you *can't* say no, because marrying me is in your best interest: QED".

Let us leave on one side Mr Collins's patronizing assumption that he can do this piece of reasoning about how Elizabeth should live better than Elizabeth herself. The main point is that his reasoning in this speech about what is good for Elizabeth is – in its own terms, and in the context of that society – really quite good reasoning. Every claim or prediction that Mr Collins makes is (for all he and Elizabeth know) a true or very probable one; every logical move that he offers is logically impeccable. In that sense, Mr Collins's answer to the ques-tion how Elizabeth Bennet should live is a rational one. Whereas *her* answer to that question simply appeals to her feelings: "I thank you again and again for the honour you have done me in your propos-als, but to accept them is absolutely impossible. My feelings in every respect forbid it. Can I speak plainer?" (*ibid.*). True, Elizabeth goes on, in the next sentence, to do what she can to make her response look like a rational one rather than a "merely feminine" one: "Do not consider me now as an elegant female intending to plague you, but as a rational creature speaking the truth from her heart". For all that, the truth about her aversion to Mr Collins is clear enough despite her polite words.

For all his rationality, it is obvious that Mr Collins is the one who is mistaken here. He is trying to determine how he (and Elizabeth) should live by mere computation. The passage demonstrates how an answer to the question "How should life be lived?" can be both rational, and also, at the same time, completely unsatisfactory.

We might have another sort of doubt about Mr Collins's rationality: the Nietzschean or Freudian doubt that his rationality is merely a mask for deeper and darker purposes that he harbours: to empower himself by disempowering others, perhaps, or to keep going some vast charade of social climbing. (In the novel, Mr Collins is a social climber of the most brazen kind.) It is very easy for seemingly rational arguments to be recruited for purposes that themselves have nothing to do with reason; *rationality* easily becomes *rationalization*, a strategy for justifying what we subconsciously want to do anyway.

Mr Collins's sort of rationality about how life should be lived is unsatisfactory: partly because it is so obviously self-serving, and partly because it is so thin and abstract. Rationality of his sort cannot possibly be responsive to the whole of our experience. In particular, Mr Collins's sort of rationality clearly cannot make good sense of the kind of emotional imperatives that Elizabeth recognizes as reasons why she must not marry Mr Collins. In his mode of rationality, her virtually explicit confession of an insuperable aversion to him can register only as an expression of perverse ingratitude and childish obstinacy (not to say bad manners). He is bound to see Elizabeth as someone who simply has not calculated right.

Compare Bernard Williams's remarks, in a survey of the features of contemporary ethics that he has most criticized in his writings:

> Often, some theory has been under criticism, and the more particular material [that is provided by considering specific examples] has come in to remind one of the unreality and, worse, distorting quality of the theory. The material … is itself extremely schematic, but it [at least brings] out the basic point that … the theory is frivolous, in not allowing for anyone's experience, including the author's own. Alternatively, the theory does represent experience, but an impoverished experience, which it holds up as the rational norm – that is to say, the theory is stupid.
>
> (1995a: 217)

Being frivolous and being stupid are two ways for an account of how life should be lived to be unsatisfactory. Both flaws are, as Mr Collins's case demonstrates, quite compatible with rationality. The suitor who woos by balance sheet is not being *irrational*. He is simply deploying an inappropriate form of rationality, and hence being frivolous, or stupid, or both.

This third case too, then, suggests only a moderate scepticism about reason in ethics. It suggests a scepticism about particular *ways* of applying reason in ethics: for example, about the mechanical and narrow-minded way that Mr Collins applies it, and the equally mechanical and narrow-minded deployments of rationality that Williams finds in certain contemporary moral theories. What the case does not suggest is a scepticism about the very idea of applying reason in ethics in *any* way. To that and other stronger forms of scepticism I turn in §4.3.

4.3 Deeper scepticism about reason in ethics: Burke, Hume, Williams, Ayer

One stronger form of scepticism about reason in ethics is a general suspicion of reason's authority anywhere. Such an attitude is often called conservatism, or (by those who do not like it) obscurantism. One of its greatest spokesmen is the English politician Edmund Burke. At the time of that triumph of reason in action, the French Revolution, Burke, in his *Reflections on the French Revolution*, addresses an imaginary French listener like this:

> We [the British] are generally men of untaught feelings ... instead of casting away all our old prejudices, we cherish them to a very considerable degree and, to take more shame to ourselves, we cherish them because they are prejudices; and the longer they have lasted and the more generally they have prevailed, the more we cherish them. We are afraid to put men to live and trade each on his own private stock of reason; because we suspect that the stock in each man is small, and that the individuals would do better to avail themselves of the general bank and capital of nations and of ages. (Burke 1931: 155)

Burke sees human tradition as a rich legacy of wisdom that has been handed down to us by our forefathers. ("Tradition" literally means "what has been handed over", from the Latin *tradere*.) Burke's striking claim echoes an equally striking claim of Aristotle's: "What *seems* to everyone, we say that this *is*; the person who takes away this conviction can have nothing more convincing to put in its place" (*Nicomachean Ethics* 1172b36–a2). A consensus or traditional belief that is sufficiently widespread and sufficiently authoritative has, in Aristotle's view, a virtually unchallengeable authority. For Aristotle, "well-established opinions" stand alongside self-evident truths as the most certain truths of all (see Aristotle, *Topics* 100a25–b25; see Ackrill 1987: 60). With this, no doubt, Burke would completely agree.

Burke continues with further arguments for his traditionalist scepticism about the scope of reason in human affairs:

> Many of our men of speculation, instead of exploding general prejudices, employ their sagacity to discover the latent wisdom which prevails in them. If they find what they seek, and they seldom fail, they think it more wise to continue the prejudice, with the reason involved, than to cast away the coat of prejudice, and to leave nothing but the naked reason; because prejudice, with its reason, has a motive to give action to that reason, and an affection which will give it permanence. Prejudice is of ready application in the emergency; it previously engages the mind in a steady course of wisdom and virtue, and does not leave the man hesitating in the moment of decision, sceptical, puzzled, and unresolved.
>
> (Burke 1931: 155)

The person who, like the French revolutionary, rejects all tradition, and tries to work out the best way to live by his own new reasoning alone, is not merely in danger of reinventing the wheel: of unnecessarily repeating the huge labours of others to get humanity to progress as far as it has. There is also (to reuse a joke of Bernard Williams's) a serious danger that the wheel that the rational innovator reinvents will be a *square* wheel; abolishing our traditions and starting again from scratch may not even get us back to where tradition has got us to. (Not all historical examples of this point are comic: think of the Cultural Revolution or Pol Pot.)

Burke hints at other dangers too in an over-reliance on reason in political and ethical decision-making. Prejudice "has a motive" and "an affection" where reason has not: our prejudices have deep roots in the things that we really care about and which really motivate us. Also prejudice "is of ready application in an emergency": it tells us straight off how to act when swift action is called for. "Naked reason" cannot compete with these advantages of prejudice. We cannot stop to calculate the best course of action when a building is burning down, however rational it might be to do so. Moreover, the fact that a course of action would be rational, rather than, say, patriotic, or an expression of my love for my family, is likely to leave ordinary people cold. The French revolutionaries did not motivate the populace by telling them that the revolution was demanded by pure reason alone (even though that is what the more cerebral and extreme revolutionaries, such as Saint-Just, believed). They got them moving by telling them that the revolution was demanded by true patriotism.

Burke's views about the scope of reason are all views for which he *argues*. So Burke gives us an example of how reason itself can suggest a fairly wide-ranging scepticism about the role of reason in human affairs in general, and in ethics in particular.

Other writers have argued for more precisely articulated forms of this general scepticism. Here, for instance, is the Irishman Burke's contemporary, the Scotsman David Hume:

> It appears evident that the ultimate ends of human actions can never, in any case, be accounted for by *reason,* but recommend themselves entirely to the sentiments and affections of mankind, without any dependence on the intellectual faculties. Ask a man *why he uses exercise*; he will answer, *because he desires to keep his health.* If you then enquire, *why he desires health,* he will readily reply, *because sickness is painful.* If you push your enquiries farther, and desire a reason *why he hates pain,* it is impossible he can ever give any. This is an ultimate end, and is never referred to any other object.   (Hume [1776] 1977: Appendix I)

Hume is not sceptical about the possibility that reason might have some role to play in *determining means to* "ultimate ends" such as avoiding pain. What reason can never do, according to Hume, is *set* ultimate ends.

'Tis obvious, that when we have the prospect of pain or pleasure from any object, we feel a consequent emotion of aversion or propensity, and are carried to avoid or embrace what will give us this uneasiness of or satisfaction. 'Tis also obvious, that this emotion rests not here, but making us cast our view on every side, comprehends whatever objects are connected with its original by the relation of cause and effect. Here then reasoning takes place to discover this relation; and according as our reasoning varies, our actions receive a subsequent variation. But 'tis evident in this case that the impulse arises not from reason, but is only directed by it.   ([1739] 1985: 2.3.3)

As philosophers like to put it, Hume has an *instrumental* conception of reason. As he sees it, reasoning is simply an instrument to ends that are not determined by reason, but by "passion": by our instincts, by our constitutions, by our reactions and emotions and by our basic preferences. From this Hume at once draws a conclusion that looked scandalous to his more moralistically inclined contemporaries:

Since reason alone can never produce any action, or give rise to volition, I infer, that the same faculty is as incapable of preventing volition, or of disputing the preference with any passion or emotion … thus it appears, that the principle, which opposes our passion, cannot be the same with reason, and is only called so in an improper sense. We speak not strictly and philosophically when we speak of the combat of passion and of reason. Reason is, and ought only to be the slave of the passions, and can never pretend to any other office than to serve and obey them.   (*Ibid.*)

Hume is sceptical about the possibility of reasoning about ends, as distinct from means to those ends, because he thinks that ends are set by "passion". All reason can do is work as a *servant* for those passions, like Jeeves butlering for Bertie Wooster: reason brings the passions what they want, and protects them from what they prefer to avoid. And unlike Jeeves, Humean reason only criticizes the passions for inefficiency: for finding poor means to their own satisfaction. Humean reason never says, to any passion, "You're just mistaken to want that".

Here the reader might object as follows. If Hume does not think that reason can set our ends, and that there cannot even be reasoning about ends, then he must think that any "ultimate end" at all is as good, as far as its rationality goes, as any other. But that is a ridiculous conclusion! Suppose one person takes his "ultimate ends" to be nicely summed up in one of the catchphrases of the film *Moulin Rouge*: "The greatest thing you'll ever learn is just to love, and be loved in return". And suppose another person has only one "ultimate end", namely, to collect as many saucers of mud as he can. Surely the first of these two persons is *obviously* more rational than the second?

So you might think. But in this same passage, Hume simply denies it:

> Where a passion is neither founded on false suppositions, nor chooses means insufficient for the end, the understanding can neither justify nor condemn it. 'Tis not contrary to reason to prefer the destruction of the whole world to the scratching of my little finger. A passion must be accompanied with some false judgement, in order to be unreasonable; and even then 'tis not the passion, properly speaking, which is unreasonable, but the judgement. (*Ibid.*)

Hume would agree with the objector that there is *something* wrong with a person who is interested in nothing but saucers of mud, or who thinks it a more important "ultimate end" to protect his own little finger than to prevent the "destruction of the whole world" (apart from that little finger, presumably). But what is wrong with such a person, according to Hume, is not *irrationality*. You cannot reason someone out of an obsession with collecting saucers of mud, or preserving his own fingers. No argument, says Hume, can show that these are bad ends to have, or the wrong ends to have. It is simply that *we* – most of us in the human community – do not find such ends at all appealing or attractive. We condemn them because we do not share them. We call them "irrational" because calling them hard names is just about our only way to discourage them.

I said that Hume is more specific in his scepticism about reasoning in ethics than Burke is, because Hume begins by restricting his scepticism to reasoning about ethical ends, not ethical means. But, as is clear from the argument just traced, Hume's final position is a scepticism about reasoning in ethics that is far more radical than Burke's. If some-one claimed that the only thing that matters in life is to collect saucers of mud, or protect his little finger, Burke would say that we can be per-fectly sure that someone with these values is unreasonable, because the whole experience of humanity supports the verdict that he is unreason-able, and never mind how this universal experience might be justified in its confidence.

Contrast Hume's view. On this, we can only criticize the reasona-bleness or rationality of the mud-saucer-fancier or the finger-lover if he makes a mistake about means. We can say to him "But that's not a good way to get hold of saucers of mud", but we cannot say to him "But saucers of mud are not worth getting hold of anyway". We can voice our preference for our ends as opposed to his, or write songs like "Nature Boy" about our ends and defiantly sing them at him. We still cannot, on Hume's view, show that he is *unreasonable*. Arguments may be available if we are discussing means to ends. But argument runs out at the level of ends: that is, at the level of values. At this level, all we have are our pref-erences and other people's preferences. It goes without saying that we prefer our preferences to theirs, and that they prefer their preferences to ours. That does not make us more *reasonable* than the saucer-fancier or the finger-lover, nor them more reasonable than us. Reason just does not enter into it until we come to the question of means.

There are a number of interesting modern analogues of this Humean argument that reason does not apply to our choice of ends or values, but only to our choice of means to those ends. (Some people think that there is an interesting ancient analogue, too: "We do not deliberate about ends, but about the things which are towards our ends" [Aristo-tle, *Nicomachean Ethics* 1112b12].) One modern analogue is Bernard Williams.

As we have seen already, Williams is sceptical about the specific form of ethical rationality that is found in moral theories. But he also has some other, deeper and more thoroughgoing, forms of scepticism about ethical rationality itself. One of these is developed in Williams's "Inter-nal Reasons Thesis", which he himself describes as a Humean view.

Williams's Internal Reasons Thesis says that the only reasons to act that we have or can have are our *internal* reasons: that is, those reasons that serve motives that we already have (see Williams 1981: 101). If we do not already have a given motive (say, to be kind to old ladies, or to look to exchange love with others), we cannot be *argued* into taking it on, unless taking it on will help us to achieve the motives that we do already have.

Of course, we might adopt this new motive anyway, without being argued into it: perhaps by conversion, that is, by a simple shift from one set of basic motives to another set. This is a possibility that John McDowell (1995, 1998) raises in criticism of Williams. But Williams is not denying that we could acquire a new motive (or indeed lose an old one) in this sort of non-rational way. His point is that where there is no *rational* route from our present motives to some new motive, no one can be *rationally* criticized for not having that new motive. So if I were only concerned about acquiring saucers of mud, and if being kind to old ladies, or looking for love, in no way served that concern, there would be no way to criticize my rationality. You might, if you liked, call me bad, callous or crazy for caring so much about plates of goo and so little about venerable senior citizens or love. But this would be nothing better than name-calling: "mere bluster", as Williams calls it. You have no good *argument* for calling me irrational. All that you are saying is that you do not like my attitudes.

A similar point is made less subtly by A. J. Ayer:

> [O]ne really never does dispute about questions of value … we do not attempt to show by our arguments that [our opponent] has the "wrong" ethical feeling towards a situation that he has correctly apprehended. What we attempt to show is that he is mistaken about the facts of the case … We feel that our own system of values is superior, and therefore speak in such derogatory terms of his. But we cannot bring forward any arguments to show that our system is superior. For our judgement that it is so is itself a judgement of value, and accordingly outside the scope of argument. It is because argument fails us when we come to deal with pure questions of value, as distinct from questions of fact, that we finally resort to mere abuse. (1936: 146–7)

The basis of Ayer's sceptical position about the rationality of ends is his "logical positivism". Logical positivism says that there are only two ways for language to have factual meaning: either it must express logical truths or tautologies, such as "2 + 2 = 4" or "If it's gone, then it's gone", or else it must express a hypothesis that we could test by experiment. All other language has no factual meaning. But ethical claims are neither tautologies nor claims that we can prove by experiment. So ethical claims cannot have factual meaning. But they do have meaning of a non-factual sort: ethical claims simply express our preferences about values.

Thus Hume's distinction between *means* and *ends* in the rationality of ethics modulates into Ayer's distinction between *facts* and *values*. There is also an analogy between Ayer's argument and Williams's, and between their arguments and the arguments of other recent philosophers such as the expressivists Allan Gibbard and Simon Blackburn. All these arguments alike have the same strongly sceptical upshot, namely, the Humean conclusion that we cannot use reason to justify our most basic values because those basic values are matters not of fact or reason, but of feeling and passion.

Is Ayer *right* to say that argument about values is simply impossible: that all we can do is cite the non-moral facts that are relevant to forming moral views, or vent our abuse on others who know these facts but do not share our moral attitude to them? Some examples surely suggest not. Suppose someone says, for instance, that it is a good thing that John raped Jane, where the speaker means by this that it is one of his values to approve of rape. In this case, we can (and no doubt will) say many things in response. Some of these will be (as Ayer predicts) factual remarks, for example that rape causes severe pain and distress. Others will be (as Ayer also predicts) "mere abuse" of the speaker for his disgusting attitudes. Other possible responses, however, will not fit either of Ayer's categories. For example, I might say, "Rape *shouldn't* be one of your values: rape is brutal, humiliating, insulting, and dehumanizing". To say this is not to "resort to mere abuse" of the speaker. But it is not exactly a factual claim, either, in the way that it is a factual claim to say that rape causes unhappiness. It is a claim about value-concepts and about how they are exemplified or instantiated: a *constitutive* claim, as we may call it. The claim is that one allegedly positive value-concept (rape) is so clearly an example of some other plainly negative value-concepts (brutality, humiliation, insult, dehumanization) that rape cannot be a positive value at all.

Such constitutive claims are a perfectly familiar part of pretty well everybody's experience, even when we consider cases that are not quite as open-and-shut as rape. Think of how we argue about bull-fighting or fox-hunting. Whether or not we put it quite this way, our question will probably be something like this: what values does bull-fighting or fox-hunting instantiate? Is it positive values, such as courage, élan and historical/contextual authenticity? Or is it negative values, such as cruelty and callousness? Or is it both? If so, which of the values matters more? Here too it is a familiar part of our experience that there can be argument about values that is not mere abuse of our opponents, nor mere recital of the facts of the matter, but which involves making and assessing constitutive claims.

Think also of how we argue about people, Diana, Princess of Wales, for example (I write this on the tenth anniversary of her death). Was she *gracious* or was she *self-absorbed*? Was she a *tragic* figure or a *pathetic* one? Were her interactions with various charities *genuine altruism* or merely *self-promoting hype*? To accept or reject any of these characterizations of the princess is to say that she instantiated the values, negative or positive, that correspond to my italics. Disagreeing about such claims is not just disagreeing about the facts about Diana, although of course the facts are relevant; nor is it just abusing our interlocutors. Such arguments about character also involve what philosophers often call "thick concepts" (Williams 1985: 140–43): that is, they involve conceptions of particular and specific values, and of the ways in which particular actions or character traits can instantiate or constitute cases of those values.

This happens on a number of levels. There are disagreements about whether a given action was an instance of one good "thick" trait (a virtue), or another closely related bad "thick" trait (a vice); about whether that action, if it instantiated both virtues and vices, was dominated by the good in it, or the bad; about whether it was in character or out of character; and so on. Moreover, claims of these sorts about the interrelation and instantiation of values and virtues do not fit at all neatly into Ayer's philosophy of language. Claims like "Diana was a good person because despite her own private griefs she was full of compassion for others" and "Rape is a dreadful crime because of its brutality" seem perfectly meaningful. Yet these claims are neither true by definition, nor the kind of thing that can be scientifically proved.

Of course, Ayer might just say that the impression of meaningfulness that such claims create is an illusion. But the more he makes that move, the less it is worth. The more of our common experience he condemns as illusory, the less we are likely to find his views credible.

So a little reflection on our own experience suggests the opposite result to the one that Ayer wants to draw from experience. It simply is not true that we never argue directly about values. On the contrary, arguing directly about values is something we do all the time, in all sorts of ways. We argue about how values relate to each other, how they are instantiated; about what constitute instances of any value; about how the instantiation of different values together affects the overall value of a particular situation, character or thing; and more.

There will be more to say about this sort of constitutive arguing about values, and the contrast between it and means–end argument, in Chapter 5, where there will be a lengthier discussion of the stronger forms of scepticism about reason in ethics, and the distinction that they presuppose between fact and value, which are argued for by Hume, Williams, Ayer and others.

Chapters 5–7 will discuss the fourth of our initial questions: the one about ethical objectivity. My discussion will serve more than one purpose, since the central question that I have raised in this chapter – the place of reason in ethics – has so far gone unanswered. This, I think, is unavoidable: the question of reason can only be answered in the light of an answer to the question of objectivity. To that latter question I now turn. We shall not come back to the question of the place of reason in ethics directly until the beginning of Chapter 8; my own answer to it will not appear until the end of the book.

5

Introducing subjectivism
and objectivism

… there is nothing either good or bad but thinking makes it so …
(*Hamlet* II.ii)

God made man simple; his complex problems are of his own devising.
(*Ecclesiastes* 7.29, Jerusalem Bible)

5.1 Ethical subjectivism and some subjectivist qualms

Chapter 1 pointed us towards four key initial questions about ethics, and Chapters 2–4 discussed the first three of these. In Chapter 5 we come to the fourth and last of these initial questions: the question of objectivity. That question will remain our focus until the end of Chapter 7.

Socrates poses the question "How should life be lived?", and urges his hearers to try to answer it. But many today will feel subjectivist qualms about even trying to give an answer. Their response to Socrates' question is something like this: "No one has the right to impose their views about how they think I should live on *me*. So I can't have the right to do that to anyone else. Who am I to tell other people how they should live?"

This common view at the level of individuals is paralleled by an equally common view at the societal or cultural level: what right has my society to impose its views of how human beings should live together on other societies? The arguments run in close parallel at the two levels. Here I shall talk mainly at the individual level, but it will not be hard to construct the parallel argument at the level of cultures.

"Who am I to tell other people how they should live?" seems to be an ultra-democratic response to Socrates' question. The idea is that it is because we are all equal that no one has the right to impose his views on others. But then, who says ethics involves an attempt to impose our views on others? I have argued that ethics is about *the use of reason* to determine how life should be lived. Using reason need not mean imposing any views on anybody. It can mean reaching agreement in the most consensual, egalitarian and democratic way possible.

Of course reasoning, or a show of reasoning, can be misused to bully or browbeat people. One way to describe what Mr Collins does to Elizabeth Bennet is to say that he misuses reason to try to browbeat Elizabeth Bennet into accepting his offer of marriage. But this is a *misuse* of reason precisely because the right use of reason is to *persuade* people to agree with you, not *force* them. When people reach agreement by the right use of reason, they agree *freely*, on the basis of good arguments that they have thought through for themselves and decided to accept. In this sense, agreeing by way of reasoned argument is the *opposite* of coercion, and there is nothing more democratic than reason.

But (it might be objected here) how are such arguments to go? What sort of facts can we appeal to, to settle a disagreement about how life should be lived? And how can we tell that we are appealing to the *right* sort of facts? We know what sort of facts are relevant to solving a specific technical problem such as "How should I keep warm in my cave at night?", or "What's the best sort of stone to use if you want to make a pyramid?" But (it might be said) there are *no* facts about how life should be lived overall. As the old journalists' saying has it, "Opinion is free but facts are sacred". You have to take care to get the facts right, but you can think what you like at the level of mere opinion. And that is the level at which we find ethics.

Here we might deploy a distinction made in §4.3. We might say that although there is something that we cannot argue about in ethics, namely ends or basic values, there is also something we *can* argue about, namely means. If someone's ends, his or her basic values, are quite different from ours, then we will indeed be stuck about how to argue with him. If what he cares about at the most basic level is just collecting saucers of mud, or protecting his little fingers from every conceivable threat at every conceivable cost, then we will not be able to argue him out of thinking that it is worthwhile to spend his life this way. (He might change his mind, of course, but that is not being *argued* out of his previous views.) Nor, conversely, will he be able to argue *us* into a change of mind about our basic values. Disagreements about basic values, on this view, will never be amenable to reason.

But now suppose that you and I agree about all our basic values, or even just about most of them. In that case (we might suggest), we will be able to argue about different ways in which we might try to realize those values. So, for instance, you and I might share "loving and being loved in return" as an end that we value. But we might disagree completely about what is the best *means* to that end. Does this kind of disagreement not appear to be one that we can resolve? After all, it usually is not that hard to see which means go with which ends. And so, the suggestion would be, there can be fruitful argument about ethics provided we restrict ourselves to arguing about means and do not try to argue about ends.

There is something to this suggestion. But it runs into two problems, both already hinted at in §4.3. The first is that it moves us away from the main difficulty: that of arguing about basic values themselves. If all we have is a consensus to pursue a set of basic values, then we cannot know that those values are anything more than what all of us in the consensus just happen to prefer. It looks as if restricting our argument to means is not solving the problem of objectivity, but giving up on it.

The second problem is that there is a difference between means–end relations (*instrumental* relations) and constituent–whole relations (*constitutive* relations). It is more often the latter sort of relation that we have to deal with in cases of ethical dispute. But, unfortunately, constitutive relations are much harder to argue about than instrumental relations.

The distinction between instrumental and constitutive relations is this. We can ask whether a particular practice *is a means to* a given end or value. For example, we can ask whether collecting saucers of mud is a means to the end of having a large saucer collection or the end of running a marathon in less than three hours. We can also ask whether some practice *is an instance of* some value. For example, we can ask whether collecting saucers of mud is an instance of intellectual enquiry, or just of irrational obsession.

When we make judgements of the means–end sort it is usually fairly easy to tell whether they are right or wrong just by asking whether the means involved reliably causes the end. So, for example, collecting saucers of mud does look like a means to the end of having a large saucer collection, because collecting saucers of mud does, in the long run, cause you to have many saucers. But collecting saucers of mud does *not* look like a means to running a sub-three-hour marathon because, as a rule, there is no causal connection between mud-saucer-collecting and marathon-running. So means–end questions are quite easy to answer because it is quite easy to tell, in most cases, what means are likely to cause what ends.

Constitutive questions are much harder. Asking whether collecting saucers of mud is an instance of intellectual enquiry is not asking to be shown how mud-saucer-collection *causes* intellectual enquiry. It is asking to be shown how mud-saucer-collection *is* intellectual enquiry. Asking how "loving and being loved in return" constitutes happiness is not asking how mutual love *causes* happiness; it is asking in what sense loving and being loved in return *is* happiness. Constitutive questions are not questions about *routes to* values or *how to get* values. They are questions about what, in detail, those values *are*. So the suggested distinction between questions about means and about ends does not help us with constitutive questions.

The trouble is that nearly all the questions that matter most in ethics are questions about constitutive relations, not means–end relations. In particular, Socrates' question "How should life be lived?" is a constitutive question. As I said in §3.1, it is easy to answer this in outline by saying "Life should be lived well". The interesting – and difficult – bit is saying what *counts* as living well: what *constitutes* living well. This is obviously a question about constitutive relations, not instrumental relations. The worry remains that we have no practicable way of arguing rationally about all the biggest issues in ethics.

This point about the difficulty of constitutive questions, and their centrality in ethics, tends to feed the subjectivist qualms mentioned above. Another thought that also feeds those qualms is about *creativity*.

For each of us, answering the general question "How should life be lived?" means answering the specific and personal question "How should *I* live?". Whatever answer I give to this specific and personal question, my answer surely will not be just waiting for me in a how-to-live manual. Answering my question "How should I live?" will be a creative process, not just a process of following someone else's instructions. So ethical answers cannot just be "out there" independently of us, waiting to be found, in the way that scientific or technical answers are generally thought to be. A good answer to "How can I keep warm at night?" or "What is the chemical formula of water?" can be the same for anybody; a good answer to "How should I live?" will have to be specifically *my* answer. This sounds like grounds for suspicion that whereas answers to scientific and technical questions are objective, answers to ethical questions are subjective.

5.2 Objectivism, and some objectivist responses to subjectivist qualms

These, then, are some of the thoughts that lead many people, both philosophers and non-philosophers, towards the view called ethical subjectivism. This view can be defined as follows:

Ethical subjectivism: No ethical judgement is objectively true.

"Objectively true" here means true as a matter of fact: not just a matter of opinion. For example, it is not just a matter of opinion that there are seven days in a week; that Columbus reached the Americas in 1492; and that the atomic number of gold is 79. All three of these statements are true as a matter of fact, hence objectively true. The ethical subjectivist's claim is that in ethics there *are* no matters of fact; everything in ethics, according to him, is just a matter of opinion.

The negation of ethical subjectivism is ethical objectivism:

Ethical objectivism: At least some ethical judgements are objectively true.

Notice the form of this view. The ethical subjectivist says that *no* ethical judgements are objectively true, but the ethical objectivist does not say that *all* ethical judgements are objectively true. The objectivist cannot say this, because it would lead straight to contradiction. "Hitler was a bad man" and "Hitler was a good man" are both ethical judgements. But

41

they cannot both be true because they contradict each other. We get a workable objectivism only when we allow that there are both objectively true *and* objectively false ethical judgements.

Notice, too, that there is nothing in the definition of ethical objectivism to prevent the objectivist from allowing that *some* ethical judgements are only subjectively true or false. Perhaps, for instance, it is no more than a matter of opinion whether the French way of greeting people by kissing them on the cheeks is ethically better or worse than the American way of greeting them by shaking their hands. From the objectivist's point of view, that there should be *some* subjective ethical truths and falsehoods is just fine.

On the other hand, it would be a strange kind of ethical objectivism that only recognized *two or three* ethical truths, none of them very important. My definition says that an ethical objectivist is someone who believes that "*at least some* ethical judgements are objectively true". This might mislead the unwary. After all, on this definition, you count as an ethical objectivist if you believe that there is just one objective moral truth and everything else is subjective. The kinds of ethical objectivism that philosophers are mainly interested in say not only that *at least some* ethical judgements are objectively true, but also that *a lot of important and interesting* ethical judgements are objectively true. (Call this "full objectivism"; "full subjectivism", by contrast, is the view that no ethical judgements at all are objectively true.)

So we can have *degrees* of ethical subjectivism or objectivism, depending on *which* ethical truths we say are objective or subjective. It is common for philosophers to talk as if full ethical objectivism and full ethical subjectivism were the only serious alternatives; indeed, I myself am going to spend most of Chapters 5–7 talking that way. This helps to keep the discussion simple, but it should not be allowed to obscure the fact that there is a whole range of more nuanced possible positions in between full subjectivism and full objectivism, depending on what we think about the objectivity or subjectivity of *particular ranges* of ethical judgements. Maybe, for instance, ethical objectivism is right about the ethics of killing, but ethical subjectivism is right about the ethics of sport. Such in-between positions are not very common, but they are perfectly possible.

A different way of nuancing our views about objectivity and subjectivity is this. We might observe that *ethical* objectivism is just one species of a wider genus, *value* objectivism: the view that there are at least some true judgements *about value*. Value is a much wider category than ethical value. There is aesthetic value, for instance – the value that is there in the *Mona Lisa*, or the view from the summit of Mont Blanc, or a graceful ballerina. Or there is epistemic value – the value that knowledge and understanding have; or comic value – the value that attaches to funniness; and so on. The truth of objectivism (or subjectivism) in any one of these areas apparently does not force the truth of objectivism (or subjectivism) in any other of them. There is nothing inconsistent in the position of an aesthetic objectivist who is also an ethical subjectivist. (Perhaps that was Oscar Wilde's position, or Nietzsche's.) This, too, is an interesting possibility that I shall not explore much here.

If this is what ethical objectivism is, what is there to be said for the view? And how might an ethical objectivist deal with the subjectivist qualms described in the previous section? In the rest of this chapter I shall take these two questions in turn.

Here, then, to begin with, are three rather simple arguments to motivate the objectivist view, and undermine ethical subjectivism:

- *Argument from rational criticism*. Ethical subjectivism makes rational ethical criticism impossible. If no ethical judgement is objectively true, then there are no objective standards for criticism. Any criticism is as good (and as bad) as any other. There is no difference between a good ethical criticism of somebody's action or character and a bad one. A moment's reflection shows that this cannot be right. Suppose you criticize Hitler for being a murdering, racist, war-crazed, fanatical monster while I criticize him for not always being as kind as he might have been to his pet Alsatian Blondi. If we know anything at all about ethics, we know that your criticism of Hitler is better than mine ("better" here meaning "more accurate and more rational"). A theory that, like ethical subjectivism, gives us no way of telling your criticism and my criticism apart, as good and bad, respectively, is surely hopeless.
- *Argument from experience*. The second objectivist argument begins from a thought about the *phenomenology* of our ethical experience: what that experience seems like from the inside; what it is like to have ethical beliefs or thoughts or opinions. The argument is that we experience our typical ethical thoughts as beliefs in facts, not as

43

attitudes or feelings. Remember here a point I made at the beginning of Chapter 2: you could say "It's wrong to steal, *and* I don't personally like people stealing" without repeating yourself. In the same way, disliking someone is fundamentally different from thinking that he is a bad person. I can like someone who I think is a bad person, and dislike someone who I think is a good person. And again, I can coherently think "I don't like bull-fighting, but that's just my attitude"; but I cannot coherently think "Bull-fighting is wrong, but that's just my attitude". As Bertrand Russell (himself an ethical subjectivist) admits: "Suppose that someone were to advocate the introduction of bull-fighting in this country. In opposing the proposal, I should *feel*, not only that I was expressing my desires, but also that my desires in the matter are *right*, whatever that may mean" (1944: 51).

Thinking that bull-fighting is wrong commits me to thinking that there is more to the wrongness of bull-fighting than my negative attitude to it. It commits me to thinking that bull-fighting would be wrong *no matter what* my attitude to bull-fighting was: negative, positive or indifferent. The wrongness of bull-fighting has the hardness and obstinacy of a fact. In a phrase of Williams's, it is part of "how the world is anyway" (1968: 65), quite apart from me and my attitudes to it. But if our ethical thoughts are typically beliefs in facts that are part of "how the world is anyway", quite apart from us and our attitudes to it, then they are beliefs in *objective* ethical facts. And if there are any objective ethical facts, then ethical subjectivism must be wrong.

- *Argument from language.* The third thought that works in favour of ethical objectivism is a thought about a phenomenon about language that I shall call *default literalism*. The simplest and most natural way to take ordinary sentences – "The grass is green", for instance – is this: to be true, the sentence must ascribe (1) a genuine property to (2) a real thing and (3) that thing must really have that property. But it looks pretty obvious that "The grass is green" *is* true. So it looks pretty obvious, too, (3) that grass really is green, (2) that grass really exists and (1) that greenness is a real property. Similarly, it looks pretty obvious that "Murder is wrong" is another true sentence. So it seems equally obvious (3) that murder really is wrong, (2) that murder really exists and (1) that wrongness is a real property. The natural way to take any ordinary sentence is as literally true (or else, as literally false). But if we take the sentences of ethics as literally true or false, then we get the conclusion that properties such as wrongness are as real and objective as greenness or any other property.

These simple arguments make a very basic case for ethical objectivism. To this case, we can add some initial responses to the subjectivist qualms described in §5.1.

Take the issue of creativity first. An objectivist can agree that ethical truth is unlike scientific truth in its close and personal relation to the individual. He can agree that the truth about how I should live is something that I have to invent, and cannot simply discover. But (the objectivist will say) we need to think harder about what is involved in inventing or creating an answer to "How should I live?". Will any old random invention do? Can I pick my creative answer to "How should I live?" out of a hat? Of course not. *Inventions are criticizable.* Some inventions are brilliant ideas, such as the internet, and some are not such great ideas, such as garlic-flavour ice cream. The mere fact that something is invented goes nowhere near showing that we cannot say, objectively, whether that something is useful or good. (In this sense, there is something to question in the title of J. L. Mackie's famous defence of ethical subjectivism, *Ethics: Inventing Right and Wrong* [1977].) Similarly, *creativity is criticizable*: it can be exercised more or less well, and there are standards for what counts as the good or the bad exercise of creativity. As long as I am exercising my own creativity, I will constantly be using these standards to assess and appraise what I have done so far, and to ask myself how I might do better in the future. But I can use these same standards to assess and appraise other people's creativity too.

Certainly – to come back to the "ultra-democratic" thoughts developed in §5.1 – I need to avoid arrogance and high-handedness in the views I take of other people's creativity. If I am allowed to criticize *them* then they are allowed to criticize *me*, and maybe I will hear some unpalatable truths when they do. But allowing us to criticize each other is not necessarily a recipe for judgementalism. It can also be a recipe for open-minded humility.

To say that we have standards for criticizing exercises of creativity, and that everyone can use those same standards, is to say that those standards are *objective* standards. So there is nothing for the ethical objectivist to fear in the idea that some sorts of ethical truth that are central to the living of good lives are invented, not discovered. He can happily agree, and just respond that what are objective are the standards that make the difference between good invention and bad invention.

Notice, incidentally, that we can put "creativity is criticizable" another way: we can equally say "creativity is *a rational process*". Putting it that way helps to bring out the connection with an important question that arose in Chapter 4: the question what sort of rationality we need for a satisfactory account of how life should be lived. If the argument just given is right, the sort of rationality that we need is, at least in part, the rationality of creativity: the application of the kinds of standards that creativity involves.

And where do the standards come from for assessing creativity? From several sources, no doubt, but the objectivist can point to one in particular. He can say that the background for the individual's question "How should I live?" is always set by the general question "How should life be lived?". One important way of assessing how well any particular human being is living is by the standard of what living well means for human beings in general.

The objectivist calls this a *standard*. The subjectivist may worry that there is not much content to the standard; perhaps not enough to provide us with a determinate answer to the question "How should life be lived?". The subjectivist might think that this question no more admits of a determinate answer than the question "How long is a piece of string?".

But, the objectivist will respond, this is an exaggeration. Of course there is *some* indeterminacy about how human beings should live their lives. In fact there needs to be some indeterminacy, to make room for the vitally important activities of individual creativity in deciding how to live. But this indeterminacy is not total. We know that a life of counting blades of grass would not be a very good answer to the Socratic question, whereas a life of loving and helping others would be. We know that the life of a talented and successful composer is a better answer to that question than the life of a hopeless alcoholic. (We also know that it is better than the life of a talented and successful composer who *is* a hopeless alcoholic.) We know that finding fulfilment in a life of worthwhile activities is better than finding no fulfilment in a life of worthless activities, while an unfulfilling life of worthwhile activities and a fulfilling life of worthless activities come somewhere in between. These familiar truths about what makes human lives go well or badly are, apparently, objective truths; they are not just matters of opinion. The ethical subjectivist does himself no favours if his theory gets him into a position where he has to deny them.

What is still missing from the objectivist story so far is any account of how to *argue* for such claims as the ones made in the previous paragraph (or as people often say, "how to prove them", although asking for claims to be *proved* is a much stronger demand than asking for claims to be *argued for*). Even if everyone does know that the life of a successful composer is a better life than the life of a hopeless alcoholic, I still have not shown how to support such a claim with reasons.

Here we seem to get back to the problem noted at the end of §4.3: that claims about basic values are beyond argument. What is more, to restate the subjectivist's other main qualm from §5.1, it is not as if most ethical claims are merely about means–end relations, like the relation between scratching someone's back (a cause) and the physical pleasure this gives him (an effect). Typically they are about constitutive relations, for example those between going to the ballet and having a good time. And as we saw, claims of this sort are much harder to argue for than means–end claims. It may look as if the subjectivist has the only good explanation of these phenomena. He explains them by saying that claims about basic values and about constitutive relations are beyond argument because they are really claims about our feelings and preferences, not claims about facts.

Here the objectivist can say that, even if we cannot prove our claims about basic values in the same way that we can prove mathematical results or scientific theories, still we are not *totally* without resources for arguing about basic values and what constitutes them. In comparing the composer's life with the alcoholic's, for example, we can point out the indignity and degradation of alcohol-dependency (a point about constitutive relations). And we can point out the ways in which alcoholism affects people's ability to control their own lives or address their own problems (a point about means–end relations). Looking, by contrast, at the composer's life, we can point out what a good thing it is to be creative, and what a privilege it is for anyone to immerse himself in the extraordinary history and the rich and various traditions of human music. We can also point out that a living can be made – sometimes, and with a bit of luck – out of music, and show the well-documented health benefits of having a master passion or enthusiasm in your life. (Here, too, there is a mix of points about constitutive relations and points about means–end relations.)

So it is not true that we have *no* resources for arguing about basic values. Very commonly we can appeal to instrumental and constitutive relations to enrich and support our picture of what the basic values are, and of the diverse and creative ways in which they can be fitted into human lives. That is, we can argue for basic values by showing how some things are means to achieving certain values and/or how other things are more specific instances of more general values.

Of course, as Hume points out (§4.3), we cannot justify *everything* by relating it back to some more general or more basic value. But that need not show what Hume thinks it shows: that our most basic values are mere preferences or desires. It might simply show that our basic values are *basic*. Hume's move from "basic values cannot be argued for" to "basic values cannot be objective" is a move that the ethical objectivist can reject. The objectivist can say, "All that Hume shows is that we haven't yet worked out how to argue for basic values". Or else he can say, "All that Hume shows is that our basic values are like mathematical axioms, or scientific data, or simple perceptions [§7.4]. They are raw data, inputs to deliberation, not outputs of deliberation." As Aristotle puts it (*Nicomachean Ethics* 1095a31), we argue *from* them, not *to* them. So the fact that we cannot argue for or prove our basic values – at least not in the same way that we argue for other things – is not, all on its own, a good enough reason for thinking that our basic values are subjective.

The trouble is, the ethical subjectivist may respond at this point, that we do not yet have a good enough reason for thinking that our basic values are objective, either. Objectivism, he will claim, comes at too high a philosophical cost. However attractive the view may be in itself, believing it forces you to believe too many other things that are not attractive at all.

To show how this claim might be made out, as part of the wider case for ethical subjectivism, will be our next task. Chapter 6 will develop and examine five arguments for ethical subjectivism.

6

Five arguments for
ethical subjectivism

My own suspicion is that the universe is not only queerer than we suppose, but queerer than we can suppose.   (Haldane 1927: 208–9)

In §5.2 we saw this definition of the position that I have been calling ethical subjectivism:

Ethical subjectivism. No ethical judgements are objectively true.

I contrasted this with the position that is the strict negation of ethical subjectivism – ethical objectivism:

Ethical objectivism. Some ethical judgements are objectively true.

As I noted, this objectivist position is not the most interesting one, since it is much too weak. *This* sort of ethical objectivism is true if there is only one completely inconsequential objective truth in ethics – say, that smiling at strangers is nice – and everything else is subjective. What we are really interested in (and what I shall be talking about from here on) is the far stronger position that Chapter 5 calls full ethical objectivism:

Full ethical objectivism. Very many important and interesting ethical judgements are objectively true.

In Chapter 5, in response to the last of the four key questions to which we were led by our initial definition of ethics as the use of reason to answer the question "How shall we live?", I began a debate between (full) ethical objectivism and subjectivism. In Chapters 6 and 7 I take this debate further. In Chapter 6 I develop and assess some more sophisticated arguments for what I call ethical subjectivism. Then in Chapter 7 I shall examine some subjectivist accounts of what moral discourse is about, criticize them and compare some objectivist accounts of what it is about.

Notice, incidentally, my words "*what I call* ethical subjectivism". Other philosophers often mean something different from what I mean by "ethical subjectivism" or "ethical objectivism". Hence they deny that they are (what *they* call) ethical subjectivists. For example, by my definition Williams and Blackburn both count as ethical subjectivists, although on their own definitions of "ethical subjectivist", both would probably reject the label. This is an essentially verbal issue; the main purpose of mentioning it is just to stop it distracting us. What is interesting is not the labels, but the content of their philosophical positions.

I turn, then, to the arguments.

6.1 The argument from relativity for ethical subjectivism

This can be stated in three or four sentences:

The argument from relativity has as its premiss the well-known variation in moral codes from one society to another and from one period to another, and also the differences in moral beliefs between different groups and classes within a complex community. Scientific disagreement results from speculative inferences or explanatory hypotheses based on inadequate evidence, and it is hardly plausible to interpret moral disagreement in the same way. Disagreement about moral codes seems to reflect people's adherence to and participation in different ways of life. The causal connection seems to be mainly that way around: it is that people approve of monogamy because they participate in a monogamous way of life rather than that they participate in a monogamous way of life because they approve of monogamy.   (Mackie 1977: 36)

There are disagreements between moral beliefs; and these disagreements cannot be explained – or resolved – in anything like the way that scientific disagreements can. The best explanation of these disagreements is that moral beliefs are merely a matter of opinion, not of fact. The phenomenon of ethical disagreement is best explained by ethical subjectivism; for which this is the first argument.

6.2 The argument from the is–ought gap for ethical subjectivism

In three quick sentences: there is an *is–ought* gap. And the best explanation of the *is–ought* gap is that there is a *fact–value* gap, an exclusive distinction between factual claims and claims about value. But to assert that no claims about value are factual claims is just to assert ethical subjectivism.

We need to spell this out a bit. In his *Treatise of Human Nature*, Hume famously writes:

> In every system of morality, which I have hitherto met with, I have always remarked, that the author proceeds for some time in the ordinary ways of reasoning, and establishes the being of a God, or makes observations concerning human affairs; when all of a sudden I am surprised to find, that instead of the usual copulations of propositions, *is*, and *is not*, I meet with no proposition that is not connected with an *ought*, or an *ought not*. This change is imperceptible; but is however, of the last consequence. For as this *ought*, or *ought not*, expresses some new relation or affirmation, 'tis necessary that it should be observed and explained; and at the same time that a reason should be given; for what seems altogether inconceivable, how this new relation can be a deduction from others, which are entirely different from it.
>
> ([1739] 1985: 3.1.1)

You cannot get an *ought* from an *is*: there is no logically sound argument that moves from exclusively non-ethical premises to an ethical conclusion. (This is the is–ought gap.)

A *logically sound* argument has two features that we should note here. First, it has a true premise or premises, such as "All men are mortal" and "Socrates is a man". Secondly, it is logically valid. That is, if its premises are true, then its conclusion has to be true as well. For example, if the premises "All men are mortal" and "Socrates is a man" are true, then the conclusion "Socrates is mortal" must be true. Hence the argument that moves from those two premises to that conclusion will be logically valid.

Equipped with these definitions, we can quickly see Hume's point that you cannot get any ethical conclusions from any exclusively non-ethical premises, even if those premises are true. Suppose, for instance, that you have these premises:

1. Whatever behaviour does not increase our chances of transmitting our genes to the next generation is unnatural.
2. Homosexuality does not increase our chances of transmitting our genes to the next generation.

It is a logically valid argument to infer from these premises to the conclusion

3. Homosexuality is unnatural.

However, your argument (1–3) will not be valid if you mean something *moral* by "unnatural" in (3): for example if you mean that homosexuality is morally wrong (which is what peddlers of this argument usually have in mind). Premises (1) and (2) only imply (3) if (3) uses the sense of "unnatural" defined by (1). And that sense of "unnatural" is biological; it has nothing to do with moral wrongness. In (1)'s sense of "unnatural", playing in symphony orchestras, writing philosophy, giving charitable donations at Christmas-time, being a monk, and a whole host of other human activities are just as unnatural as homosexuality. But no one thinks these things wrong for that reason.

Here is a second example. Suppose we have the premise that

1. Lucy is causing pain to Sophie.

Can we infer validly from (1) to

2. Lucy is doing something morally wrong?

No, we cannot: not without further premises. We might of course add the premise

3. It is wrong to cause people pain,

and (given that Sophie is a person) we could then validly infer (3) from (1) and (2). But then we would not have an argument that crosses the is–ought gap. No argument crosses that gap unless it has *exclusively* non-moral premises that entail a moral conclusion. And the argument (1), (2), (3) does not have exclusively non-moral premises, because (2) is obviously a moral claim.

This is the phenomenon of the is–ought gap. It is a striking phenomenon, which evidently needs an explanation. The explanation offered by the ethical subjectivist is that there is an is–ought gap because there is a fact–value gap: the reason why we cannot argue from non-moral facts to moral facts is because there are *no* moral facts. And if there are no moral facts, ethical objectivism cannot be true. This is the second argument for ethical subjectivism.

6.3 The argument from naturalism for ethical subjectivism

The striking fact that there is an is–ought gap deserved an explanation, according to the second argument. That explanation invoked a fact–value gap. Maybe the fact–value gap deserves an explanation too. That it does is the point of the third argument for ethical subjectivism.

We should be curious about the metaphysical foundations of the fact–value gap. *Why* are there two categories of facts and values, and what can we say about what makes anything a member of either category? According to the third argument for ethical subjectivism, there is a clear and precise answer to this question. The facts that we are talking about are the *scientific* facts. Science – total science – gives us a systematic theory of everything. It is no accident that the English word "science" comes from the Latin word *scientia*, which just means "knowledge", for science is the only real knowledge we have of the only real nature or reality that there is.

Now science is all about explanation: rigorously confirmed, repeatable, universal and experimentally tested explanation. The only true facts are the "naturalistic" facts, which means the facts that can do explanatory work within a scientific framework. But moral "facts" do no such explaining. So they are not really facts at all. And so we get from naturalism to ethical subjectivism, for which this is the third argument.

6.4 The argument from motivation for ethical subjectivism

The fourth argument for ethical subjectivism, a little more complicated than the first three, emerges from another excerpt from Hume's *Treatise Concerning Human Nature*:

> Since morals have an influence on the actions and affections, it follows, that they cannot be derived from reason; and that because reason alone can never have any such influence. Morals excite passions, and produce or prevent actions. Reason of itself is utterly impotent in this particular. The rules of morality, therefore, are not conclusions of our reason. Reason is the discovery of truth or falsehood. Truth or falsehood consists in an agreement or disagreement either to the real relations of ideas, or to real existence and matter of fact. Whatever, therefore, is not susceptible of this agreement or disagreement, is incapable of being true or false, and can never be an object of our reason. Now 'tis evident our passions, volitions, and actions, are not susceptible of any such agreement or disagreement. 'Tis impossible, therefore, they can be pronounced either true or false, and be either contrary or conformable to reason. ([1739] 1985: 3.1.1)

The argument of this passage begins from a pair of claims that we have seen Hume make before (§4.3):

1. Only passions motivate.
2. Reason does not motivate.

In the words just quoted: "Morals excite passions, and produce or prevent actions. Reason of itself is utterly impotent in this particular." Which reminds us that Hume is also making a third claim here:

54

3. Moral judgements motivate.

It should be clear from (1–3) alone that a problem is looming for the ethical objectivist. But let us take the longer and more careful route to that problem, as Hume himself does, in order to get clearer about its exact nature.

What Hume tells us next gives us a little more information about what he means by "reason":

4. "Reason" means the formation of beliefs by way of rational processes.

(As it says in the *Treatise* quotation above: "Reason is the discovery of truth or falsehood" [*ibid.*].)

Then (4) in turn leads Hume to tell us some more about what he means by "belief":

5. Beliefs are true or false in so far as they represent or misrepresent either of two kinds of fact: (a) logical or conceptual relations, (b) matters of fact in the world. There are no other kinds of fact besides (a) and (b).

("Truth or falsehood consists in an agreement or disagreement either to the real relations of ideas, or to real existence and matter of fact" [*ibid.*].)

Now Hume adds this point about passions:

6. Passions cannot represent either of these two kinds of fact.

("… 'tis evident our passions, volitions, and actions, are not susceptible of any such agreement or disagreement" [*ibid.*])

(5) and (6) together imply that nothing can be both a passion and a belief. For if anything is a belief, then it will represent the facts about logic or matters of fact (if true), or misrepresent them (if false). But if anything is a passion, then it will not represent *any* kind of fact. No passion is a belief, and no belief is a passion. And only beliefs can be true or false. Hence, no passion is either true or false.

Now remember what (1), (2) and (3) told us:

1. Only passions motivate.
2. Reason does not motivate.
3. Moral judgements motivate.

Claims (1–3) already set up a problem for the ethical objectivist because they imply that moral judgements are "passions", not "reason". Spelling Hume's line of thought out as far as (6) enables us to put the argument more sharply. *Whatever can be true or false cannot motivate, and whatever can motivate cannot be true or false. But moral judgements do motivate. So moral judgements cannot be true or false.*

This is how Hume's argument in the quotation above from the *Treatise concerning Human Nature* uses the plain fact that our moral beliefs motivate us as evidence that our moral beliefs are not genuinely *beliefs* at all. Those moral judgements may *look* like beliefs. But the fact that they motivate shows that they are not really beliefs, but passions: emotions, reactions, attitudes. As such, they can be neither true nor false objectively speaking.

Not only does Hume's argument lead us to the conclusion that our moral *judgements* are not really moral *beliefs*, because our moral judgements characteristically motivate us. It has the further upshot that even if there *were* moral beliefs strictly so called, they would not do the work that (Hume thinks) the ethical objectivist wants them to do, namely motivate us. Even if there were moral judgements that deserved to be called *beliefs* in the proper sense, because they were judgements that involved representing how the world is, they would be motivationally irrelevant in a way that our most characteristic moral judgements most certainly are not. *Not only are there no such things as moral facts, but moral facts would be irrelevant even if they existed.*

That is the fourth argument for ethical subjectivism: Hume's argument from the motivational power of moral judgements. The argument remains influential today. It is, for instance, the cornerstone of the argument of Michael Smith's contemporary classic *The Moral Problem* (1994) (even though that book ends up rejecting Hume's ethical subjectivism).

6.5 The argument for ethical subjectivism from the Internal Reasons Thesis

In his famous paper "Internal and External Reasons" (1981: 101–13) Bernard Williams presents a claim that we have already looked at briefly in §4.3, and which I shall now give more careful examination. This is "the Internal Reasons Thesis". The Internal Reasons Thesis is a view about how to read sentences that say that someone has reason to do something: sentences of the form "*A* has reason to do *x*". We can read such sentences as implying that:

> *Internal reading*: "*A* has some motive which will be served or furthered by his doing *x*" (*ibid.*: 101),

so that, if there is no such motive, it will not be true that "*A* has reason to do *x*". We can also read sentences of the form "*A* has reason to do *x*" as not implying this, but as saying that:

> *External reading*: *A* has reason to do *x* even if none of his motives will be served or furthered by his doing *x*.

On this *external* reading of such sentences, Williams argues, they are all false.

The basic idea of the Internal Reasons Thesis is that we cannot have genuine reasons to act that have no connection whatever with anything that we care about. Since, apparently, people might care (or fail to care) about just anything, this presents a challenge to the objectivist way of thinking about ethics. When we tell someone that he should not rob bank vaults or murder bank clerks, we usually understand ourselves to be telling him that he has *reason* not to rob bank vaults or murder bank clerks. If the Internal Reasons Thesis is true, the bank-robber can prove that he has no such reason simply by showing that he does not have any motives that connect with anything that is achieved by abstaining from robbing banks. He can just say, "But I don't *care* about the considerations you cite. For me, they just aren't motives." So we reach the disturbing conclusion that the rules of ethics are like the rules of some sport or parlour game: they apply only to those who choose to join in. There are no external reasons; and the best explanation of that fact is that ethics is subjective.

There are echoes of this view of Williams's in Mackie. Mackie too believes that there are no reasons to act that do not come from our own motivations, and that this fact is evidence for ethical subjectivism:

[T]he objectification of moral values [is] primarily the projection of ... wants and demands. As Hobbes says, "Whatsoever is the object of any man's appetite or desire, that is it, which he for his part calleth *Good*" [*Leviathan* 6.7] ... We get the notion of something's being objectively good, or having intrinsic value, by reversing the direction of dependence here, by making the desire depend upon the goodness, instead of the goodness upon the desire. (1977: 43)

For Mackie, the world does not give us reasons. Our reasons come from within us, from our desires or wants. The ethical objectivist's mistake is to find these reasons so compelling that he thinks they *cannot* have come from within us: they must be reasons that apply to us "in the nature of things", as part of the way the world is, not conditionally, depending on what we happen to want. But this is a mistake, according to Mackie (and Williams). Once we understand how the mistake happens, we understand that what we have here is a fifth argument for ethical subjectivism.

And that is the last of the arguments that I promised for ethical subjectivism: the arguments from relativity, from the is–ought gap, from naturalism, from motivation and from the Internal Reasons Thesis. In §6.6 I offer a summary, and in §6.7 an assessment, of all five arguments.

6.6 The five arguments for ethical subjectivism as abductive arguments

All five arguments for ethical subjectivism presented in §§6.1–6.5 are best understood as examples of what philosophers call *abductive* arguments, or *inferences to the best explanation*. I pause to explain this notion.

Abductive arguments are philosophically interesting for all sorts of reasons. For one thing, they seem like good arguments; yet they are not logically valid arguments! Given that all the silverware is missing, and that there are new footprints in the rose-bed by the open kitchen window, we may infer that the best explanation of these two facts is that there has been a burglary. This is a perfectly good piece of abduction. But it is patently not a deductively valid argument, as we can see by trying to express it as one:

1. All the silverware is missing.
2. There are new footprints in the rose-bed by the open kitchen window.
3. Therefore, there has been a burglary.

As we saw above (§6.2), an argument is deductively valid when, if its premises are true, then its conclusion *must* be true. We can hardly say that about this little argument. There might be no connection at all between (1) and (2). Perhaps the silverware is missing because the cook has taken it off to be security-tagged, while there are footprints in the rose-bed because the gardener has been weeding there. Even if there is a connection between (1) and (2), it could so easily not be the connection that (3) makes. (Perhaps the kitchen door has jammed, so that the cook who was taking the silverware for security-tagging had to leave through the window.) There are all sorts of other possible conclusions besides (3) that we might draw from (1) and (2). So whatever reason there may be for accepting abductive arguments – and there surely is *some* sort of reason – the reason is not that they are deductively valid.

My point here is not to raise questions about abductive argument as such. It is just to observe that the five arguments for ethical subjectivism in §§6.1–6.5 are all instances of abductive argument.

Thus the first argument starts with the fact that different societies have different ethical codes, values and priorities, and offers an explanation of this phenomenon: namely, that these differences arise because there is no reason why they should not. There are no ethical truths for ethical views to converge on; that is why they do not converge. In short, we should believe ethical subjectivism because it offers a good explanation of the phenomenon of moral relativity.

The second argument exhibits the same abductive structure. It begins from the phenomenon that there is no logically valid argument from non-moral premises alone to moral conclusions, and offers an explanation of this phenomenon: there is an is–ought gap because there is a fact–value gap. There is no way of making out a logically valid argument from non-moral facts to moral facts because there *are* no moral facts. Likewise the fifth argument exhibits a phenomenon – the non-existence of external reasons – and suggests an explanation of that phenomenon: the subjectivity of ethics.

The third and fourth arguments are slightly different in structure, but can still be seen as examples of abduction. Thus the third argument begins from a worldview widely accepted among philosophers: philosophical naturalism. Roughly, this is the view that there is nothing real outside science and the nature that science studies. If naturalism is true, as the third argument assumes, then we need an explanation of the status of ethical claims that will be consistent with naturalism. The explanation on offer in the third argument is that ethical claims are consistent with naturalism because they do not involve us in asserting that there is anything real outside science. There are no ethical facts or anything like that. There is just the world and the facts that science posits, and our reactions to that world and those facts. According to the third argument our reason for taking this ethical subjectivist view is, once more, that it is the best explanation on offer of the phenomenon of a world where naturalism is true, but also, where people offer ethical claims.

Similarly with the fourth argument. According to Hume and his contemporary disciples, Blackburn and Gibbard for example, we have the three phenomena that "passions" motivate, that "reason" does not motivate and that "morals" do motivate. The most obvious and simplest way to explain these phenomena is to place "morals" with "passions", not with "reason": that is, to deny that ethical "beliefs" are really beliefs at all rather than reactions to the world.

Now any abductive argument moves from a description of some set of phenomena to an explanation of those phenomena. So to assess any abductive argument, we should ask two basic questions:

(a) Does the abductive argument describe the phenomena accurately, or does it misrepresent or omit any important phenomena?

(b) Does the explanation on offer really explain those phenomena as well as it claims to: is it really the *best* explanation, a *good* explanation, or even an explanation at all?

In the next section I apply these two questions to the five arguments for ethical subjectivism that this chapter has developed.

6.7 Criticizing the arguments for ethical subjectivism

Let us begin with the first argument, the argument from relativity (§6.1). So (a) is that argument right to claim that there is extensive moral relativity between societies, classes, ages and even individuals?

This is actually rather hard to assess. It would be pointless to deny that there is *some* moral relativity between societies and other groups. The difficulty is: how much? Less, I am inclined to suspect, than the moral relativist needs to make a convincing case. Of course there are differences in detail, often very striking ones. But underlying these, there is a discernible core of basic moral orientations that are shared by pretty much every society. For instance, every society that I have heard of – not that I am a comparative anthropologist – recognizes moral commitments to reciprocity ("do as you would be done by"); to justice and fairness, or something very like them; to friendship, love and care for others; to the importance of truth and trust; to the universal need for respect and dignity; to the place of the divine/uncanny/supernatural/sublime in human experience; and to the centrality of sexuality, physical vulnerability and weakness, and mortality to human life.

One important recent philosopher who agrees about this is Martha Nussbaum, whose "capability approach" explicitly aims at producing a defensibly universalistic ethics on the basis of just such a list of universally recognized areas of moral concern: the eponymous capabilities (Nussbaum 1992a). The list of capabilities that Nussbaum offers is strikingly similar to the list of areas of basic moral concern that I have just offered: "(1) Mortality; (2) The human body; (3) Capacity for pleasure and pain; (4) Cognitive capability: perceiving, imagining, thinking; (5) Early infant development; (6) Practical reason; (7) Affiliation with other human beings; (8) Relatedness to other species and to nature; (9) Humour and play; (10) Separateness" (*ibid.*: 219). It is similar, too, to the lists offered by writers such as Aristotle (*Rhetoric* 1300b), and by many modern writers such as John Finnis (1980: ch. 4). As the evidence of these similar lists accumulates, so should our doubts about whether there is, in fact, as much moral relativity around as moral relativists imagine.

Even if there is lots and lots of moral relativity around, the relativist still needs to answer the second sort of challenge for abductive arguments, by showing that ethical subjectivism is the best explanation of the phenomenon of relativity. This can be doubted. Maybe *progressivism* is a better explanation of moral relativity: maybe ethical views differ over time and space because they form different parts of a continuing story of moral development in human beings. Or perhaps *original sin*, also known as sheer bloody-mindedness, is a good explanation of relativity: maybe some societies are just very *obstinate* in the ethical mistakes they insist on making. To make a convincing abductive case for his position, the relativist needs to be able to rule out, or at least show the relative unattractiveness of, such alternative possibilities. And that is a tall order.

The same questions apply to the second argument for ethical subjectivism, from the is–ought gap (§6.2). (a) The ethical objectivist can query the phenomenon, then (b) he can query the subjectivist's supposed explanation of it.

At both steps, the second argument for ethical subjectivism encounters much severer problems than the first argument. The argument is supposed to begin from the phenomenon of the is–ought gap: that is, the phenomenon that no valid arguments with only non-moral premises have moral conclusions. But we can question whether this "phenomenon" is there at all. There seem to be at least two sorts of valid argument that *do* move from only non-moral premises to moral conclusions. Here is one (first pointed out by Arthur Prior):

Premise: Tea-drinking is common in England.
Conclusion: Therefore, tea-drinking is common in England or all New Zealanders ought to be shot.

This argument is valid. It is an inference from "*p*" to "*p* or *q*", and any inference of that form is valid. (Logicians call this form of argument *or-introduction*.) The premise is plainly non-moral: it has no ethical content. But the conclusion *does* have ethical content, for the conclusion is a disjunction in which one of the two disjuncts is a moral claim ("All New Zealanders ought to be shot"). Moreover, the premise is true, and the conclusion is true as well. (I hasten to add that the conclusion is true because "Tea-drinking is common in England" is true, not because "All New Zealanders ought to be shot" is true.) So here, apparently, is an argument that crosses the is–ought gap.

No doubt there is something tricksy about this argument. To bring it out, we could distinguish *a moral conclusion* from *a conclusion with moral content*. A moral conclusion, we might say, is (roughly) one that actually tells us to do something, for example shoot New Zealanders. A conclusion with moral content is something weaker: it is a conclusion with a part that, if it stood on its own, *would* tell us to do something. And this is all Prior's argument gives us. "Tea-drinking is common in England or all New Zealanders ought to be shot" does not really tell us to do anything. At most, it tells us to shoot all New Zealanders *if* tea-drinking is not common in England – as in fact, fortunately for New Zealanders, it is. So, a defender of the second argument for ethical subjectivism might insist, there is no real breach here in the barrier between is and ought.

Perhaps that is right. But even if it is, there are other ways of making such a breach. Here is another form of counter-example to the is–ought rule:

1. Everything Alfie says is true.
2. Alfie says "Murder is wrong".
3. Therefore, murder is wrong.

This argument does not seem tricksy like Prior's argument. The conclusion follows validly from the premises. The premises are straightforwardly non-moral. (We might say that premise [2] "has moral content", because it reports Alfie's moral view. But *reporting* a moral view falls on the is side of the is–ought distinction, not the ought side. After all, *reporting* that Jones holds some moral view is different from *recommending* Jones's moral view.) And the conclusion is straightforwardly moral: it tell us not to murder. This seems as plain a counter-example to the is–ought rule as can be imagined.

You could retort that even if this sort of argument is *valid*, it is not going to be *sound*, because premise (1) is so likely to be false: it is hard to imagine circumstances in which *everything* anyone said would be true. But the argument is easily restricted to avoid this flaw:

1*. Everything Alfie said between 2 and 3 pm today is true.
2*. At 2.30 pm Alfie said "Murder is wrong".
  3. Therefore, murder is wrong.

You might also reply to the argument by asking: What if Alfie says "Achoo!", or "Sugarcane elephant"? Then it does not follow that achoo, or that sugarcane elephant. For anything that Alfie says to be *true*, it has to be something that is *capable* of truth. It has to be the statement of at least a supposed fact. But bodily reflexes such as sneezes, or lists of words such as "sugarcane elephant", are not supposed by anyone to be statements of facts. So argument (1–3) is presupposing that "Murder is wrong" is the statement of a fact. But that, you might say, is wrong: we know from subjectivism that *no* ethical claims state facts.

However, there is an obvious problem with this reply. It is supposed to support an argument for ethical subjectivism. But for the reply to work, it has to assume that we already know that ethical claims do not state facts. Unless we already know that ethical subjectivism is true, we *do not* already know that ethical claims do not state facts. In other words (as defenders of ethical subjectivism will say), this argument can only work as part of a larger cumulative case for ethical subjectivism. Or to put it another way (the way opponents of ethical subjectivism will put it), it is question-begging.

So much for the problems about the phenomena, or alleged phenomena, from which the second argument for ethical subjectivism begins. Suppose the ethical subjectivist finds a way to fix these problems, so that the original is–ought rule remains intact, or else just builds such apparent counter-examples to the is–ought rule into an amended version of the rule, as exceptions that it allows. Can the ethical subjectivist move on to the next part of his abductive argument: the part that offers "the best explanation" of the phenomenon about the is–ought gap that he thinks he has detected?

Not easily, because it is far from obvious that the ethical subjectivist's explanation *is* the best explanation of the phenomenon in question; or, indeed, that it is an explanation at all. Tricksy arguments and exceptional cases aside, what the ethical subjectivist has located is the phenomenon that it is usually impossible for a valid argument with non-moral premises to have a moral conclusion. But we do not need ethical subjectivism to explain this phenomenon. For as a number of writers including Francis Snare (1992) have noted, the phenomenon is just one instance of a wider truth about logic: that most forms of valid argument cannot mention *anything* in the conclusion that they do not mention in the premises.

For example, there are very few valid argument forms that have hedgehogs in the conclusion without having hedgehogs in the premises. Consider the following argument:

1. There is something in the middle of the road.
2. The middle of the road is a dangerous place to be.
4. Therefore, there is a hedgehog in a dangerous place to be.

This is invalid. And there is almost no way of making (4) follow logically from (1), (2) or any number of extra premises, unless those extra premises refer to hedgehogs. For example, an added premise might say:

3. If there is something in the middle of the road, then it is a hedgehog.

So the general rule "No hedgehog-invoking conclusions from non-hedgehog-invoking premises" seems fairly reliable: about as reliable, in fact, as the rule that says "No moral conclusions from moral premises", that is, the is–ought rule. After all, hedgehog references can apparently be introduced into *some few* conclusions of valid arguments with no hedgehog references in their premises. These two arguments, for instance, are both valid:

1. Tigers are fierce.
2. Therefore, tigers are fierce or hedgehogs are prickly.

1. Everything Alfie says is true.
2. Alfie says "Hedgehogs are prickly".
3. Therefore, hedgehogs are prickly.

So there is a non-hedgehog–hedgehog gap just as much as there is an is–ought gap. But the non-hedgehog–hedgehog gap does not need an explanation that has anything specially to do with hedgehogs. It does not force us to regard hedgehogs as "metaphysically queer" or "spooky" entities, in the way that moral values are sometimes said, most famously by Mackie (1977), to be metaphysically queer. The explanation is a simple point about entailment. So why not say exactly the same about the is–ought gap? That gap does not need an explanation that has specially to do with the nature of ethics. The true explanation of the gap comes from logic, not from moral metaphysics. Alongside this explanation, the ethical subjectivist's proposed explanation of the is–ought gap is at best unnecessary.

The third argument infers ethical subjectivism as the best explanation of the supposed phenomenon of a naturalistic world, a world where there are no facts except scientific facts (§6.3). Here, again, we can dispute whether this supposed phenomenon is real. Is it really the case that the only facts in the world are the ones known to science? I think I know that the best train for Dundee leaves Milton Keynes at 17.40; is that a scientific fact? I think I know that Shakespeare's sonnets get much of their effect from their combination of a superficial clarity with a deeper obscurity; is *that* a scientific fact? Saying that the only facts are the scientific ones seems to commit us to ignoring all sorts of other phenomena that are no less plainly true than the alleged phenomenon of a naturalistic world: the existence of cultural, psychological and personal facts, for instance. To say that someone does something in order to write a symphony, or so as to pay a favour back to his friend, is to offer an explanation of a form quite unknown to "science" (in the sense of that word that people most often mean).

Suppose that the ethical subjectivist can resolve this difficulty, and convince us that we have the phenomenon of people engaging in moral discourse in a world where only scientific statements are true. Even then, the subjectivist still needs to show that his explanation of this phenomenon is the best or the most compelling one. And that is not easy. Perhaps ethical claims *are* scientific statements. If so, then an alternative and easier explanation than the ethical subjectivist's will be available for the phenomena that he wants to explain. There is a familiar problem here about how to define "science" (or "naturalism") so that these notions are tight enough to exclude something interesting – for example the moral – without being so tight that they implausibly exclude many other things as well. Unless we know what naturalism means, it is very hard to say what it excludes; and naturalists generally seem to struggle to say clearly what naturalism means. (A good book about this struggle is Rea [2002]. David Papineau is one leading naturalist who in "Naturalism" [2007] interestingly makes no attempt to define naturalism: he restricts himself to listing some typical naturalist commitments, and defending these one by one.) What is more, the case for thinking that there is anything objectionable to a naturalistic metaphysics in moral objectivism can, it seems, be undermined quite easily; for my own way of undermining it, see §7.4. For all of these reasons and others, I suspect that it is much harder than many philosophers suppose to make this third argument for ethical subjectivism run.

I turn to the fourth argument (§6.4). This started from the phenomenon that all three of the following claims seem true:

1. Only passions motivate.
2. Reason does not motivate.
3. Moral judgements motivate.

The fourth argument offered to explain these phenomena by way of the thesis that moral judgements are instances of passion, not of reason, and therefore cannot be true or false.

But we can dispute these phenomena. If any one of (1–3) is false, the fourth argument fails immediately. And, I suspect, all three of (1–3) are false. Claim (1) is false because there are plenty of motivations that are not passions in any interesting sense. Take a case where you do something because you regard it is as your duty (not necessarily your moral duty: perhaps your professional duty, or your duty as club captain, or whatever). In most such cases, it is perfectly clear and familiar from introspection that you do not act on a passion, but on a belief. (You do not act on what Hume calls a *"calm* passion" either: this is a term he invented to cover, in a rather *ad hoc* way, cases of motivation that do not look like motivations by passion.) Claim (2) is false by the same argument: acting on a belief is a case of what Hume means by being motivated by reason. And (3) is false because moral judgements do not always *motivate*; that is at least as familiar a fact about them as the fact that they normally do motivate. What moral judgements do always do, I suggest, is *give us reasons*.

Or at least, *some* moral judgements always give us reasons. The moral judgement that "Napoleon was a wicked man" has little or no tendency to motivate most people in AD 2009; the moral judgement that "Kent and Cordelia are the only true innocents in *King Lear*" has never had much tendency to motivate anyone, and never will have. What could these two judgements motivate anyone to do? And yet it seems pretty obvious that they are moral judgements. There are plenty of other moral judgements that have little or no more connection with motivation than these ones. But there is a class of moral judgements that characteristically begin with the words "What I ought to do now is ..." (or some such phrase). Provided, of course, that they are true, these *directive* moral judgements, as we might call them, do give us reasons.

However, giving us reasons is one thing, and motivating us is quite another. Generally speaking, people are actually motivated by their own directive judgements, moral or otherwise, only in so far as they are rational. (I offer that as a point of definition; this is what "rational" *means*.) And the pattern of motivation is something like this: I form the belief that I have a reason to act, and – being rational – I act on that belief. Hence I suggest, contrary to Hume, that rational moral motivation is *paradigmatically* a matter of being motivated by a belief. The way in which (3) is false sheds light on the ways in which (1) and (2) are also false.

Once we grasp the distinction between a belief's motivating force and its justificatory force, the fourth argument apparently collapses. It comes to seem that the phenomena that the fourth argument purports to explain by way of ethical subjectivism are not phenomena at all; the real phenomena have simply been misdescribed. If this is right then we do not even get as far as the second question: whether the fourth argument offers a compelling explanation of those phenomena. There are too many problems with the "phenomena" themselves.

Finally, the same two questions again can be used against the fifth argument for ethical subjectivism. This was the abductive argument from the Internal Reasons Thesis (§6.5). (a) Are the phenomena really as the argument says: that is, are there really no external reasons? (b) If there are no external reasons, is ethical subjectivism really the best explanation of that fact?

In response to (a), an ethical objectivist could just dispute the phenomena that the fifth argument claims to detect, and argue that there *are* external reasons: reasons to act that do not necessarily have any connection at all either with our actual motivations, or with any motivations we could come to have. Many contemporary objectivists are attracted by this strategy, and I shall not exclude the possibility that it is the right way for an objectivist to respond to the fifth argument. What I shall do, instead, is argue that *even if* there are no external reasons, ethical subjectivism is (b) not the best explanation of this phenomenon.

To see what it would mean to deny that there are any external reasons, we need a clearer grip on what it takes for something to count as an external reason. I said above that my reason to do *x* is an external one if I still have that reason even if it does not connect with my motives at all: even if my reason to do *x* has no connection whatever with anything that I care about. What kinds of "connections" are we talking about here?

Williams himself stresses that the Internal Reasons Thesis is not the view that, unless I *actually* have a given motive *M*, I cannot have an internal reason corresponding to *M*. The view is rather that I will have no internal reason unless either:

(i) I actually have a given motivation *M* in my "subjective motivational set" ("my *S*"), or

(ii) I could come to have *M* by following "a sound deliberative route" from the beliefs and motivations that I do actually have in my *S*: that is, a way of reasoning that builds conservatively on what I already believe and care about.

So the Internal Reasons Thesis is not falsified by the case of someone who is motivated to drink gin and believes that this is gin, hence is motivated to drink this, where "this" is in fact petrol (Williams's own example [1981: 102]). We are not obliged to say, absurdly, that this person has a genuine internal reason to drink petrol, nor to say, in contradiction of the Internal Reasons Thesis, that this person has a genuine external reason not to drink what is in front of him. It is rather that, even though he is not *actually* motivated not to drink the petrol, he *would* be motivated not to drink it *if he realized that it was petrol*. He can get to the motivation not to drink it by "a sound deliberative route" from where he already is. Hence, by (ii), he has an internal reason not to drink the petrol. That is the sort of connection that is in question here: the connection of one motive to another by a sound deliberative route.

This notion of "sound deliberative routes" might seem to prompt the question how big a threat the Internal Reasons Thesis really is, in practice, to ethical objectivism. Going back to the bank-robber, we might point out how very unlikely it is to be true that he does not care about *anything* that is achieved by not robbing banks, or lost by robbing them. Does the bank-robber not want, like anyone else, to be part of society? Does he not want, like anyone else, the love and respect of others? If he has either of these motivations, or any of a galaxy of other similar ones, then there will very probably be a sound deliberative route from the motivations that the bank-robber actually has, to the conclusion that even he should be motivated not to rob banks; hence, that even he has internal reason not to rob banks. But then, of course, it seems likely that we can extend and generalize this pattern of argument, and thereby show that just about anyone has the reasons that (a sensible) morality says they have. For just about anyone will have internal reason to do all the things that morality says they should do, provided only that they have any of the kind of social and extroverted motivations that we located in the bank-robber, and used to ground his internal reason not to rob banks. Hence, we might conclude, the Internal Reasons Thesis is no threat *in practice* to ethical objectivism: not, at least, once this is shorn by critical reflection of various excrescences that really are unreasonable. (To take one of Williams's own examples, I might feel under family pressure to pursue a military career because my father and all my uncles did that, even though I have no wish at all to be a military man myself. Here it is obvious that I really do not have any reason to go into the military, and that the reason why I do not really is because going into the military does not connect at all with anything that I actually want.)

On one line of thought, then, ethical objectivists can respond to the threat posed by the Internal Reasons Thesis by just saying "In practice people *will* all have the same motives, so the problem doesn't really arise". This response is found in many ethical objectivists, from Plato's *Republic* to Philippa Foot's "Moral Beliefs" (in Foot 1977). However, this response is not entirely satisfactory. It is rather like another unsatisfactory response that we saw in §5.1, where we developed the subjectivist qualm that in ethics we might not be able to argue about anything, and found that we were not entirely satisfied with the objectivist response that it was only *ends* we could not argue about: we could argue about means. The trouble with that response was that it did not ward off the main subjectivist threat, which was precisely about the possibility of arguing about ends as well as means. Likewise, the present response to the challenge of the Internal Reasons Thesis does not ward off the real threat. The real issue is not whether there are motivations that we can share in practice; obviously, there are. Rather, it is whether there are any motivations that we *must necessarily* share. The problem is that the applicability of ethical reasons is still conditional on people's actual motivations, and local to those people who have the right motivations.

The best way of responding to this continuing threat is to find an argument for saying that everyone has, at least fundamentally, the same reasons, and that there is not even a theoretical possibility that someone might fail to share in these reasons. The most likely argument to this effect might go either of two ways: I shall call them the *virtue-ethical* and *Kantian* forms of the argument. (More about them in Chapters 8 and 10, respectively.) The virtue-ethical form of the argument will say that we all have the same reasons because we are all the same sort of creatures. The Kantian form will say that we all have the same reasons because of certain crucial facts about reasons themselves, and about what any creature would have to be like to be capable of responding to reasons. On either conception, the basic point is that everyone has the same reasons to act because the human good is necessarily the same for everyone.

If that is right then there will be a possible form of moral argument that no one can just ignore, or say they do not care about because it does not connect with any of their own motivations. If the human good is necessarily the same for everyone, there will *always* be a sound deliberative route from anyone's subjective motivational set to the specific moral reasons, whatever they may be, that follow from the answer to that question. (It is another issue whether we will be able to get anyone actually to take that sound deliberative route. But that is a problem about their rationality, not about the rationality of ethics.)

If it is possible to show, by either the Kantian or the virtue-ethical route, that everyone has fundamentally the same reasons, that will undercut Williams's distinction between external and internal reasons. For the Kantian or the virtue ethicist, the point will not be that the agent has any external reasons: any reasons that bear no relation at all to the motivations he presently has, or might come, by some sound deliberative route, to derive from his present motivations. The point is rather that, necessarily, there are some internal reasons that *are derivable from any set of motivations whatever.* And this fact is enough for ethical objectivism to be true. So ethical objectivism simply does not need external reasons, even if they are available.

Thus even if the fifth argument is right that there are no external reasons, it is wrong to conclude that this phenomenon abductively supports ethical subjectivism. Or, at least, it is wrong *provided* there are reasons of something like the universal sorts that Kantians or virtue ethicists believe in. Reasons of those kinds would give ethics the kind of universality that external reasons are supposed to provide, without sharing the features of external reasons that are supposed to be problematic. In that case, this fifth argument for ethical subjectivism does not succeed either.

That concludes this chapter's discussion of the five main arguments for ethical subjectivism. The strategy common to all five arguments was to persuade us that we must be ethical subjectivists by ruling out ethical objectivism. The upshot of this chapter is that these arguments do not succeed; unless a large number of apparently possible positions can be excluded from the argument, ethical objectivism remains a possible option.

We turn next to a different question about ethical subjectivism and objectivism. This time the question is not, as it has been in Chapters 5 and 6, what sorts of evidence can be given for either position. Rather, the question is: on either the subjectivist or the objectivist account, what is ethics *about*? For more on the meaning of this question, and some suggestions about how it might be answered, see Chapter 7.

7

The content of ethics: expressivism, error theory, objectivism again

Knowing is seeing.
(John Locke, *Of the Conduct of the Understanding*, §24)

When we talk about ethics, what are we talking about? This simple question might seem especially pressing for the ethical subjectivist, whose view is that there is – basically – no moral reality, no ethical truth or falsehood. If so, then the subjectivist needs to help us to understand what is going on in ordinary life, where we often seem to talk fairly confidently as if there *were* such a thing as moral reality.

The same question is an important one for the ethical objectivist too. If ethical objectivism is true, then there is such a thing as moral reality, moral truth and falsehood. But we naturally want to know more than that. We want to know something about the nature of this alleged moral reality. We want the ethical objectivist to tell us, not just that some ethical judgements are objectively true, but also what *makes* them objectively true: what reasons or grounds there are for the claim of objective truth.

It is this question of the content of ethical claims, a question that faces subjectivists and objectivists alike, that I shall focus on in this chapter. I shall begin with the two main subjectivist answers to this question, which can be explored under the headings *expressivism* and *error theory* (§§7.1–7.2). Then I shall turn to five kinds of answer that ethical objectivists have offered: the *divine-command view* (§7.3), *perceptualism* (§7.4) and *biological naturalism, welfarist naturalism, and rationalism* (§7.5). First, then, expressivism.

7.1 Expressivism

Expressivists are probably the majority party among ethical subjectivists. They include David Hume, A. J. Ayer and, more recently, Simon Blackburn, Allan Gibbard and others. In answer to the question what ethics is about, expressivists say what we have already seen said by Hume (as quoted at the start of §6.4): that moral judgements are not really statements of beliefs at all, but expressions of our attitudes, feelings, emotions or reactions. Here are Ayer and Blackburn:

> "Stealing money is wrong" ... expresses no proposition which can be either true or false. It is as if I had written "Stealing money!!" – where the shape and the thickness of the exclamation marks show, by a suitable convention, that a special sort of moral disapproval is the feeling which is being expressed ... In saying that a certain type of action is right or wrong, I am not making any factual statement, not even a statement about my own state of mind. I am merely expressing certain moral sentiments ...
> ... [Moral utterances] are pure expressions of feeling and as such do not come under the category of truth and falsehood.
> (Ayer 1937: 142, 144)

> [W]e might say that the speech-act of putting forward a moral opinion is not one of asserting that some state of affairs obtains, but one of evincing or expressing an attitude, or perhaps of encouraging others to share an attitude.   (Blackburn 1984: 167)

Let us fix the central expressivist idea in the following definition. Many expressivists would want to qualify it in one way or another, but this definition gives us the basic idea of expressivism:

> *Expressivism*: No ethical judgement is objectively true, because ethical judgements do not admit of objective truth or falsehood; they are expressions of attitudes, not (attempted) statements of fact.

If expressivism is to succeed as an account of the nature of moral judgements, by giving us a plausible picture of what moral judgements are, then it needs to deal with a number of questions. First, is expressivism too narrow in what it says about the point of moral judgement or utterance? Here is Blackburn again:

When we voice our ethics we have distinct conversational dynamics. People are badgered. Reproaches are made and rejected. Prescriptions are issued and enforced. Resentments arise and are soothed. Emotions are tugged. The smooth clothing of statements produced as true or denied as false disguise the living body beneath. (1998: 51)

Fundamentally, moral utterance has a single point for expressivists. All moral utterance is, to reuse the word I used in discussing the fourth argument for subjectivism in §6.4, *directive*: that is, in moral utterance we express our feelings in order to influence people's attitudes and actions. Some expressivists may lay more stress on the expressing side of this formula: Ayer, for instance. Others may lay more stress on the influencing side: Hume and Stevenson, for instance. Some expressivists, such as Blackburn himself, may stress different sides of the formula in different contexts. All remain committed to a basically unitary account of the single purpose of moral utterance as directive.

But why must moral discourse have any single purpose, whether this is directive or anything else? Why can't moral discourse, like any other sort of discourse, have all sorts of purposes? To quote a recent discussion by Alan Thomas:

Here are some ethical uses of language: first, contemplating the wrong you did a friend, who is now dead, by misinterpreting his actions as selfish when in fact he was acting for your own good in a way you could not, at the time, appreciate ... Secondly, thinking to yourself about the destruction and loss of something of value. Thirdly, the contemplation, in a disinterested way, of the goodness of a person far from you in time and space ... Are these instances of the ethical use of language? I would say that they were. But whereas [Blackburn] only gives examples where a person tries to change another person's attitudes, in none of these cases do you try to change another person's attitudes. Indeed, these cases do not seem to have much to do with action or the practical at all.

(2006: 122–3)

Expressivism is in danger of getting tied to an implausibly narrow account of the point of moral utterance. Ethical objectivists, by contrast, typically think that moral utterance, when correct, is fact-stating. This is much less narrow. As evidence of its breadth, notice that while the question "What is the point of ethical statements?" might seem in order, there is evidently something wrong with the question "What is the point of factual statements?". The question seems an odd one, not because stating facts is pointless, but because fact-stating could have all sorts of points. It would be absurd to insist that there must be some interesting sense in which all statements of facts have one and the same point. One worry about expressivism is that this may well apply as much to ethics as to anything else.

A second worry is that what the expressivists are trying to show is a thesis about the *meaning* of moral discourse. But they are arguing for their thesis by way of claims about the *point* or *use* of moral discourse. And despite the well-known Wittgensteinian slogan "Meaning is use" (1951: I, 43), this seems to be something quite different. What a word or set of words means is one thing, what you (or anyone) might use them for is quite another. I might come up to you in a towering rage and tell you something that I know you already know: "They lost *eight–nil*!", "They gave *Jones* a knighthood!" My words here are expressive of emotion all right: I am simply furious. The fact that my purpose in saying them is to express my emotion in no way precludes those words from also forming a factually true proposition. So even if the expressivists were right that the point of moral utterance is to express emotion, it seems not to follow that moral utterance cannot have a meaning that comes from the facts that it states.

Thirdly, by making moral argument simply a matter of expressing my emotions in order to work on other people's emotions, expressivism seems to be in danger of underplaying the contrast between arguing with others about ethics, and browbeating, hypnotizing, or hyping others into adopting my ethical views. ("Emotivism entails the obliteration of any genuine distinction between manipulative and non-manipulative social relations" [MacIntyre 1981: 23]; cf. Blackburn's own words quoted above – "badgering", "soothing", "emotion-tugging" [1998: 51].)

Fourthly, expressivism can seem to be in danger of entailing relativism. This is a consequence that expressivists would like to avoid; but it can be argued in more than one way that they cannot avoid it. Here is one way of arguing it. (For another see Pettit & Jackson [1998].) Expressivism tells us that the real meaning of moral utterances is not the propositions that they misleadingly appear to be, but the attitudes that they express. "Stealing is bad" does not really have the content of ascribing a property, badness, to a thing, stealing. Rather, its real content is best expressed by "Boo (stealing)!", or as we might also put it, "[Disapproval of stealing]". But there is this crucial difference between facts and attitudes: facts are only incidentally connected to the people who state them, whereas attitudes are essentially connected to the people who express them. The fact that the Taj Mahal is in India remains the same fact on your lips, on mine or on anybody's: we do not need to attach that fact to any particular person to make sense of it. By contrast, when we start talking about "the attitude of disapproval of stealing", we immediately want to know *whose* disapproval of stealing we are talking about. It might be hard to pin down the exact sense in which facts do not essentially attach to anyone, but attitudes do; but there does seem to be such a sense. If so, then when expressivism analyses moral utterance as expression of attitudes, it builds a reference to the speaker into the full analysis of every moral utterance.

This tends to push expressivism towards a relativistic account of rightness or truth for moral judgements. For the expressivist, the difference between true and false moral statements is not the difference between statements that do and do not state the facts correctly. It is the difference between statements that do and do not express the right attitudes. But then, which attitudes are right? As I said in the previous paragraph, attitudes, unlike facts, essentially have owners. And it is hard to avoid the suspicion that, for expressivism, the attitudes that we call "right" will just be *our* attitudes. Expressivism thus seems to be in danger of losing touch with any notion of moral truth that goes beyond our own approval of our own attitudes of approval.

Or so it seems, although Blackburn protests:

[T]he last word is never that this is "just us". For we can go on to describe the "us" whom we are. In the case of science we might say: that is just us, informed, able to test drugs reliably, inheritors of a long and reasonably successful tradition ... In the case of logic we can say: that is just us, able to distinguish truth from falsehood, able to distinguish better from worse inferences ... In the case of ethics, we have an even longer list of virtues. We can say that it is indeed just us: liberal, humane, sympathetic, imaginative, able to admire attitudes and policies useful and agreeable to ourselves and others, capable of selecting what is better and rejecting what is worse, capable of bringing other genders, races, or even species within the folds of our concern ...   (2004: 11)

Does it help the expressivist to describe the "us" that we are in this sort of way? We might wonder about that; we might wonder whether Blackburn's further descriptions just give us a wider variety of ways of approving of ourselves. It then becomes hard to see how expressivism, developed this way, can fail to entail relativism.

A fifth question facing the expressivist account of the subject matter of ethics touches on a notorious difficulty about how expressivist moral arguments can work. Philosophers usually nowadays call this *Frege's Puzzle.* Consider the following argument:

1. If lying is wrong, then getting your brother to lie is wrong.
2. Lying is wrong.
3. So getting your brother to lie is wrong.

On the face of it this argument is obviously valid (and also sound, provided we accept (2), the wrongness of lying). Indeed, it is no less valid than the following closely parallel argument:

4. If grass is green, then the lawn in the front quad is green.
5. Grass is green.
6. So the lawn in the front quad is green.

This argument is also not only valid but sound.

Of course the expressivist has no more trouble than anyone else about recognizing (4–6) as valid and sound. But how can the expressivist preserve the validity of the apparently entirely parallel argument (1–3)? His problem is that valid and sound arguments require *propositions* as inputs. But according to him, moral "propositions" like those in (1–3), despite appearances, are not really propositions at all; they are, roughly speaking, exclamations. The deep logical form of "Lying is wrong", according to the expressivist, is "Boo for lying!" or something of that sort. But when we translate argument (1–3) into the terms that the expressivist thinks it really involves, this produces chaos:

1*. If (boo for lying!), then (boo for getting your brother to lie!).
2*. Boo for lying!
3*. So (boo for getting your brother to lie)!

Now (1*–3*) is not just invalid (and therefore unsound); it does not even make grammatical sense, except in so far as we construe it as an eccentric way of rewriting (1–3).

There is a huge and still-expanding literature about Frege's Puzzle, containing many sophisticated attempts to solve this difficulty for the expressivist. I shall not go into that highly technical literature here. (Readers who want to are encouraged to begin with Miller [2003].) I simply comment that it is a difficulty for expressivism that it raises this problem at all, and that it cannot offer the most obvious treatment of (1–3) as straightforwardly parallel to the argument (4–6), just as it seems to be.

A sixth question about expressivism will also lead us into some technicalities. This is the question whether expressivism can explain how sentences like this one work:

(M) Murder would still be wrong, even in the case where it is no one's attitude that murder is wrong.

Unless you are an out-and-out relativist – and expressivists claim not to be relativists – you will probably find (M) deeply intuitive: you will find it hard to imagine how (M) could fail to be true. How can an expressivist capture its truth? Expressivism, remember, says that typical first-order moral utterances do not state facts, they express attitudes. So, presumably, the expressivist parses (M) as something like this:

(ME) The correct attitude would still be "Boo to murder", even in the case where "Boo to murder" is no one's attitude.

However, (ME) still has "correct" in it. So to be acceptable to expressivists it needs further parsing, perhaps like this:

(MEE) The Hurrah-able attitude to murder would still be "Boo" even in the case where "Boo to murder" was no one's attitude.

This still will not do: "hurrah-able" is a gerund, a to-be-done word, and thus implicitly moral. So the parsing needs a further step for a fully expressivist form of claim to emerge from it. Perhaps this:

(MEEE) Hurrah to Hurrah to "Boo to murder", even in the case where no one says "Boo to murder".

Now (MEEE) *is* fully expressivist. When we arrive at it, do we finally have an acceptable expressivist paraphrase of (M)? Apparently not: (MEEE) seems not to mean the same as (M). And it is hard to see how further to modify it to bring it into line with what it is meant to translate from realist into expressivist terms.

It seems that none of the paraphrases (ME, MEE, MEEE) tells us, as (M) itself does, that reality is thus and so, no matter how our beliefs about reality may stand. At most, apparently, the expressivist can tell us that we are currently resolute in a given attitude, even though there is the possibility that, later on, we might take a different attitude, and indeed might be resolute in that attitude too. What the expressivist seems to be in danger of losing is the idea that one of these attitudes is not just an attitude that we are (at present) inclined to endorse, but one that is *actually correct.*

It is this idea of correctness that seems under pressure when Blackburn offers the following comment on the present question: "[When I say that murder is wrong] I have taken in all the facts, seen the situation in the round, and I am reasonably sure that no hidden subjective agenda, such as a desire for my own advantage, is driving the attitude. This is all that objectivity is, or can be" (2004: 9). The present question about expressivism is whether it can make sense of the idea that there is a difference between our best opinion about ethics and the way things really are ethically speaking. Blackburn here seems simply to deny that there is such a difference. It is hard to square this denial with Blackburn's "quasi-realist" ambition: his ambition, that is, to show how the expressivist can do everything worthwhile that the objectivist can do, and at a lower metaphysical cost. (Presumably the way out is for Blackburn to deny that it is "worthwhile" to maintain the difference between best opinion and the way things are in ethics.)

My first question about expressivism was whether it is too narrow to say that the point of all moral judgement or utterance is to motivate. My seventh and last question about expressivism is whether it is, in another way, too broad, namely in its claim that moral judgements are basically expressions of approving or disapproving attitudes. This might seem too broad because there are so many different kinds of approval and disapproval. Think of the approval and disapproval that football fans bestow on each other, for example. This is one of Blackburn's own examples of approval/disapproval in his discussion of moral attitudes (1984: 194). The example seems incongruous, because football fans' attitudes, while evaluative all right, are clearly anything but *moral* attitudes of approval or disapproval.

What more is required for an attitude of approval to count as an attitude of *moral* approval? In the words of Mackie:

It is a very natural reaction to any non-cognitive [e.g. expressive; more about "non-cognitive" in a minute] analysis of ethical terms to protest that there is more to ethics than this, something more external to the maker of moral judgements, more authoritative over both him and those of or to whom he speaks … Ethics, we are inclined to believe, is more a matter of knowledge and less a matter of decision than any non-cognitive analysis allows.

(1977: 32–3)

Moral approval, it seems, is not just like preferring Celtic to Rangers or sago to semolina. As Mackie points out, when you *morally* approve of something, you make two crucial assumptions. The first is the *categoricality* assumption. Moral approval is not *mere* approval; it is not just a matter of taste or dependent on your brute preferences, as approving sago over semolina or Celtic over Rangers typically is mere approval and dependent on brute preferences. You assume, rather, that there is some sense in which your approval *matches reality*. Accordingly, the second assumption (the *universalizability* assumption) is that anyone else similarly situated to you must share your approval: if they see what you see, and do not morally approve it, then they are *wrong*. (Here, too, notice the contrast with mere approval. Whatever football fans may sometimes say, no one sane and clear-headed who approves of Celtic and not Rangers, or sago and not semolina, is seriously committed to thinking that supporters of the other team or dessert are actually wrong or bad.)

Now these features of our moral judgements, as Mackie notes, are not just ways in which moral judgements are unlike other attitudes of approval. More than that, they are ways in which moral judgements are not like attitudes at all but, rather, like *beliefs*. This makes Mackie a *moral cognitivist*, that is, someone who holds the view that moral judgements are, basically, beliefs. The opposite is *non-cognitivism*, the view that moral judgements are, basically, something other than beliefs. Mackie's point in the last quotation is that non-cognitivist theories such as expressivism fail to make good sense of the nature of moral judgement and assertion. Here, then, is a seventh worry about expressivism's answer to the question what moral judgements can be, if they are not what the objectivist says they are.

Having presented these worries about the expressivist answer to that question, I now turn to the other main answer that is offered by ethical subjectivists (the answer that Mackie, for one, presents): namely, error theory.

7.2 Error theory

Expressivism and error theory offer very different answers to the question "What are we talking about when we talk about ethics?". The contrasts can be brought out in Table 1.

The contrast between the ethical objectivist and the ethical subjectivist who is an expressivist is the contrast between the top left-hand box and the bottom right-hand box. Expressivists are irrealists and non-cognitivists: they deny that there are any true moral beliefs because they deny that there are really any moral beliefs at all.

The contrast between the ethical objectivist and the ethical subjectivist who is an error theorist is the contrast between the top left-hand box and the bottom left-hand box. The error theorist is a cognitivist, but he is still a subjectivist because he is an irrealist. Although he does

Table 1

	Cognitivist	Non-cognitivist
Realist	Ethical assertions are genuine propositions, and some important and interesting ethical assertions are true *All or nearly all objectivists*	??? ???
Irrealist	Ethical assertions are genuine propositions, but none of them are true *Subjectivists who are error theorists*	Ethical assertions are not genuine propositions, so they are neither true nor false: they just express feelings, so cannot be right or wrong *Subjectivists who are expressivists*

not deny that there are moral beliefs, he does deny that there are any *true* moral beliefs.

(What about the top right-hand box, incidentally? Could there be a non-cognitivist realist position? Some philosophers might be read this way: possibly Richard Hare, for instance. The problem is that a realist non-cognitivism would have to say something like this: "Ethical assertions are not genuine propositions, so they are neither true nor false: they just express feelings, but they can be right or wrong, because feelings can be right or wrong." But then, what *makes* them right or wrong? Either they are right or wrong because there is a fact of the matter about what they say; or they are right or wrong in virtue of further feelings that people have. But the former position while realist is also cognitivist; and the latter position while non-cognitivist is also non-realist. So there does not seem to be a stable realist non-cognitivism.)

For an expressivist such as Blackburn, non-cognitivism is key to his position: ethical assertions do not state true beliefs because they do not state beliefs at all. For an error theorist such as Mackie, by contrast, ethical assertions do state beliefs: it is just that they all state false beliefs. *Every ethical assertion or belief is untrue*, according to Mackie:

The denial of objective values will have to be put forward ... as an "error theory", a theory that although most people in making moral judgements implicitly claim, among other things, to be

pointing to something objectively prescriptive, these claims are
all false.   (1977: 35)

When you think about it a little, this might seem a bizarre claim.
How can *every* ethical assertion or belief be untrue? Maybe "The Holocaust was a good thing" is a false ethical belief. But is that not just
because "The Holocaust was a bad thing" is a true ethical belief? Not
according to Mackie. For him, "The Holocaust was a bad thing" is *also*
a false ethical belief. On his view both sentences in this pair are false: it
is just as wrong to say that the Holocaust was a bad thing as to say that
it was a good thing. If any philosophical claim puzzles our intuitions,
this one does.

The last quotation shows how Mackie answers the puzzle. The reason
why he thinks that it is just as wrong to say that the Holocaust was a bad
thing as to say that it was a good thing is because he thinks that both
claims, even though they have the cognitive status of beliefs, not mere
expressions of attitudes, are infected by the same error: false presuppositions.

At the end of §7.1 I suggested, following Mackie, that moral approval
always involves two crucial assumptions: the *categoricality* assumption
(there is some sense in which your moral approval matches reality),
and the *universalizability* assumption (if you morally approve of X, then
anyone else similarly situated to you must also morally approve of X,
and if they do not, they are wrong). Mackie is a cognitivist because he
thinks, like the objectivist, that these two assumptions are built into
the way we think and talk about ethics. He is a subjectivist because he
thinks that both these assumptions are false.

[O]rdinary moral judgements include a claim to objectivity, an
assumption that there are objective values in just the sense in
which I am concerned to deny this. And I do not think it is going
too far to say that this assumption has been incorporated in the
basic, conventional meanings of moral terms. Any analysis of the
meanings of moral terms which omits this claim to objective,
intrinsic, prescriptivity is to that extent incomplete.   (*Ibid.*: 35)

It is part of the nature of ethical judgement that, in every such
judgement, we presuppose that our judgements match some aspect

of reality, and that anyone who judged differently would be not just different from us but also wrong. But, says Mackie, these presuppositions, universal though they may be, are both quite mistaken. There is no aspect of reality that our moral judgements could match, and so there is no sense in which those who make different judgements from us are *really* wrong. So we are in error every time we make a moral judgement. The falsity of these presuppositions infects our entire moral practice.

To put it another way, Mackie's point is that the sentence-pair "The Holocaust was bad"/"The Holocaust was good" is rather like a sentence-pair that intrigued Bertrand Russell: "The King of France is bald"/"The King of France is hairy". It is false to say that "The King of France is bald", not because the King of France is hairy, but because there is no king of France: France has been a republic, or succession of republics, since 1791. Discourse about "the" King of France is infected by systematic error, because there is no such person. Likewise, according to Mackie, with "The Holocaust was bad"/"The Holocaust was good". Not just one of these contradictory claims is false. Both are false, because both rest on a foundation of systematic error.

Here is a definition that fixes the error theorist's central idea:

Ethical subjectivism 2 – error theory: No ethical judgement is objectively true, because all ethical judgements are objectively false: they all involve false presuppositions.

What are we to make of this idea? Let us try out on it the questions we raised about expressivism in §7.1.

Since error theory is a cognitivism, unlike expressivism, it does not raise the worries that we noted for expressivism about unduly restricting "the point" of moral judgement, or making moral utterance indistinguishable from emotional manipulation, or from any other kind of expression of approval.

However, error theory does share some of expressivism's problems. For one thing, error theory seems to struggle just as much as expressivism to deal with Frege's Puzzle. If all moral judgements are false, then it is false that lying is wrong. So in the error theorist's terms, apparently, the argument labelled (1–3) in §7.1 cannot be sound, because it does not have premises that are all true. For similar reasons (1–3) cannot be valid, either. It is hard to see what it could mean to describe (1–3) as an argument "in which the conclusion must be true if the premises are", given that, according to error theory, the premises *cannot* be true.

For similar reasons, error theory's problems seem just as bad as expressivism's when it has to deal with sentences such as (M) "It would still be true that murder is wrong even if it was no one's attitude that murder is wrong". In fact, error theory's problems look worse, because error theory says that it is *false* that murder is wrong, whatever people's attitudes may be. So apparently sentences like (M) simply cannot be translated at all from the ethical objectivist's terms into the error theorist's terms. This is quite a big bullet for the error theorist to bite.

A different problem for error theory, which expressivism does not share, brings us back to the seeming bizarreness of the whole idea of saying that there is no true–false distinction in ethics: that *every ethical judgement alike* is equally false. Even when we keep it in mind that Mackie's point is only about the over-ambitious presuppositions of moral judgements, we are still left with the result that, according to error theory, there is no distinction as to truth between "Hitler was an evil man" and "Hitler was a saint". A number of philosophers (notably Wright 1995) have urged that there must be *some* distinction between those sentences – a distinction as to acceptability, palatability or what you will – and that, *pace* Mackie, it is hard to see why we cannot just call this a distinction between truth and falsity. Of course, we can then go on to discuss whether this true–false distinction has deep metaphysical roots. But to deny the distinction itself, as the error theorist does, seems to many to be a step too far away from the dictates of common sense.

Some recent philosophers (e.g. Kalderon 2005) have developed Mackie's error theory by supplementing it with a *fictionalist* move at this point. As the name suggests, the idea of moral fictionalism is that there are truths about ethics just as there are truths about fiction, provided you state them in the right form. The claim "Hamlet was prince of Denmark" is, just as it stands, plain false, because Shakespeare's character never existed in history. (Even if there was a real prince of Denmark really called Hamlet, that historical Hamlet was not Shakespeare's character Hamlet.) Contrast the claim "*In Shakespeare's play* Hamlet was prince of Denmark", which is true because it puts us into the fictional context of the play *Hamlet* before advancing its claim about the character Hamlet. Just likewise, the fictionalists suggest, "Murder is wrong" is false as it stands, for the kind of reasons that Mackie identifies. But the claim "*In the moral fiction*, murder is wrong" is true: morality as a whole is still false, according to the fictionalist, but it is undeniable that it is part of the system that we call morality to see murder as wrong.

The fictionalist revival of Mackie's error theory raises further questions. One obvious question is how the moral fictionalist can tell the difference between two different activities: *making moral claims* and *describing the content of moral systems*. (Another important contemporary version of fictionalism, about mathematical "truths", faces a parallel problem.) When I say things such as "In the moral system, murder is wrong" this sounds like *description*; it does not sound as if I am *advocating* the view that "Murder is wrong". "In the moral system" is a phrase that naturally prompts the question: in *whose* moral system? Hence the claim that begins with the preface "In the moral system …" seems more similar to claims such as "*In the Vikings' moral system*, murder was not wrong" or "*In the Mafia's moral system*, murder is sometimes obligatory" than to what we ordinarily mean by saying, with no preface, that "Murder is wrong". The effect of the preface is, apparently, to turn an ethical claim into an anthropological or sociological one. The only way to avoid this effect, it seems, is to drop the preface altogether. But does dropping the preface not mean dropping moral fictionalism?

Sections 7.1–7.2 have raised a series of questions for two sorts of ethical subjectivism, expressivism and error theory. These questions have been about how expressivism and error theory can offer a positive account of the nature of moral judgement: of what we are talking about when we make ethical claims. If expressivists and error theorists cannot give good answers to these questions, then perhaps no kind of ethical subjectivist will be able to give a convincing positive account of the nature of moral judgement.

But then, what positive account of the nature of moral judgement can the ethical objectivist give? I have already said that the ethical objectivist just treats moral judgements as expressing beliefs: beliefs that are capable of objective truth. But that on its own hardly adds up to a substantive positive account of the nature of moral judgement.

What more can an ethical objectivist say, and how can he answer the problems that ethical subjectivists pose for him? In the remaining sections of this chapter, I shall explore some alternatives.

7.3 Divine command theory

According to the ancient form of ethical objectivism known as divine command theory, what we are talking about when we talk about ethics is *God's will*. The real content of moral discourse consists in claims about what God commands, what God permits and what God forbids. So if we want to understand why some things are right, others wrong, and others again neither right nor wrong, it is God's will that we need to understand.

One very familiar objection to the divine-command view of the content of ethical discourse is the so-called "Euthyphro dilemma". According to this objection, in Plato's dialogue the *Euthyphro* the sceptical Socrates meets the credulous Euthyphro, a rather sanctimonious divine-command theorist, and sets him this question: "Is what is good, good because God loves it? Or does God love it because it is good?". But Euthyphro – so the objection goes – cannot take the first alternative: that what is good is good because God loves it. For if that were true, then the content of the good would be set by God's loving it, which would make the nature of the good arbitrary. Nor, however, can Euthyphro take the second alternative: that God loves what is good because it is good. For then the nature of goodness is already set before God's love comes into the picture, and so we do not need God's commands to know what goodness is. Either way, the conclusion is, divine commands cannot set the content of ethics.

Although the "Euthyphro dilemma" is a popular objection to the divine-command view, it seems to face two major problems of its own. First, the "Euthyphro dilemma" is arguably not in the *Euthyphro*. Secondly, the "Euthyphro dilemma" is arguably not a dilemma.

The first of these problems raises exegetical issues about Plato that I do not want to go into here. I will just note that, for one thing, Socrates seems like the last person to oppose divine-command ethics, since he himself spends his life obeying a divine command (see *Euthyphro* 3a10–b5). And for another thing, the proposal that Socrates and Euthyphro are discussing in the dialogue is not a proposal to give an account of the content of ethics in terms of "what [the Judaeo Christian] God wills", but a proposal to give a definition of the virtue of holiness in terms of "what the [ancient Greek] gods love". We should be wary of thinking that a good argument against the latter proposal is equally convincing against the former.

As for the second problem: if theistic ethicists are asked to choose between saying "God's will determines the good" and saying that "The good determines God's will", it seems that they are not trapped in a dilemma at all, because they can take either horn with impunity. There need be no serious problem for theistic ethicists in saying that "God's will determines the good", provided they do not also say that God's will is (what we would call) arbitrary. But any intelligent and civilized theist is hardly likely to say that anyway. Nor need there be any serious problem for theistic ethicists in saying that "The good determines God's will", provided they do not also say that the good is something that pre-exists God, or that we do not need God's commands to know what goodness is. But, again, it is hard to see why a theistic ethicist would have to say the former; and the latter is unlikely to be true if God is omniscient and we are not.

What's more, theistic ethicists have a third option that looks better still. The "Euthyphro dilemma" presupposes that we have to choose between one order of determination, from ethics to God's will, and the opposite order, from God's will to ethics. But why should we accept either order? Compare triangles with three equal sides and three equal angles. Are these triangles equilateral because they are equiangular, or are they equiangular because they are equilateral? Both, in the sense that our minds might come to understand either property by understanding the other property first; and neither, in the sense that the two properties are necessarily and essentially conjoined. Get one, and you are bound to get the other as well, as you will see as soon as you understand either property properly. Likewise, the theist can say, with the properties "what God wills" and "what is good". By starting with either, you can get to the other; but neither of them "controls" the other in such a way as to give us a single clear direction of determination holding between them. (Still less should we presuppose, as many presentations of the "Euthyphro dilemma" seem to, that there must be an order of *temporal* priority between God's will and ethics, as if God might at some time have said, "What shall I do today? Oh, I know, I'll create ethics".) The "Euthyphro dilemma" clearly opens up some interesting questions for divine command theories of the content of ethics. But, it seems, we may reasonably doubt that it really raises much of a difficulty.

However, that is not to say that divine command theories face no difficulties. The obvious difficulty about the claim that the content of ethics is determined by God's commands is simply: which God, and which commands? To choose *which God* (or gods) we are talking about as issuing the commands in question is to choose between the world's religions. To choose *which commands* we take to be divinely issued is to choose between different interpretations of one or more of these religions. Neither is a choice that I propose to try to take in a book on ethics.

All religions that claim to involve a revelation need methods of deciding what God's commands actually are. Some of these methods are specific to religion, for example investigating the correct interpretation of a holy text, and so I have nothing to say about them here. But another method of determining God's commands is to assume the goodness of God and then ask whether some supposed divine command is ethically good or acceptable. (If there is anywhere where anything like the "Euthyphro dilemma" *does* have some genuine bite, it is presumably here: in the predicament of the believer who, like Abraham with his knife poised over Isaac (Genesis 22), has to decide whether to obey what he thinks is God's command, or instead to do what seems to him to be right.) In this sense, divine command ethics seems not to stand on its own as an account of the content of ethical discourse. It points us beyond itself, to other ways of thinking about ethics. And we shall follow this direction.

7.4 Moral perception

It seems, then, that the ethical objectivist should not look to divine command theory to give him his answer to the question "What are we talking about, when we talk about ethics?"; or, at any rate, that he cannot get everything he needs by looking to divine command theory alone.

So where else might he look? Well, one place he might look is to the notion of moral perception. Since this is the main place where I myself think he should look, I shall indulge myself by developing this notion a little here. (For a longer and slightly more technical version of the argument, see Chappell [2008].)

As we have seen, moral objectivism is widely supposed to have a problem with ontological extravagance: it is accused of giving us too many properties, too wild and exuberant a profusion of kinds of thing and kinds of property, compared with the sober ontology of "science" (or, rather, of philosophical naturalism). But this charge seems not to be well placed; apparently we can rest quite a strong form of moral objectivism on an extremely thin ontological basis. We can do this even if we begin with maximal ontological parsimony: say, with a world in which nothing exists except the void and, in it, the following sixteen-dot matrix:

What ontology could be more minimal (except, presumably, one with fewer dots)? But notice that even this ontological minimalism sustains an indefinite multiplicity and complexity of patterns. If these sixteen dots exist thus arranged, then it is immediately not the case that *only* these sixteen dots exist. There also exists every pattern that these sixteen dots constitute. After all, a capacity that perceived the sixteen-dot matrix as four four-dot squares would be picking up a pattern that is genuinely there in the matrix, whether you notice it or not. So would a capacity that perceived it as a four-dot square inside a twelve-dot square; and a capacity that perceived it as a twelve-dot cross against a background sketched in by the four corner-dots; and one that perceived it as three vertical or three horizontal corridors; and so on. There is no limit to the patterns that we can find in the diagram, beyond those set by our ingenuity, imagination or mathematical/geometrical aptitude. And find, not create, seems to be the right word: the patterns would still be there even if we did not see them.

Obviously, the world is a good deal more ontologically complex – even on the simplest and most reductive reading of what counts as "the world" – than a sixteen-dot matrix. So the world contains far more patterns than those in the sixteen-dot matrix. And these patterns are really there in the world: or at any rate, they are just as much really there in the world as the dot patterns listed in the previous paragraph are really there in the sixteen-dot matrix.

Notice that we can treat patterns as *properties* of such matrices; and that recognition of such patterns is a kind of *perception.* Perhaps not all properties are patterns (or *vice versa*), and perhaps not all perception is pattern-recognition (or *vice versa*). Still, certainly some pattern-recognition is perception. For example, seeing a face is perception, and so is reading; seeing something as a group of four is perception, and so is understanding another speaker; and so on for many other cases of pattern-recognition.

This sort of perception can be contrasted with what we can call *inference.* Inference is active, perception passive. In inference, I set my mind to work something out, whereas in perception, something "just comes to me": I am subject to an occurrence that I do not make happen, except in the minimal sense in which I can, for example, choose in which direction I look. Inference is experienced as structured, perception as simple: to perform an inference is, normally, to run through a number of steps of reasoning, whereas perceiving something is a step-less, instantaneous whole. So perception is quick where inference is slow: perceiving something can happen instantaneously, inferring something normally takes time.

Furthermore, a series of inferential moves may be available that explain *why* I have a given perception. For example, going back to the sixteen-dot matrix, it is the configuration of the dots that explains why I perceive four four-dot squares, or one twelve-dot cross, if I do. However, there is more phenomenologically speaking to either perception than there is to the inference. Inference does not have any characteristic *feel* to it; there is nothing in particular "that it is like" to work out why I see a twelve-dot cross in the sixteen-dot matrix. By contrast, there *is* something "that it is like" to see that cross: seeing the cross in the matrix *does* have a particular experiential feel.

Perception, in this sense, is a quick, "analogue" route to many of the same epistemic destinations as can also be reached via the "digital" route of inference. It gets us there with a useful speed, directness and a vividness that grounds, and in favourable cases justifies, a sense of certainty.

For all we can tell, then, the instantiation-base of some remarkably complex and recherché types of patterns or properties might be remarkably metaphysically minimal. It might be like this, for instance, with the patterns that form *moral properties*. As David McNaughton suggests:

> We might suppose that the only properties that can be observed are the "proper objects" of the five senses: touch, shape, and texture; hearing, sound, and so on. If we adopt this austere account of what can be perceived it is clear that not only moral properties but a great many of the things we normally take ourselves to perceive will be, strictly speaking, unobservable. If, on the other hand, we are prepared to allow that I can see that this cliff is dangerous, that Smith is worried, or that one thing is further away than another, then there seems no reason to be squeamish about letting in moral observation. (1988: 57)

As McNaughton says, there is no profit in restricting perception to sensation in the way that he describes. For this restriction on perception excludes not only moral perception, but many other sorts of perception in the wide sense of pattern-recognition or *Gestalt*-uptake (*representational* perception, as we may call it). Nor, I suggest, is that restriction well motivated by a concern for ontological modesty. If at least some properties are patterns, and at least some perception is pattern-recognition, then there can be perception of properties that has a very modest ontological base indeed: maybe even as modest as my sixteen-dot matrix. Since such perception is so modestly based, it does not face the worry about ontological extravagance. If moral perception is one example of this sort of perception, then there is no good reason why moral perception should face the ontological-extravagance worry any more than any other example of the kind.

This picture of moral epistemology and metaphysics is not just a bare possibility for the realist. It is an attractive possibility, because it gives him good answers to some of the most familiar problems that he faces, including some of those already discussed here and in Chapters 5 and 6. Here, in Mackie's words, are two of the best-known:

> If there were objective values, then they would be entities or qualities or relations of a very strange sort, utterly different from anything else in the universe. Correspondingly, if we were aware

93

of them, it would have to be by some special faculty of moral perception or intuition, utterly different from our ordinary ways of knowing everything else.   (1977: 38)

Mackie sets the realist a puzzle about moral metaphysics: what could moral properties possibly be? And he sets the realist a puzzle about moral epistemology: how we could possibly know about moral properties? On the picture of properties and perception that I have just sketched, neither of these puzzles seems very puzzling at all. Moral properties can be just what many other properties are: patterns in reality. And our knowledge of moral properties can be representational perception, in just the sense that, in McNaughton's example, seeing that a cliff is dangerous can be representational perception.

If we ask where moral properties are supposed to fit into a scientific world-picture, the answer is that there is nothing in a scientific world-picture to exclude the possibility that the world's constituents should be reasonably perceived as standing in patterns that are not themselves used in scientific explanations. Likewise, if we ask how moral properties relate to the properties that science does use in its explanations, the answer is simply that moral properties and scientific properties are two different types of pattern that are both found in the same world. Of course, there will be no perceiving these patterns without an evolutionary and cultural history that is suitable for the emergence of the requisite perceptual capacities. But given obvious and familiar facts about our own culture, which is easier to say: that we cannot conceive how these perceptual capacities might possibly have developed; or that just such perceptual capacities apparently *have* developed – so obviously *can* have developed?

If all this is correct, then it gives us a clear and distinctive objectivist answer to the question "What are we talking about, when we talk about ethics?". The answer is that we are talking about moral perceptions. Perhaps not exclusively about them, but they are one of the things that we are talking about. What else might we be talking about? I say a little about that in §7.5.

7.5 Three other bases for ethical objectivity

In the previous section I argued briefly for what we may call *perceptualism*, the position that I myself think constitutes the best answer for the objectivist to give to the question "What is moral discourse about?":

Perceptualism: The real content of moral discourse consists in claims about what beings that are capable of moral perception may or may not morally perceive they should do, think or be.

Perceptualism is not the only possible answer that the objectivist might give to that question. Here, in very quick summary, are three other possible answers:

- *Biological naturalism:* The real content of moral discourse consists in claims about what contributes to the well-being of human beings, considered broadly as a species in biology (and possibly to other similar species).
- *Welfarist naturalism:* The real content of moral discourse consists in claims about what contributes to the happiness/pleasure/preference-satisfaction of human beings (and possibly to other beings capable of happiness/pleasure/preference-satisfaction).
- *Rationalism:* The real content of moral discourse consists in claims about what beings that are responsive to reasons have reason to do, think or be.

Whichever way we choose between them, one or two points about these four alternatives are worth noting. First, the alternatives are not exclusive of each other. Ethics could be about what contributes to human biological well-being, *and* also about what reason-responsive beings have reason to do, think and be; for these could be the same. Likewise, ethics could be about *both* what contributes to happiness, *and also* about what we morally perceive; for these could be the same too. In fact all four alternatives could get us to the same subject matter for ethics; indeed, all four of these alternatives *plus* divine command theory (§7.3) could get us to the same subject matter. These and other alternatives do not have to compete against each other (although, as we shall see, they often end up in competition).

A second point to notice is that there are interestingly close cor-relations between these different views about what ethical objectivity comes to and different views in normative ethical theory. By saying that, I do not mean to imply that ethical subjectivists cannot hold positive views about normative ethical theory; of course they can. Nonetheless, there are some clear connections and affinities between these four ways of spelling out ethical objectivism, and four or more styles of ethical theory. Thus biological naturalism fits well together with virtue ethics; welfaristic naturalism fits well with utilitarianism; rationalism fits well with Kantianism or contractarianism; and perceptualism fits well both with the moral theory called intuitionism, and also with the anti-moral-theory view that I shall eventually develop in Chapter 11.

In that sense, this chapter's discussion has paved the way for my dis-cussion of these alternatives in normative ethical theory in the rest of this book. In Chapter 8 I turn to the first of them that I shall consider: virtue ethics.

8

Virtue ethics

[We might] look for "norms" in human virtues: just as *man* has so many
teeth, which is certainly not the average number of teeth men have, but is
the number of teeth for the species, so perhaps the species *man*, regarded
not just biologically, but from the point of view of the activity of thought
and choice in regard to the various departments of life – powers and fac-
ulties and use of things needed – "has" such and such virtues: and this
"man" with the complete set of virtues is the "norm", as "man" with, e.g.,
a complete set of teeth is a norm.

(G. E. M. Anscombe, "Modern Moral Philosophy",
in Geach & Gormally 2005: 188)

8.1 Introducing normative ethics

The central question of ethics, with which I began this book, is "How
should life be lived?". That question raises further questions about truth
and falsity, subjectivity and objectivity, the meaning of ethical claims,
and what the world has to be like for them to be capable of being true.
These questions form the agenda of meta-ethics, which I have been
pursuing in the previous three chapters especially.

The last of these meta-ethical questions was "What are we talking
about when we make moral assertions?". Among the possible ways
of answering this, as we saw, are the views that the content of moral
discourse is shaped by our nature as a zoological species (*biological*

naturalism); by what contributes to our happiness (*welfarist naturalism*); by what reason tells us to do, think, or be (*rationalism*); and by what moral perception tells us to do, think, or be (*intuitionism*). As I pointed out, alongside these possible views about the content of moral discourse there stand possible views about the shape of normative ethical theory: virtue ethics, utilitarianism, Kantianism or contractarianism, and intuitionism, respectively.

In this way our discussion of meta-ethics brings us back to the central ethical question, "How should life be lived?". In Chapters 8–10 I shall be asking whether there is a moral theory that gives a good answer to this question. To assess this I shall describe and examine four moral theories in turn: virtue ethics, utilitarianism, Kantianism and contractarianism. My conclusion, to be developed in full in Chapter 11, will be that all four theories have something to teach us; but none of them can teach us everything. For an adequate answer to the question how to live, we need to look elsewhere than to moral theory; we need to develop the (broadly intuitionist) idea of what I shall call *an ethical outlook* (see §11.3).

But first, the moral theories. Here is how I briefly summarized them in §3.1:

- *Virtue ethics:* An action is right iff it is what a virtuous agent would characteristically do in the circumstances. Virtuous agents characteristically act in accordance with the virtues (in the West, the traditional list is: courage, self-control, justice, wisdom, faith, hope and love), and never act in accordance with the vices (the traditional list is: pride, avarice, lust, envy, gluttony, wrath and sloth).
- *Utilitarianism:* An action is right iff it promotes the greatest happiness of the greatest number.
- *Kantianism:* An action is right iff it is in accordance with a universalizable principle, and not contrary to any universalizable principle. So we should never do anything that we cannot rationally will could be done by anyone, and we should treat other people as ends in themselves, never merely as means.
- *Contractarianism:* An action is right iff it is required by the code that all rational persons would agree to in a free negotiation. So we should never do anything to others unless they could reasonably

agree to our doing it to them. Conversely, we should not let others do to us what we cannot reasonably agree to their doing to us.

A preliminary point about all four of these definitions is that they all focus on *right action*. But any worthwhile moral theory will need to be more general than this, in two ways. First, it will have to tell us not only what is right, but also what is wrong and what is permissible. Secondly, it will have to tell us not only about action, but also about response, emotion, character, outlook and way of life in general.

The first of these two generalizations seems quite easy to accommodate. Wrongness and permissibility can both be defined in terms of rightness: what is wrong is what it is right not to do, and what is permissible is what it is neither right nor wrong to do.

The second generalization is a little more controversial, especially in virtue ethics. Some virtue ethicists (e.g. Annas 1993) think that it is a mistake to focus moral theory on action at all, and have called their own theory "agent-centred", and other theories "act-centred", to bring out their own emphasis on character-assessments rather than act-assessments. This redirection of our attention to the importance of character is a useful corrective to the tendency of some moral theory earlier in the twentieth century, Hare's for example, to think about the moral assessment of actions almost exclusively, and hardly ever say much about character. It is of course possible to go too far the other way, and think about character only and never about actions.

These preliminaries aside, I turn to the first of these theories: virtue ethics.

8.2 "Act in accordance with nature"

How should life be lived? At the heart of virtue ethics lies a simple but (when you unpack it) surprisingly powerful answer to this book's basic question, which we can express in a two-word slogan: *act naturally*. This slogan is ambiguous. "Act naturally" can mean "act in accordance with nature" (a motto of Cicero's; *de Finibus* 1.56). It can also mean "act spontaneously". Virtue ethicists have both meanings in mind, and there is a good deal to say about both. Let us begin with the idea of acting in accordance with nature.

As I spell out what virtue ethics has to say about this, it should become obvious how this idea enables virtue ethicists to answer the previous chapter's question, "What are we talking about when we engage in moral discourse?", with a *biological naturalist* account: we are talking about what contributes to the welfare of human beings, considered as a zoological species.

If you want to know how life should be lived, then an obvious place to start is by thinking about what kind of creature you are, and what kind of life suits a creature like you: what kind of life satisfies the sort of needs (on the one hand) and goals (on the other) that creatures like you typically have.

For instance, if you are a blue whale, the answer to "How should life be lived?" that works for you will include plenty of plankton, cool deep unpolluted oceans, the company of other blue whales, and a complete absence of Japanese fishing vessels. Or if you are a male cheetah, the applicable answer to "How should life be lived?" will specify the company of hardly any other cheetahs except at mating time (when a good supply of females and a short supply of males will be desirable), the availability of gazelles or other suitable prey, wide-open unpolluted savannahs or forests, and so on.

Likewise if you are a human being, at least part of the answer that you should give to the question "How should life be lived?" will be about the things that accommodate and fulfil human nature, that facilitate or enhance typically human strengths or aspirations, and that deal with or correct for typically human weaknesses: "The virtues are concerned with what we find *difficult*" (Aquinas, *Summa Theologiae* 2a2ae.58.12.3; cf. Aristotle, *Nicomachean Ethics* 1105a9); "Men need the virtues as bees need their stings" (Geach 1977: 17).

We have a pretty good idea what sort of things the characteristic human weaknesses, needs and goals are. Indeed we have a better idea, given the "inside knowledge" that comes from the fact that we *are* human beings, than we do for blue whales or cheetahs. The facts about blue whales and cheetahs that I have just mentioned are obvious facts of zoology or natural history. It is also an obvious fact (if you like, it is also a fact of natural history) that human beings are by nature intelligent, playful, curious, adventurous, aggressive, social, land-dwelling, diurnal, omnivorous, sexually reproducing, impatient, self-assertive animals who do not cope well with extremes of heat, cold, humidity or aridity, nor with extremes of loneliness or crowdedness, excitement or monotony, exertion or inactivity.

Just to specify these simple zoological or quasi-zoological facts is already to be well on the way to at least an outline account of a life in accordance with human nature. To complete that account, we can add more detail of this species-specific sort. We can also add some details of the kind that seem to be true for almost any species. Whatever species a creature may belong to, pleasure, health, opportunities to eat and to satisfy other bodily needs, contentment, interest/stimulation and so forth are pretty certain to be ingredients of the life that accommodates and fulfils its nature. And pain, disease, hunger, fear and boredom are pretty certain not to be. Any species' natural needs and goals feed into our account of what sort of life is good for that species; including the human species. As Foot likes to point out:

> It is necessary for plants to have water, for birds to build nests, for wolves to hunt in packs, and for lionesses to teach their cubs to kill … human defects and excellences are similarly related to what human beings are and what they do. We do not need to be able to dive like gannets, nor to see in the dark like owls; but our memory and concentration must be such as to allow us to learn language, and our sight must be such that we can recognise faces at a glance; while, like lionesses, human parents are defective if they do not teach their young the skills that they need to survive. Moreover, in that we are social animals, we depend on each other as do wolves that hunt in packs, with cooperation such as our own depending on special factors such as conventional arrangements.   (2001: 15–16)

For Foot's style of virtue ethics, the starting-point for understanding how life should be lived is the fact that we are human beings, individuals of one particular zoological species. The sort of life we ought to live is the life that fulfils *human* needs and goals; the good life is the good life for human beings, considered as one kind of animals among others. And the virtues are the character traits (dispositions, as philosophers call them) that we need to live this good life. Here is Foot again:

It seems clear that the virtues are, in some general way, beneficial. Humans do not get on very well without them. Nobody can get on well if he lacks courage, and does not have some measure of temperance and wisdom, while communities where justice and charity are lacking are apt to be wretched places to live, as Russia was under the Stalinist terror, or Sicily under the Mafia.

(1977: 2–3)

If Foot is right, then dispositions such as courage, temperance (i.e. self-control), wisdom, justice and charity stand to living well as dispositions such as strength, agility and speed stand to playing tennis well. The former are the dispositions that you need for a good human life, just as the latter are the dispositions that you need for a successful tennis career. Just as we might call strength, agility, speed and so on the *tennis-playing* virtues, so we can call courage, self-control, wisdom and the rest the *human* virtues; or, since we are human beings, just the virtues, full stop.

Two questions arise at this point:

(i) Why *these* dispositions, particularly? Why should we say that the virtues are courage, self-control, wisdom, justice, and charity (or love) – rather than any other dispositions?

(ii) Why *dispositions,* particularly? If we are looking for a way to connect our choices with the ideal of the good life that they aim at, why not just aim our choices *directly* at that ideal? That is, why do we need the intermediate link via the sort of qualities and character traits that I have just been talking about?

The answer to question (i) is not a simple matter. In part, the virtue ethicist will need to answer it by explaining why courage, self-control, justice, wisdom and love are the virtues, and ferocity, self-indulgence, injustice, calculation and selfishness are *not* the virtues. To explain this is to address another form of the why-be-moral problem, which I have discussed already in Chapter 3.

Another part of what the virtue ethicist will need to do to answer question (i) is to show us how virtues are different (if they are) from other dispositions "without which the good life will not be accessible". Not all of these dispositions fit our intuitive sense of what counts as a virtue. For example, the good life will not be accessible – not at all easily, anyway – to any human being who suffers from deep long-term depression. Being free from deep long-term depression is (I suppose) a kind of disposition, or a collective term for a range of dispositions. But it surely does not deserve to be called a *virtue*; nor does being depressed deserve to be called a *vice*. Again, whether or not there is life after death, the human good life is not accessible to the dead. And being alive is also (I suppose) a kind of disposition. But it looks absurd to say that being alive is a virtue, or that being dead is a vice. And so on for many other dispositions, including some of the ones that I called "tennis-playing virtues" above. Being agile, having strength and stamina and good hand–eye coordination, are all dispositions that are likely to help us to access the good life. It might be right to call such things *tennis players'* virtues, but it hardly seems right to put them in our list of *human* virtues: the list of virtues, *period*.

Whether virtue ethicists have the right to exclude these counter-intuitive examples depends on how they define virtue. Some phil-osophers have offered definitions of virtue that actively encourage an (over-?)generous list of virtues. Hume, for example, famously defines virtue as whatever dispositions observers approve of: "The hypothesis which we embrace is plain. It maintains that morality is determined by sentiment. It defines virtue to be whatever mental action or quality gives to a spectator the pleasing sentiment of approbation; and vice the contrary" ([1776] 1977: Appendix 1). As his critics immediately pointed out, this suggests that Hume must count dispositions like not being depressed, hand–eye coordination, and being alive as virtues.

Other philosophers with an interest in the virtues, Foot and Aristotle among them, have suggested that our notion of what counts as a virtue will be more useful if it is narrower than the notion that Hume suggests. These philosophers point out that we do not just find virtues *agreeable*. We also base praise and blame on them, which we do not do with being alive or being depressed or having good hand–eye coordination. The virtues presuppose *responsibility*; as Foot puts it, "virtues belong to the will" (1977: 4).

Now I turn to question (ii): why should it be *dispositions*, particularly, that make the link between our choices and the concept of the good life? This interesting question brings us on to the second sense of "act nat-urally" that I distinguished earlier in this chapter: "act spontaneously". I turn to it now.

8.3 "Act spontaneously": the modularity of practical choice

Obviously enough, virtue ethics gets its name from the fact that virtue ethicists are particularly interested in the virtues. They think that having the right dispositions, the virtues, is a crucial part of what you need to get the good life; either because the virtues are a *means* to the good life, or because the virtues are a *constituent* of the good life, or for both reasons. (This is the instrumental–constitutive distinction again, which we saw in §5.1.)

Of course, virtue ethicists need not say that the virtues are *all* you need to get the good life. A disposition is a tendency to act or behave in a certain way. As Aristotle remarks (*Nicomachean Ethics* 1098b34–1009a3), it is no use having that tendency if you never activate it. This is one reason why an "agent-centred ethics" (§8.1) would seem to be missing something if it had nothing at all to say about acts: because a "virtue" that never leads to virtuous action is not really a virtue at all. Compare our tennis player again. There is no point saying that he has really good hand–eye coordination, except that it lets him down every single time he actually plays tennis. If the tennis player cannot reliably *act* on the dispositions involved in good hand–eye coordination he cannot claim to *have* them.

What virtue ethicists are committed to is an idea that I shall call the *modularity of practical choice*. To explain what I mean by that label, here are four little stories: "War", "Hospital", "Desert" and "Immigrant".

- *War.* A good person finds himself in a war. His friend has just been wounded by gunfire in no-man's-land. The wound is serious, there is no one else to bring his friend back behind the lines for medical treatment, and the enemy artillery is beginning to bombard the sector where the wounded man lies, so that to leave him there is almost certainly to leave him to die. In this situation, a good person will act spontaneously. He will crawl out into no-man's-land, and come back with his wounded friend on his back if he comes back at all. By so doing, the good person will display the virtue of *courage*.
- *Hospital.* A good person learns that his friend is in hospital. Spontaneously, the good person will feel a rush of pity and concern for his friend, and dash off to visit him. By so doing, the good person will display the virtue of *love*. (Compare Stocker's hospital-visiting example, as discussed in Ch. 4.)

- *Desert.* A good person is alone in the desert with his friend, with very little water to share between them. Despite his raging thirst, there is something that the good person will spontaneously *not* do: he will not take more than his share of the dwindling water supply. Indeed, until he is truly desperate with thirst, it will not even occur to him to do so. By so doing, the good person will display the virtues of *self-control* and *justice*.

- *Immigrant.* A good person is hoping to give consolation and a listening ear (there being nothing more practical that he can do) to an immigrant friend who, like far too many immigrants to Britain these days, is facing the brutal routine of 4 am arrest and forcible deportation. The good person knows that the immigrant is in this plight, but the immigrant does not know that he knows, and is liable to be secretive about his difficulty because he feels ashamed about it. The good person happens to know, also, that the immigrant has been to see the authorities about his case today, so innocently asks him, "I saw you in town today; were you out shopping?" Hesitantly, the immigrant replies "Yes, … yes, shopping; that's right". The good person, correctly seeing this as a sign that the immigrant does not want to talk about his troubles, again spontaneously will *not* do something: he will not barge in and contradict his immigrant friend ("No you weren't, you were talking to Immigration. Tell me about it"). By not barging in and contradicting him, the good person will display the virtue of *wisdom* (or, if you like, discretion).

In each of these four cases, someone acts virtuously, in a praiseworthy or desirable or meritorious way – in "War" and "Desert", even in a heroic way – without having to think or reason his way to the conclusion that this is what he should do. The good action, as we say, *comes naturally to him*. That it comes naturally is the work of his virtues in him: his virtues "programme" him for good action, and leave bad actions as ones that "go against the grain" for him. The bad actions that he could have done in these situations have become out of character, unnatural or simply unappealing to him. Or, more radically, they have become options that are not on his radar at all: options that would not even occur to him. At the extreme, the good person can see certain options as *unthinkable* or *impossible* even if they are proposed to him by someone else (he would never propose them himself). If you suggest to him that he leave his friend to die in "War", or poison his friend to ensure that there is enough water for himself in "Desert", the good person will not only not have thought of doing such a thing: he will be appalled that *you* have thought of it. And if you can get him so much as to contemplate your proposal, his only response will be to tell you – fiercely – that such a deed is absolutely out of the question.

And this is the point of the idea of "the modularity of practical choice". The scope of a good person's deliberation will often be radically narrower than a certain sort of moral theorist might be predisposed to imagine. Perhaps, in "Hospital", the good person will decide that it is a good idea to take a gift to his bedridden friend, and so have to decide whether he should take (a) chocolates, (b) grapes, (c) roses, or just (d) an amusingly vulgar card. But in "Hospital" there is also the possibility that the good person should take his friend (e) *poisoned* chocolates, or (f) *exploding* grapes, or (g) a dead badger, or (h) *Trainspotter's Weekly*, and so on indefinitely. There are many other possibilities about what he might take his bedridden friend, perhaps infinitely many.

What the modularity of practical choice means is that a good person, as the virtue ethicist understands him, does not even need to raise the possibilities from (e) onwards for deliberation. If anyone else raises possibilities such as (e–h), he will treat them with the bemusement that they deserve.

In this, once more, he bears comparison with the tennis player. Sometimes a tennis player does deliberate. Perhaps, for instance, his opponent has put a high angled lob to the back of the court behind him, and there is time to decide, while back-pedalling to field the shot, whether to play it on the backhand, or run round it and take it on the forehand. Our tennis player might have time to work out, by conscious calculation, which of those two alternatives is the better option. What he almost certainly will *not* do is reason that – since he could also deliberately top-edge the ball, or play it off his racquet-handle, or through his legs, or see if the umpire notices if he kicks it back over the net (etc.) – therefore he had better think about these alternatives too before making his shot. He will not reason like this because these are *poor* alternatives. In all probability they will not even enter a good tennis player's head.

Contrast the understanding of how a good person should deliberate that you would get if you asked a moral-theory-minded advisor whom

I shall call the *ethical rationalist*. According to the ethical rationalist, no choice can be a rationally defensible one unless it involves you in think-ing through *all* the possibilities, and having a good reason for rejecting *all* the possibilities that you do in fact reject. (This is what I mean by calling him a *rationalist*.) Every possible alternative is one that the good person should at least consider. As far as the stupid or wicked possibili-ties go, he should dismiss them, no doubt; but he should consider them *before* he dismisses them. After all, if he does not consider them, how can he know whether or not to dismiss them?

By the definition of his position, the ethical rationalist is committed to the view that reason should concern itself with *everything*; should fix, in every situation, on the thing to do out of *all* the alternatives; and should arrive at its conclusions about what to do on the basis of reason alone. So it looks as if the ethical rationalist's good person has a big deliberative task ahead of him. The virtue ethicist can just *help himself* to the idea that the good person will deliberate only between a small range of good alternatives, because those are the alternatives that his good dispositions naturally point him towards. A person who has a virtue will make his choices between the options that the virtue makes salient to him. So in "Hospital", a good person will be asking himself a question such as "Shall I take my friend roses or grapes or chocolates?" The possibility of taking his friend poisoned chocolates is simply not on the good person's deliberative agenda. By contrast, the ethical rational-ist is stuck with the idea that the good person will have to consider and evaluate even the craziest options, with just the same seriousness as he considers and evaluates the best and wisest options, before he makes his choice between them.

The point is not that ethical rationalism makes the wrong predic-tions about which options good people will choose. The ethical ration-alist is entitled to say that the good person (or at any rate, the *ideally* good person) will come out, in the end, with the right conclusion. The point is rather that the ethical rationalist's picture of how the good per-son gets to good conclusions is completely unrealistic, in that no one actually *does* reason in anything like the way that the ethical rationalist supposes. Perhaps it is actually impossible, in that no one even *could* reason like this because, in any actual situation, there are just too many out-of-the-way possibilities for action for it to be practicable for us to do the reasoning to eliminate them all.

More generally (the virtue ethicist will say), ethical rationalism praises the wrong things, and virtue ethics praises the right things. Ethical rationalism praises the deliberator who works his way rationally through all the options, and comes up with the right answer about which one he ought to be taking, by sheer computational power. Virtue ethics, by contrast, praises the deliberator who deliberates *virtuously*: that is, in ways that are prompted by, and that exemplify, the virtues.

To say that, for virtue ethics, good deliberation is *virtuous* deliberation might seem empty. But we can now see how it has content. The real content of the concept of virtuous deliberation rapidly appears when we start to put the adjectives corresponding to particular virtues into the place held by the adjective "virtuous". Attributes such as courage, self-control, love, wisdom and justice are the kinds of attributes that we praise people for having, and for displaying in action and in deliberation. Virtue ethicists can say that their moral theory gives a very plausible account of these points: much more plausible than the account suggested by ethical rationalism.

Hence one interesting consequence of the modularity of practical choice is that virtue ethics will often tell us to praise two ways of acting that are frequently condemned, namely acting on our emotions, and acting without thinking. Virtue ethics says, for instance, that the right way for the good person to act in "Hospital" is *on his emotions*. He feels a surge of compassion and love for his bedridden friend, and according to virtue ethics, it is entirely right for him to be carried away by that surge. He *should* dash off and visit his friend simply on the basis of that emotion, and he would act less well if he acted on any other basis.

The virtues give us a natural way of accommodating the modularity of practical choice. For it is the role of the virtues to make ethical deliberation modular, by dividing it into two separate modules. Ethical deliberation, according to virtue ethics, is not a matter of consciously looking at all the possibilities on the same footing, and deciding between them by evaluating them all at once. Rather, a different mental "module" – our virtues or our vices, depending on whether we are good people or bad – *pre-selects* which possibilities, out of all the indefinitely many that are available for deliberation, the agent will actually deliberate between (if and when the agent needs to deliberate at all). Only after the virtues have made this pre-selection do we get to the second module: the quite different stage of conscious deliberation (see Table 2).

Table 2

Options actually available: →	Options selected for deliberation by virtue: →	Option selected for action by deliberation:
Giving my friend roses Giving my friend chocolates Giving my friend a rude card that will make him laugh Giving my friend poisoned chocolates Giving my friend a bag of horse-manure → Giving my friend all of the above Giving my friend nothing Giving my friend a copy of *Trainspotters' Weekly* (even though he has no interest in trainspotting) Giving my friend a dead badger ...	Giving my friend roses Giving my friend chocolates Giving my friend a rude card that will make him laugh Giving my friend some or all of the above Giving my friend nothing	→ Giving my friend chocolates and a rude card that will make him laugh
In the world →	In deliberation →	In decision

Before we even get to the conscious process of choosing our actions, which is the business of deliberation, our virtues have, in a quite different and modularly separate way, already done a great deal of *unconscious* choosing for us. They have eliminated all but a tiny proportion of our possible alternatives, on the grounds that those alternatives are stupid (such as giving my friend horse manure) or wicked (such as giving my friend poisoned chocolates or shooting him) or irrelevant/inappropriate (such as giving him *Trainspotters' Weekly* or a dead badger). Since all this option-elimination goes on *unconsciously*, we do not even notice it. (You have just had the option of using this book as a missile to throw out of the window. If you are reading this, you did not take that option. And it is almost certain that, before you began this parenthesis, you had not even *noticed* that you had this option, unless of course you really dislike this book.)

For virtue ethics, deliberation is a conscious process of choice that takes place, when it needs to take place at all, against the background set by the unconscious choices that our virtues have already made for us. Such a view of deliberation could not be more different from the view that you find in ethical rationalism, according to which each and every choice needs to be made on explicit deliberation if it is so much as to count as rational.

But who holds the view I call ethical rationalism? You might expect that no serious theory of normative ethics would really hold that *every* rational choice must be preceded by an *explicit* act of deliberation. However, there are famous moral theorists who at least *can* be read this way: Kant and Bentham, for example. More about them in later chapters.

Actually it does not matter even if no moral theorist worth reading has ever really believed what I call ethical rationalism. Even if ethical rationalism is a fiction, thinking about it is useful because it brings out what the virtue ethicist means by telling us to "act naturally", in the sense of "spontaneously". Virtue ethics's modular account of deliberation shows us why we should sometimes prize spontaneous and unthinking action and, in many cases, should actually prefer it to carefully calculated and rationalized action. It also helps us to see why the virtue ethicist is so focused on the virtues, the good dispositions, in the first place. He is focused on them because the world is such a complicated place that the "modularity" that the virtues bring into our practical choices and deliberative processes is an indispensable means to the end of acting well at all.

This modularity, however, raises certain questions about virtue ethics. One question raised by philosophers such as Gilbert Harman and John Doris is whether, as a matter of empirical fact, the virtues do any real modularizing work at all (e.g. Harman 1999). According to Harman and his allies, it is the "fundamental attribution error" to think that character contributes more to agents' choices and behaviour than context does. They cite evidence from experimental psychology (Milgram's famous experiment is often mentioned here) tending to show that individual people are highly plastic, and mostly behave alike in similar contexts. In short, there *are* no virtues, just contexts. Harman's and Doris's opponents question their empirical data, and point out (first) that it is predicted by virtue ethics itself that agents will often fail to act virtuously, and (secondly) that it is a matter of common sense that people often act heroically, in ways that have everything to do with their characters, and nothing to do with their contexts; if social-psychology experiments cannot be designed to replicate that commonsensical result, then so much the worse for social-psychology experiments. This is an interesting debate, but a complex and (so far) inconclusive one, and I shall not pursue it further here.

There are other questions about the modularity of choice that we need to look at soon; also still awaiting our attention are some questions about virtue ethics that arose from the biological naturalism that I described in §8.2. In §8.4 I shall consider questions about biological naturalism, and in §8.5 questions about modularity.

8.4 Questions for virtue ethics I: naturalism

We might say that virtue ethics has a tendency to *smooth away differences.* Its response to this book's opening question, "How should life be lived?", is to focus on the whole of life, not just on some special sub-part of life, or on some special sort of assessment of our lives. On the virtue ethical approach, ethics just *is* thinking as clearly and as rationally as we can about our lives "in the round". There is not some special sort of ethical or moral assessment that can be radically separated from that kind of holistic practical thinking; ethical assessment just *is* holistic practical thinking. The supposed difference between them has been smoothed away.

At the other extreme from virtue ethics on this are ethicists such as Prichard, who does not smooth away this difference between moral thinking and practical thinking in general. Instead he makes it as stark as he can. In his famous essay "Does Moral Philosophy Rest Upon a Mistake?" (in Prichard 1949), Prichard tells us that it is a mistake even to raise the question "Why should I be moral?", because moral motivation is special and different from all other motivation. You either have it or you do not, and either way there is no point asking *why* you should be motivated that way. If you do not see that you have special moral reason to be moral, then no argument is going to get you to see it.

For virtue ethicists, by contrast, the question "Why should I be moral?" *has* to be asked, because moral rules and demands can only have any point if they are part of living well overall. Prichard's whole idea of a special sense of "moral" is a mistake. Morality or ethics becomes a matter of what Christopher Coope, commenting on the twentieth-century reception of Aristotle's foundational discussion of these issues in the *Nicomachean Ethics*, simply calls *good sense*:

> [G]ood sense was clearly the fundamental thing for the Greeks. They considered practical wisdom the master-virtue: man was a rational animal, and his excellence lay in rationality ... For years people had been saying: "But that can't have anything to do with ethics – it is just a matter of prudence!" [After the twentieth-century revival of virtue ethics we] were now to say (more or less): "That is not a matter of prudence – so it can have nothing to do with ethics!" ...
>
> ... The *Nicomachean Ethics* ... starts, and indeed ends, by taking up the tremendous question, what it is to be truly fortunate ... The notion of good sense in acting must be related to the answers we give. It has always been one of the key advantages of [virtue ethics] to have revived this issue. And it has been important that our account of flourishing and good fortune be uncontaminated with contemporary thoughts of "morality".   (2006a: 21–2, 24)

Ethicists such as Prichard – and Kant, with his separation between "action on inclination" and "action on duty" – see a huge gulf between moral motivation and other sorts of motivation. Virtue ethics denies that there is any such gap at all. An ethicist of Prichard's sort will say that the reason why we ought to be just, or loving, or truthful, is simply because this is what morality or duty demands. For virtue ethics, by contrast, there is a basis in human nature for claims such as "You ought to be just/loving/truthful". The reason why we should be just, or loving, or truthful, is because being like that is either instrumental (a *means*) to the good life for human beings, or constitutive (a *part*) of the good life for human beings, or quite possibly both (§5.1). It is the biological naturalism underlying virtue ethics that creates its tendency to smooth away the supposed difference between moral and other sorts of motivation or reasons.

Foot's meta-ethics is one clear example of this biological naturalism, so I shall focus on it in my discussion here.

"*There is no change in the meaning of 'good' between the word as it appears in 'good roots' and as it appears in 'good dispositions of the human will*'" (Foot 2001: 39, original emphasis). On Foot's view, human defects and excellences are related to what human beings are and do in something like the way in which a plant's or a bird's or a wolf's or a lioness's defects or excellences are related to what these things are and do. "[I]t is necessary for plants to have water, for birds to build nests, for wolves to hunt in packs, and for lionesses to teach their cubs to kill", and so an excellent wolf will not be a loner, and a lioness that does not teach her cubs to kill will be defective in something like the way in which a morally bad human being is defective. Here too a difference is being smoothed away by virtue ethics; this time it is the difference between moral badness and zoological dysfunctionality.

Foot's idea of deriving the moral from the zoological in this smooth fashion may seem vulnerable to that familiar philosopher's weapon, a trivial-or-false dilemma. To put her choices at their starkest, Foot might be saying either:

(i) that moral properties are the very same category of properties as zoological properties, or

(ii) that in the human species, moral properties have emerged or developed, historically, out of zoological properties.

Option (i) seems false. As Foot herself agrees (2001: 66), a wolf that walks alone is not a *morally bad* wolf, even if its behaviour is not statistically normal or species-characteristic wolf behaviour. Walking alone, in any case, might turn out to be a behaviour that brings this particular wolf an evolutionary advantage over other wolves, in which case either what counts as normal wolf behaviour will change over time or a new and better-adapted species (super-wolves?) will emerge to compete ecologically with wolves. Conversely, a human being who tells many lies does not seem to be a *zoologically dysfunctional* human being, any more than a monkey that hides fruit from other monkeys is zoologically dysfunctional. It is not abnormal or uncharacteristic for human beings to tell lies (however morally regrettable it might be). And here, too, there is the possibility that telling lies might give liars an evolutionary advantage, so that – even if lying *was* zoologically abnormal for human beings – there could come to be a new species of super-humans for whom lying is not zoologically abnormal, and who come to compete ecologically with human beings.

So there is a question about whether (i) is true. The question about (ii), by contrast, is not whether it is true, but whether it is too obviously true to be any use to Foot. It does not seem at all controversial to say that human beings' moral properties have developed out of their zoological properties. Given the known facts about the origins of the human species in evolution, there is nowhere *else* that human beings' moral properties could have come from. But this does not seem to close the gap between moral assessment and zoological assessment.

Foot evidently sees this difficulty, and so ends up defending the thesis that moral assessment is *in some ways* like zoological assessment, even though it is different in others. But – a critic might persist – while it is useful to be reminded of the continuities between zoological and ethical assessments, it is also useful to remember the differences. Here are three differences that the critic might home in on.

- *The Mafioso.* There does not seem to be anything wrong, *zoologically speaking*, with a robber baron or a Mafioso, or (to take a less grandiose example) someone who makes a living by credit-card fraud. But there plainly is something wrong *morally speaking* with these characters. It is not clear how this fact can be squared with Foot's claim that moral assessments are continuous with zoological ones.

    Foot is, of course, aware of this difficulty, and she discusses it more than once. In a passage already quoted, she remarks that a society dominated by Mafiosi is apt "to be a wretched place to live". (For those outside the magic circle, perhaps. But what is that to the Mafioso and his family as they sit on their balcony overlooking the Straits of Messina and sip their cocktails?)
- *The existentialist wolf.* There cannot be an existentialist wolf, that is, a wolf that says to itself "What is the purpose of my existence? What am I here for? What shall I do with my life?", and goes on to create the best answers it can devise to its own questions. The reason why not is that the purpose of a wolf's life is completely set by the facts

of lupine zoology. By contrast, existentialist human beings certainly seem possible. Many people have devised, and tried to live by, their own answers to existential questions like the ones just listed. Indeed, the leading question of this book, "How should life be lived?", is itself an existential question. When we try to devise answers to these questions, are we just overlooking a simple truth about how human beings ought to live that we can get straight from human zoology, in the way that a wolf can get a simple answer to its question straight from lupine zoology? It seems not. But if not, then moral truth will not derive as directly from biological facts as Foot suggests.

- *The cockroach objection.* According to Foot, truths about what it is good or bad for human beings to do or be depend on truths about what counts as biological flourishing for human beings. Human beings live by hunting and gathering in their pre-cultural state, and by political life or something like it in their acculturated state. So, according to Foot, it is the facts about what we need to do well as hunter-gatherers, or as participants in a political society, that ground what is good and bad for human beings.

  Here a critic might ask: why not just run the same pattern of argument for cockroaches? As we all know, cockroaches live by scavenging dirt and refuse. So presumably a good cockroach is one that eats dirt and refuse with particular avidity, and a cockroach that is fastidious about dirt, and likes to keep things tidy, is a defective cockroach. If it is morally good for human beings to do what makes for human well-being, there seems to be the same argument for saying that it is morally good for cockroaches to do what makes for cockroach well-being. This seems a pretty strange conclusion! But how, the critic will ask, is Foot to avoid it?

  Foot seems to have something like the cockroach objection in mind when she writes as follows:

  [T]here is no room for [the notion of the goodness of states of affairs] in the theory of natural normativity. Where, after all, could "good states of affairs" be appealed to in judging the natural goodness or defect in characteristics or operations of plants and animals? In evaluating the hunting skills of the tiger do I start from the proposition that it is a better state of affairs if the tiger survives than if it does not? What about pestilential

115

creatures such as mosquitoes, to which the pattern of natural
normativity also applies?   (2001: 49, original emphasis)

Here Foot identifies the problem: there is no place in what she calls
"natural normativity" for claims such as "It is a good thing, or state of
affairs, if the tiger survives or does well". For that means that there's
no place in "natural normativity", either, for claims such as "It is a
good thing, or state of affairs, if the human survives or does well".
But if *that* is so, then, the critic might say, all we can get out of Foot's
notion of "natural normativity" is the thought that some states of
affairs are *good for tigers*, or *good for human beings*, or *good for mos-*
quitoes, or *good for cockroaches*. If these species-relative notions of
goodness are all we can have, and there is no such thing as a notion
of *good overall*, then we might find it hard to say why we should prefer what is good for human beings to what is good for mosquitoes,
cockroaches or tigers. More exactly, while it is not hard to predict
that we *will* have this preference – after all, we are human beings,
not mosquitoes or cockroaches or tigers – we might find it hard to
say why we would be *justified* in this preference.

Some philosophers would say that the cockroach objection is
just a version of the problem raised for ethical naturalism by the
is–ought gap: the problem that will face anyone who says "This is
how things *are* with human nature, so this is how things *ought to*
be with human nature". I myself have not put the problem quite that
way, partly because, as we saw in Chapter 6, I think there are serious problems with the whole idea of an is–ought gap. But there is
a good point, and one that makes trouble for virtue ethics in Foot's
style, somewhere in the vicinity. If you can argue that "Human
beings are by nature sociable; so sociability is a good thing", you
can equally well argue (i) that "Tigers are by nature man-eaters, so
man-eating is a good thing", and (ii) that "Human beings are by
nature aggressive; so aggression is a good thing". An unrestricted
appeal to human nature founders on the very ambiguous *goodness*
of human nature.

These three contrasts between moral assessment and zoological assessment raise real difficulties for Foot's project of grounding her virtue
ethics in biological naturalism. One way for a virtue ethicist to avoid

them is, of course, to give up on biological naturalism, and base her virtue ethics on some other account of what we are talking about when we talk about ethics. The virtue ethicist might return, for instance, to Hume's suggestion that the basis of the virtues is simply our feelings of approval towards various sorts of disposition. Or we might take up a suggestion of Zagzebski's (2006), and start our account of the virtues from a range of *exemplars* of the virtues: "saints and heroes" whom everybody or nearly everybody recognizes as paradigms of moral goodness. Such suggestions naturally raise worries about relativity: how do we know that *we* approve the right dispositions, or the right "saints and heroes"? On the other hand, these suggestions avoid the difficulties for biological naturalism that I have discussed in this section.

However the virtue ethicist decides to base his account of the virtues, there are still further questions to answer. These come under the second broad heading that I used in my description of virtue ethics in §§8.2–8.3: *spontaneity*.

8.5 Questions for virtue ethics II: deliberation and modularity

There is a very general question that we might ask about any of the four ethical theories summarized in §8.1. These summaries tell us, at least roughly, what an ethical theory is. But we must ask: what is an ethical theory *for*? How are we supposed to use an ethical theory, and how is using one supposed to help us?

As the reader will recall, the first sentence of our summary of virtue ethics in §8.1 went like this:

> *Virtue ethics*: An action is right iff it is what a virtuous agent would characteristically do in the circumstances.

This gives us a (skeleton) account of what rightness is. What are we supposed to do with this skeleton account? The most obvious suggestion is that we are supposed to use it in deliberation: we are meant to use this account *to decide what to do*. And then the second sentence of the summary of virtue ethics in §8.1 comes in, to give us more information about how to use it to decide:

Virtuous agents characteristically act in accordance with the virtues (courage, self-control, justice, wisdom, faith, hope, and love), and never act in accordance with the vices (pride, avarice, lust, envy, gluttony, wrath, and sloth).

Compare this suggestion with what I said in §8.3 about the modularity of practical deliberation in virtue ethics. The point about modularity was that the virtuous agent often does better not to deliberate. He acts in accordance with the virtues *spontaneously*, perhaps without deliberating at all. Or even when he does deliberate, his deliberation is far simpler and more focused than it would be if he were an ethical rationalist. He does not need to go back to first principles to take every decision, and he does not need to consider *everything*. Like the person considering what present to get for his friend in hospital, there will probably be only a handful of options that he needs to take seriously; everything else he can, and will, disregard.

So we can ask: what use will the virtuous agent have for our summary of virtue ethics in §8.1? If the point in §8.3 about the modularity of practical deliberation was right, then what I have just called "the obvious suggestion" seems likely to be wrong: the virtuous agent will not need to have that summary of virtue ethics in his thoughts when he deliberates. In fact, not only will he not need to think about it; he will often need not to think about it. He will, apparently, fail to be a virtuous agent if he *does* always think about it while deliberating. If this is so, then the summary of virtue ethics that I have provided does not just fail to help an agent to deliberate well; it actively prevents him from deliberating well.

If this is right, and you cannot use that summary of virtue ethics to deliberate, what *can* you use it for? Well, perhaps you can use it for reflection. Perhaps it comes into play when you step back from your deliberations and assess how you are doing as a moral agent, review whether you chose aright at this or that node of choice, wonder if you have the right sort of character, ask whether this or that historical person was really an admirable person, and so on.

As philosophers like to say: virtue ethics, as a moral theory, offers us a *criterion of rightness*, but that is not at all the same thing as offering us a *decision procedure*. (Virtue ethics offers us a decision procedure as well, which I described in §8.3 when discussing modularity. Notice the

differences between the criterion of rightness and the decision procedure.)

This answer looks feasible, so long as there is no necessary conflict
between decision procedure and criterion of rightness, or between
the theoretical materials that we use for this sort of reflection, and the
non-theoretical materials that we use for actual deliberation. Whether
such a conflict *is* necessary, and what, more generally, are supposed
to be the psychological and logical relations between "off-line" reflection and "real-time" deliberation, are still open questions, and perhaps rather puzzling ones. I shall say more about them in Chapter 11,
and before that in Chapter 9, where we shall look at their bearing on
utilitarianism.

8.6 Questions for virtue ethics III: moral weightlifting

Some further questions for the moral theory of virtue ethics arise simply because different actions are appropriate for good people and for
less good people. Suppose that the beautiful Joanna has failed her exam,
and is distraught. We recall that an action is right, according to virtue
ethics, iff it is what a virtuous agent would characteristically do in the
circumstances. And we see that a virtuous agent would characteristically go and see Joanna, console her, tell her that it is not the end of
the world, feed her chocolate and so on. So according to the virtue
ethical account of rightness, going and consoling Joanna is the right
thing to do.

But is "what the virtuous agent would do" the right thing for *anybody*
to do? Suppose that, unfortunately, I am not a fully virtuous agent: I am
a tactless oaf, or a lecherous swine, or both. If I go and see Joanna, as
virtue ethics's account of rightness tells me to, what will happen next?
Maybe my tactlessness will get the better of me, and I will say "Joanna,
don't worry; lots of girls have made it who are even thicker than you
are". Or maybe my lecherousness will get the better of me, and I will leer
and wink at her and say "I'm getting a great idea about how to cheer
you up". Either way, the result of my acting on the advice of virtue ethics
looks likely to be unfortunate.

From this little story we might draw the moral that, if I am lecherous
or tactless, then I ought *not* to do what a virtuous agent would char-

acteristically do in these circumstances. Certainly *the virtuous agent* should go and see Joanna; but that is irrelevant to what *I* should do (namely keep away from her), because I am not virtuous. Hence, we might argue, the virtue ethical account of rightness is not a general account of rightness. It is only an account of rightness for virtuous agents, and anyone else who follows it will quickly get into trouble, just as a novice climber who tries to copy what an expert climber characteristically does will quickly get into trouble.

To this a virtue ethicist can respond: "But of course you shouldn't apply the account of rightness to only *one* decision. You have to keep on applying it, like any account of rightness. So you *should* go and see Joanna, as a virtuous agent would (that's one decision); and you *should* avoid the tactless remark, as a virtuous agent would (that's another); and you *should* refrain from making a pass at Joanna, as a virtuous agent would refrain (that's a third). Not to mention the obvious fact that you should never have become a lecherous and tactless person in the first place, a character that you have because of dozens of *earlier* wrong decisions."

No doubt this is all very plausible. But does it solve the problem? The problem (which Williams has called the "moral weightlifting problem") is that virtue ethics defines "the right thing to do" as "what the virtuous person would do". But quite often, it seems, the right thing to do for someone who is not virtuous is *not* what the virtuous person would do. Is this not still a problem for the virtue ethical account of rightness?

Well, maybe that account of rightness can be adjusted to meet the problem. Maybe what we need is something like this?

> *Virtue ethics 2*: An action is right iff it is *either* what a fully virtuous agent would characteristically do in the circumstances, *or* the closest approach to what a fully virtuous agent would do that a less than fully virtuous agent can manage.

This account may meet the previous problem, but it also seems to raise new problems. For one thing, "the closest approach" is an indeterminate notion. Is going to visit Joanna and upsetting her "a closer approach" to what the virtuous agent does than just sending her flowers, or than keeping right out of her way until I have learned to behave myself with the ladies? Unless we can tidy up what sort of closeness we are talking about, we will not have an answer to this sort of question

Even if we can tidy it up, it still seems that an action that we might naturally call "the closest approach" to what the virtuous agent does can be a bad idea for a less than virtuous agent. It sometimes seems wiser for such an agent to go *nowhere near* trying to do what the fully virtuous agent does. Maybe the lecherous and tactless person should not only not visit Joanna in case he is tempted to insult her or make a pass at her in person, but not even write her a card in case he is tempted to do the same remotely.

Also, consider Heinrich Himmler. Himmler is not only a less than fully virtuous agent, he is so steeped in evil that the best *he* can manage is only to murder 200 Jews today instead of 2000. *Virtue ethics 2* implies that Himmler acts rightly in murdering 200 Jews, just so long as this is the best he can manage. Any account of rightness that implies *that* seems to be in trouble!

So perhaps the virtue ethicist should retreat to something like this?

Virtue ethics 3: An action is *perfectly* right iff it is what a *perfectly* virtuous agent would characteristically do in the circumstances.

This third formulation has the advantage that it looks very likely to be true. Unfortunately it also has the disadvantage that it seems irrelevant to anyone who is not perfect. It does not even apply to anyone who is *trying* to be perfect, and in any case we have already seen some reasons why we might think it a bad idea to try for perfection.

But maybe *Virtue ethics 3* can be augmented to include the less than perfect?

Virtue ethics 4: An action is *perfectly* right iff it is what a *perfectly* virtuous agent would characteristically do in the circumstances; and an action is *approximately* right iff it is what an *approximately* virtuous agent would characteristically do in the circumstances; and an action is *minimally* right iff it is what a *minimally* virtuous agent would characteristically do in the circumstances.

This fourth formulation has a different flaw; as it stands, it does not tell anyone what to do. But suppose we take it as read that perfectly virtuous people should do the perfectly virtuous thing, and approximately virtuous people should do the approximately virtuous thing, and anyone else should do the minimally virtuous thing.

On that supposition, *Virtue ethics 4* tells us what to think about the lecherous and tactless person, and why it is right for him not to visit Joanna even though that is what the fully virtuous person would do. The reason is because he is only minimally virtuous, or perhaps even actually vicious. So what he should do is what a minimally virtuous person would do, which is *not* visit Joanna, but recognize the reasons, arising from his own personality, why visiting Joanna would be a poor idea.

However, our fourth formulation still does not say that the minimally virtuous and the approximately virtuous should not rest content with minimal or approximate virtue; they should also have some ambition to become better people. Surely it should say this?

Virtue ethics 5: An action is *perfectly* right iff it is what a *perfectly* virtuous agent would characteristically do in the circumstances; and an action is *approximately* right iff it is what an *approximately* virtuous agent would characteristically do in the circumstances; and an action is *minimally* right iff it is what a *minimally* virtuous agent would characteristically do in the circumstances; and the minimally virtuous should seek to become approximately virtuous, and the approximately virtuous should seek to become perfectly virtuous.

This formulation gives the minimally and approximately virtuous a kind of double agenda. They have to aim both at doing the actions that fit within their categories, and also at moving up to the next category. It might not always be obvious, in practice, which of these aims is the one to prioritize. But then, if you were training as a weightlifter, it might not always be obvious, in practice, whether you should try for heavier weights today, or spend the day consolidating at your present level. Moreover, the problem of choosing between different good aims seems to be one that virtue ethics will have to face anyway. It seems fairly clear that the different virtues will often give us different aims, and it will not always be obvious which of these aims to prioritize either.

A different kind of question that arises for *Virtue ethics 5*, and indeed for all the formulations I have suggested, is this. Suppose I am (and know that I am) a perfectly virtuous person. Then what kind of practical guidance do I get from any of these formulations (either in on-the-spot deliberation, or in later reflection on how I deliberated when I needed to)? The original formulation of virtue ethics tells me that the right thing to do is "what a virtuous person would characteristically do in the circumstances"; *Virtue ethics 5* tells me that the perfectly right thing to do is "what a perfectly virtuous person would characteristically do in the circumstances". Given that I know I am myself a perfectly virtuous person, what are these formulations telling me? Apparently, they are telling me to do what *I* would characteristically do in these circumstances. But, we might say, that is not a *solution* to my problem about knowing what is right. It *is* my problem about knowing what is right!

Fortunately for virtue ethics, there is an obvious way to deal with this problem. It is to bring back in the second sentence of the first summary of virtue ethics, which tells us that:

Virtuous agents characteristically act in accordance with the virtues (courage, self-control, justice, wisdom, faith, hope, and love), and never act in accordance with the vices (pride, avarice, lust, envy, gluttony, wrath, and sloth).

When we remember this second sentence, we can see that, even if I am perfectly virtuous, I am not necessarily reduced (as it were) to looking into my own navel to find out what to do. The virtues themselves can give me some independent purchase on what I ought to do.

Or at least, they can give me this independent purchase, so long as we do not do what some virtue ethicists do, and define the virtues in terms of the virtuous agent, for example by saying that "courageous acts are just those acts that a virtuous person characteristically does in alarming situations". If we do that, then the virtuous person really is stuck with looking into his own navel. But fortunately, we do not have to do that.

There again, another and more radical response is possible for virtue ethicists, in the face of problems of these sorts about how to define virtue ethics. Virtue ethicists can also respond that there are indeed these problems about their definition; but that what the problems show is not that virtue ethics is not feasible, but that it cannot neatly be captured in any simple formula such as *Virtue ethics, Virtue ethics 2* and the rest of them. The search for any such formulas (they might say), indeed the search for a way of living that depends on simple formulas like these, is *itself* a mistake; an adequate response to the complexities of life just cannot be captured in this way. No doubt many who call themselves virtue ethicists would be inclined to offer this sort of response to the problems raised in this section. In so doing, they are moving away from the whole idea of systematic moral theory. We shall see more about what sort of view of ethics you might get, if (like me) you are inclined to follow them in this direction, in Chapter 11.

This completes my examination of some questions and problems about virtue ethics. What emerges from the examination, apparently, is at least this: that virtue ethics has the great advantage that it makes it possible for us to keep action, and at least most of our ethical deliberation or reflection, more or less together in an undivided mind. Does every moral theory manage as much as this? More about that as we turn, in Chapter 9, to utilitarianism.

9

Utilitarianism

"I don't want to! Why should I?"
"Because more people will be happier if you do than if you don't."
"So what? I don't care about other people."
"You should."
"But why?"
"Because more people will be happier if you do than if you don't."
(Katherine Tait, *My Father Bertrand Russell*, 1970: 184–5)

9.1 Moral theory and deliberative practice again

What place in a good person's deliberations can a moral theory have?
Towards the end of Chapter 8, we explored this question as it arises for
the moral theory called virtue ethics. We noted that the virtue ethical
account of rightness says this:

Virtue ethics: An action is right iff it is the action that a virtuous
agent would characteristically do in the circumstances.

(Or something like that. We developed some complications about what
the exact formula should be in §8.6, but we need not revisit these now.)
    We also noted in Chapter 8 that any plausible moral theory is bound
to be about more than simply action. It needs to have something to

say, for instance, about emotion, response, choice and deliberation as well. Hence we can produce formulas like the following that parallel the account of rightness:

An emotion is right iff it is the emotion that a virtuous agent would characteristically feel in the circumstances;

A response is right iff it is the response that a virtuous agent would characteristically produce in the circumstances;

A choice is right iff it is the choice that a virtuous agent would characteristically make in the circumstances;

A deliberation is right iff it is a deliberation that a virtuous agent would characteristically perform in the circumstances;

and so on.

This last formulation raises again the interesting question for virtue ethics that I first raised in §8.3: will a virtuous agent's deliberation ever include materials such as the virtue ethical account of rightness itself? In other words, will the theory itself be explicit in the deliberative life of the sort of agents that the theory says there ought to be?

This relation between moral theory and actual deliberative practice seems to be a very important one for normative ethics. The reason why is because any moral theory needs to have a stable relation to deliberative practice. That is, if we cannot explain how a moral theory is supposed to help us deliberate, or if the contents of the moral theory are contradictory to the contents of deliberative practice, then it is hard to see a use for the theory.

Of course, we do not have to suppose that the moral theory is involved in deliberation directly: it might be involved only indirectly, by being part of how we reflect on our deliberations "in a cool hour", as I suggested was possible for virtue ethics. But if it cannot even be involved in that sort of reflection, then the moral theory's usefulness is questionable, even if it is true.

These questions about a moral theory's relation with actual deliberative practice are important ones for every moral theory. One thing that will emerge from this chapter is the importance of these questions for utilitarianism. But before we get to that, let us begin with a review of what utilitarianism says.

9.2 Utilitarianism in outline

Utilitarianism has a basic form, and then many variations designed to deal with objections to the basic form. One way of stating the basic form of utilitarianism has already been offered in §8.1:

> *Utilitarianism*: An action is right iff it promotes the greatest happiness of the greatest number.

A somewhat fuller statement of the basic form of utilitarianism sees it as the conjunction of four separable theses:

Utilitarianism = maximalism + welfarism +
aggregationism + consequentialism

where the component theses are defined as follows:

Maximalism: It is always obligatory to take the best option available.
Welfarism: What is good is happiness/welfare.
Aggregationism: We can measure and quantify happiness/welfare, both within lives and between lives.
Consequentialism: The goodness of any option depends only on the goodness of its consequences.

Here maximalism tells us that we may never aim at less than the best. Welfarism and aggregationism together tell us what "the best" is, and how to measure it. In Mill's famous phrase, "it is the greatest happiness of the greatest number", which we find by comparing the amounts of happiness/welfare that various alternative possible states of affairs will contain for various numbers of people. And consequentialism tell us that "the best" is a state of affairs, a set of consequences, that is achievable by action.

(A note on the word "consequentialism": there are other ways of using the word besides the one laid down by my definition. The term is sometimes no more than a rough equivalent to "utilitarianism". It can also mean, as I think Brad Hooker intends it to mean in *Ideal Code, Real World* [2003], "a position family-related to utilitarianism, only more plausible". In Anscombe's original sense – she invented the term in "Modern Moral Philosophy" [Geach & Gormally 2005: 184] – the word means something else again, namely, the denial that there is any morally significant distinction between actually intended and merely foreseen consequences. This variety of usage need not be confusing, provided the reader is aware of it.)

All four of utilitarianism's component theses have such a strong and obvious intuitive appeal that, to many moral theorists, utilitarianism seems like "the only game in town". It can seem like the only moral theory worth taking seriously, or the default moral theory, the starting-point from which all departures need to be justified by argument:

- *Maximalism*: If you *can* do the best, it is hard to see why you would settle for less.
- *Welfarism*: Happiness can hardly be a *bad* thing; if moral theories do not contribute to human happiness, what is the point of them?
- *Aggregationism*: We may not be able to measure happiness scientifically, or use instruments to detect and compare happiness levels in different people. But we do generally know when one person is happier than another, how much of one sort of happiness is a fair exchange for how much of another sort, and so on. And we must know this kind of thing, not just in order to run utilitarianism, but in order to be able to say what distributions are fair.
- *Consequentialism*: It would obviously be mad not to consider the consequences of what you propose to do. And why, more generally, would anyone do anything *except* to bring about this or that consequence?

Something like the theory that we get by combining these theses can be found in many philosophical texts, including the writings of Francis Hutcheson and Adam Smith in the eighteenth century, and Spinoza's *Ethics* in the seventeenth century. Long before these writers, something similar is already visible in Socrates' proposal in *Protagoras*:

> Like a man who is skilled in measuring weights, put pleasures in the scale together with pains, bearing in mind their distance or

proximity; then say which side weighs more. If you are weighing pleasures against other pleasures, choose the larger and weightier ones; if you are weighing pains against other pains, choose the lesser and the smaller ones. If you are weighing pleasures against pains, then the right choice depends on whether or not the pains are outweighed by some pleasures which follow on them. Are near pains outweighed by distant pleasures, or distant pains by near pleasures? If so, the action to be done is the one that displays those features. But if, in the case of some action, near or distant pleasures are outweighed by near or distant pains, then don't do that action.   (356b–c, my translation in Chappell 1996: 98–9)

Here Socrates is suggesting alterations to the virtue-based view of ethics that came naturally in his society towards a view that will, supposedly, make it easier to decide between alternatives. The theory that he sketches is one in which we treat all goods and all evils as pleasures and pains. This gives us a moral "currency" in which everything can be priced against everything else (everything is *commensurable*). Socrates is thus rejecting a view that comes naturally to a virtue ethicist: *value pluralism*, the view that there are many different goods and no way of making them commensurate. Socrates here rejects value pluralism in favour of something like aggregationism. Socrates also, apparently, collapses the distinction, important in virtue ethics, between means–end and constitutive relations (§5.1): he suggests that every action is a way of bringing about a state of pleasure or pain (or both). This moves him away from the variety of different sorts of possible action that a virtue ethicist will want to recognize, towards the more uniform view of action as instrumentality that I call consequentialism. Finally, on Socrates' proposal (which may or may not be Plato's proposal, or a proposal that Socrates is offering seriously, or one that he offers elsewhere) there would always be something irrational about preferring a lesser sum of good to a greater one. There is nothing in virtue ethics to oblige us to take this view, which is very close to what I call maximalism. (Socrates' suggestion is a view about rationality, and maximalism is a view about moral obligation; but the two views clearly go naturally together.)

Utilitarianism, then, not only is a very intuitively appealing moral theory but also has a long history of attracting the adherence, or at least the interest, of some very eminent philosophers. Its four constituent theses raise all sorts of interesting questions. In the next four sections I examine them in turn.

9.3 Welfarism

Utilitarianism's historical development out of something very like virtue ethics is clear from the passage I have just quoted from Plato's *Protagoras*. It is also evident from the typical (if not universal) utilitarian commitment to a naturalistic theory of the good, in some ways rather like – and in others rather unlike – the one I described in §8.2 as a key feature of most versions of virtue ethics. Utilitarians too typically answer the question "What are we really talking about in ethical discourse?", which we saw in Chapter 7, by a form of naturalism: as I have called it, welfaristic naturalism. This is the view that the real content of moral discourse is given by claims about what contributes to human welfare or happiness or pleasure. As to what human welfare, happiness or pleasure might be, more on that shortly. But notice that there is no necessary commitment in utilitarianism to anything like the biological naturalist account of these notions that is usually found in virtue ethics.

Apparently this naturalism about the good is both a strength and a weakness of utilitarianism, for the same sort of reasons as it is both a strength and a weakness of virtue ethics. On the one hand, it helps utilitarianism to avoid the meta-ethical problems that are supposed to result from recognizing a non-natural, "special moral reality". On the other hand, it makes utilitarianism prone to the usual objection to ethical naturalism: that if people just happened to want something different from what they actually want, or to take pleasure in something different, then we would have to say that *that* was the good, possibly with very counter-intuitive consequences. (What if everyone started enjoying seeing other people in pain?)

In parallel with the point about virtue ethics that we noted at the end of §8.4, it is technically possible for a utilitarian to avoid these characteristic problems of ethical naturalism, simply by dropping the naturalism. Utilitarianism can be, and often is, presented simply as a theory about *what everybody wants*, no matter whether anyone takes that to be good or not. This form of utilitarianism – *preference* utilitarianism – has seemed very attractive to many moderns, since it does not commit us on the difficult issues of meta-ethics. This way, we can have a form of utilitarianism that is consistent with any degree of meta-ethical subjectivism or relativism.

However, the account of the good that the classical utilitarians offered was an objectivist and a naturalist one. Besides facing the usual questions for objectivism and naturalism, that account faces specific questions of its own. Let us look to Mill to clarify these questions.

Mill takes "pleasure and freedom from pain" and "happiness" to be equivalent terms, and both names for the human good:

> The creed which accepts as the foundation of morals, Utility, or the Greatest Happiness Principle, holds that actions are right in proportion as they tend to promote happiness, wrong as they tend to produce the reverse of happiness. By happiness is intended pleasure and the absence of pain; by unhappiness, pain and the privation of pleasure. ([1863] 1962: 257)

Indeed, in *Utilitarianism* Mill offers what he calls a proof that happiness is the good. According to Mill, happiness is proved to be the good by the fact that it is what we desire; indeed, it is the only thing that we *can* desire. In Mill's own words:

> The only proof capable of being given that an object is visible, is that people actually see it. The only proof that a sound is audible, is that people hear it … In like manner, I apprehend, the sole evidence it is possible to produce that anything is desirable, is that people do actually desire it … no reason can be given why the general happiness is desirable, except that each person … desires his own happiness. [Here] we have not only all the proof which the case admits of, but all which it is possible to require, that happiness is a good. (*Ibid.*: 289)

Note that last indefinite article. This passage takes us only as far as the first step of Mill's argument: that happiness, that is, pleasure and freedom from pain, is *a* good. This on its own is not very controversial; almost anyone will agree to it. The view that happiness is *a* good is not the utilitarian view. Utilitarianism involves the different and stronger view that happiness is *the* good: as Mill himself puts it, that "happiness is desirable, and the only thing desirable, as an end; all other things being only desirable as means to that end" (*ibid.*).

So Mill needs to do more than this to prove utilitarianism. In his own words, he needs "to show, not only that people desire happiness, but that they never desire anything else" (*ibid.*). To do this, Mill broadens his notion of happiness. It started out (see the extract above) as meaning the same as "pleasure and freedom from pain". It now seems to mean something much less specific than that:

> The ingredients of happiness are very various, and each of them is desirable in itself, and not merely when considered as swelling an aggregate. The principle of utility does not mean that any given pleasure, as music, for instance, or any given exemption from pain, as for example health, is to be looked upon as means to a collective something termed happiness, and to be desired on that account. They are desired and desirable in and for themselves; besides being means, they are part of the end.
>
> ([1863] 1962: 289–90)

We can find happiness, Mill is arguing, in all sorts of ways; all sorts of things are instances or constituents of happiness (cf. the distinction we saw in §5.1 between means–end and constitutive relations). Desiring any of these things – music, or health, or whatever – is desiring an instance of happiness. Therefore, it is desiring happiness.

We might wonder whether this proves that happiness (in the sense that Mill gives the word) is the only thing we ever desire or can desire. Why could someone not choose to be miserable? In fact, do people not choose misery all the time? Or alternatively, why could someone not choose something that is not opposite to happiness, like misery, but simply different from it: for instance, might someone not want to be the person who discovers the proof of Fermat's Last Theorem, without particularly *caring* whether he was happy or unhappy? "If one has one's *why* in life, one can put up with almost any *how*", commented Nietzsche; "man does not strive after happiness, only the Englishman does that" ([1889] 1968: 12).

This point that someone could systematically choose things other than pleasure or happiness – including, at the limit, pain and unhappiness – is not addressed very explicitly by Mill. There are two things that we might say on his behalf. One is to claim that people who choose things other than pleasure or happiness can still be choosing in a way that makes sense from a welfarist point of view. It makes sense because the welfarist can simply accept the *paradox of hedonism* – the familiar fact that, often, the best way to find happiness, or pleasure, is not to look for it or focus on it, but to go after something else instead. Your happiness or pleasure will then be all the greater, because you are not fixating on happiness or pleasure. This might look plausible of someone who is absorbed in the routine of his sailing, not in the pleasure that sailing gives him, but finds his pleasure in sailing precisely in this absorption. But even here, there is a doubt about whether someone who sails for this sort of reason is truly described as aiming at pleasure, rather than at sailing. And that doubt is magnified in the case of someone who explicitly says, as the mathematician bent on proving Fermat's Last Theorem or the self-destructive person might, that he "doesn't care about his own happiness".

The other thing we might say is this. Mill's real point is not that it is *impossible* for people to choose to be miserable or unhealthy, or to choose to sacrifice a good deal of possible happiness in pursuit of a mathematical proof. His real point is that it is *unintelligible*. Action, on Mill's view, is only intelligible in so far as it is directed at some instance or other of happiness. If we want to explain to people why they should aim at music or health or proving a theorem, not at being depressed or ill, the only possible way of doing it is to point out to them that music and health and proving a theorem will all, in their different ways, make them happy, whereas being depressed or ill will not make them happy. Thus all explanation of our reasons for doing anything refers back, ultimately, to happiness; actions that cannot be explained in this way cannot be explained at all.

If this is Mill's real point, then one standard criticism of him, deriving from G. E. Moore, seems mistaken. Moore's criticism fastens on Mill's (admittedly rather loose) use of the word "desirable" in the sentence quoted above: "the sole evidence it is possible to produce that anything is desirable, is that people do actually desire it". Moore claims to detect an equivocation in this: Mill, he says, mixes up "desirable" in the sense of "*capable of* being desired" with "desirable" in the sense of "*such as ought to* be desired", and hence commits a version of what is sometimes termed the is–ought confusion (§§6.2, 6.6). (Or, in Moore's own terminology, Mill commits the "naturalistic fallacy"; see Moore [1903] 2002: ch. 1. Moore is one of the chief originators of our modern difficulties in being quite sure what we mean by "natural" and "naturalism", which is one reason why I do not use his terminology.)

Moore thinks that Mill's mistake is to infer from a premise about what *is* desired to a conclusion about what *ought to be* desired. But if I have reconstructed Mill's argument accurately, this seems to be a misguided criticism, because Mill does not make this mistake. What Mill does is move from the premise that all rationally intelligible action is aimed at happiness to the conclusion that happiness is the good. If we add the plausible premise that the objective of all rationally intelligible action is the good, then we can credit Mill with a valid and persuasive argument:

1. All rationally intelligible action is aimed at happiness.
2. Whatever all rationally intelligible action is aimed at, is the good.
3. Therefore, happiness is the good.

So Mill seems to escape Moore's criticism. But perhaps he still faces a different problem about the notion of happiness. We saw above how Mill broadens his conception of happiness to include pretty well everything that anyone could pursue: "The ingredients of happiness are very various", he tells us, and "They are desired and desirable in and for themselves". (Notice Mill's phrasing here, by the way. Does the fact that he can write "desired and desirable" show him conflating these notions, as Moore charges, or distinguishing them?)

The difficulty about this broadening, a critic might say, is that it puts Mill in danger of emptying the notion of happiness of any particular content. When happiness or welfare is *this* broadly conceived, it just becomes another word for "whatever people aim at". So saying "All rationally intelligible action is aimed at happiness" just means "All rationally intelligible action is aimed at whatever it is aimed at". But that is an empty claim. There is no more content to it than there would be to saying "All cars are going wherever they are going". And so, the charge would be, Mill's argument becomes empty.

To this the utilitarian can reply that it is not empty to say that "All rationally intelligible action is aimed at whatever it is aimed at". Another way of putting that is to say "All rationally intelligible action has some aim", and this claim is clearly not an empty one. (Any more than it would be empty to say "All cars are going somewhere", which is more or less the same claim as "All cars are going wherever they are going".) We might agree with the critic that Mill has widened the notion of happiness so far that virtually anything can go into it, except that there is still one important constraint on what can be an ingredient of happiness. This, of course, is the requirement that actions that are part of happiness have to have *rationally intelligible* aims. Happiness has become whatever we can *reasonably* and *comprehensibly* aim at.

This is not such a broad conception of happiness that there is no content to it at all. But surely it is a much broader conception than Mill started with. After all, on his original conception of happiness, "happiness" was a near-synonym with "pleasure". And "pleasure" surely cannot mean all the things that "happiness" now seems to mean for Mill.

Actually it can, if you choose to use the word that way. Like "happiness", "pleasure" is a deeply ambiguous word. At one end of its range of meanings, "pleasure" can mean a specific physical sensation. At the other end, it can mean something much less specific, such as "enjoyment" or, even less specifically, "what you find worthwhile". ("Why are you doing 100 press-ups?" "For pleasure." This reply can make sense even if the person doing the press-ups is in a lot of pain!) It would obviously not be a very promising theory that claimed that everything we do is done as a means to pleasure in the physical-sensation sense. But a very different theory, and a much more promising one, will result if we claim instead that everything we do is done either as a means to something that we enjoy or find worthwhile, or as an instance of something that we enjoy or find worthwhile (cf. §4.3).

Most of the time, "pleasure and the avoidance of pain" in the physical-sensation sense seems not to be the objective of our actions. But that does not stop pleasure in some broader sense from being our objective. When I do the crossword, I am not aiming at "pleasure or the avoidance of pain" in the sense that I am when I take an aspirin or ask someone to scratch my back; I am aiming at completing the crossword. All the same, if you ask me whether for me doing crosswords is "business or pleasure", my reply will be "pleasure". And if you ask me why I do crosswords, I may well reply "because I enjoy them". I do not mean by this that doing crosswords is a *means* to enjoyment for me; I mean, rather, that doing crosswords is an *instance* of enjoyment for me. Nonetheless, when we explain my reasons for action, pleasure (in the sense of enjoyment) is firmly in the picture.

So in fact "pleasure" is not necessarily a different concept from "happiness". Interestingly, both concepts are ambiguous in the same sort of way. At one end of the spectrum both words mean one particular kind of feeling, but at the other end, they both mean something much more general and much vaguer: perhaps just that an activity is done *with enjoyment*. However, neither term is completely empty of meaning, even at this general or (as it is sometimes called) "adverbial" end of their respective spectrums of meaning. So Mill can be justified in equating happiness with pleasure, and in claiming that happiness and/or pleasure is the point of all action, provided it is the general senses of the two words that he has in mind.

The same goes for Mill's predecessor Jeremy Bentham, who defines his technical term "utility" like this:

> By utility is meant the property in any object, whereby it tends to produce benefit, advantage, pleasure, or happiness (*all this in the present case comes to the same thing*) or (*what comes again to the same thing*) to prevent the happening of mischief, pain, evil, or unhappiness.   ([1789] 1962: 34, emphasis added)

Mill and Bentham are perfectly entitled to speak of the objective of action as "happiness", or "pleasure", or "utility", or "welfare" in this broad and inclusive sense. For as we have seen, all that is meant by "happiness" (or the other terms) in this broad sense is "whatever makes any action worthwhile or rationally intelligible". So long as we think that actions *can* be worthwhile or rationally intelligible, there is no need for anyone to dispute this.

9.4 Aggregationism

What might be questioned is Mill's and Bentham's claim that happiness in this broad sense can be aggregated. Aggregationism, recall, is the distinctively utilitarian claim that we can measure and quantify happiness or welfare, both within lives and between lives. It is important to utilitarianism, as normally understood, that this claim should be true, because utilitarianism is a *maximalist* view: it tells us to do the best. But we cannot do the best unless we can work out what the best *is*; and working out what the best is will usually involve us in measuring and comparing amounts of pleasure or happiness or welfare both within and between different lives.

How are we to do this measuring and comparing? If "pleasure" or "happiness" means a sensation or a feeling, it might not be too hard to measure this feeling. We do not yet have a scientific instrument that can scan the brain and detect physical pleasure levels, or other sensations, within. But such technology is quite possibly not too far away from being invented. And if and when it comes along, a scientist will be able to *tell* us when one person is in a state of greater or lesser pleasure than another person, or than himself at some other time.

The difficulty is that, as we saw in §9.3, this is not what Mill and Bentham mean by "pleasure" or "happiness". What they mean – or are best understood as meaning – by "pleasure" is "whatever makes any action worthwhile or rationally intelligible". But this does not look like something that can be measured with brain-scanning scientific instruments! Worthwhileness/rational intelligibility is much too diverse for that. There are so many different things that can make an action worthwhile or rationally intelligible that it is very hard to see how we might get them all on the same scale of measurement.

The utilitarian has a response to this difficulty. It is to suggest that the measurements and comparisons of different degrees of happiness or pleasure are not supplied by scientific instruments. Instead, they are supplied by *us*. *We* compare possible sources of pleasure or happiness, and say what we find gives us more pleasure than what, and by how much. The rankings that maximalism needs are supplied by general agreement.

One obvious question about this suggestion is: what if people do not agree about how to rank pleasures or forms of happiness?

The utilitarian can go in one of two ways here. One way is for him to say "If people don't agree, then there is no answer". This is to allow the possibility that the rankings of degrees of happiness or pleasure have gaps or indeterminacies in them. By looking to see what people agree on, we can know that two pleasures *A* and *B* are both pleasanter than any of the pleasures *X*, *Y* and *Z*, and both less pleasant than any of the pleasures *P*, *Q* and *R*; but we cannot know which of *A* or *B* is more pleasant. The result of taking this option is an aggregationism that allows indeterminacies. It is also something like a pure subjective preference-utilitarianism: a view that bases its values solely on what people actually prefer, whether or not they are in some sense right to prefer it. Bentham seems close to this sort of position when he famously claims that "prejudices apart, the game of push-pin is of equal value with the arts and sciences of music and of poetry" (1825: ch.1).

The other way is for the utilitarian to say "If people don't agree, then we need to find an expert who can determine the answer". The utilitarian who goes this way is likely to claim that there are *no* gaps or indeterminacies in the pleasure rankings. Or at any rate he is likely to claim that there are fewer gaps than you might expect, and that where there really is a gap in the rankings this is not just because people disagree about how to rank two pleasures, but because even an expert ranker cannot find a reason for ranking them one way or the other. This gives us a utilitarianism that is more objectivist, and less purely preference based (and more elitist). On this view, it is possible to be *wrong* in my preferences, because the expert judge of pleasures provides a criterion of right and wrong preference. Mill seems close to this sort of position when he famously argues, against Bentham, for a distinction between "higher" and "lower" pleasures. To adjudicate between these sorts of pleasure, Mill appeals to the expertise of those who have experienced both sorts, who (he tells us) will report that even a small amount of higher pleasure is better than a large quantity of lower pleasure:

> It is better to be a human being dissatisfied than a pig satisfied; it is better to be Socrates dissatisfied than a fool satisfied. And if the fool, or the pig, are of a different opinion, it is because they only know their side of the question. The other party to the comparison knows both sides. ([1863] 1962: 260)

A further question about aggregationism fastens on the difference between *intra*personal and *inter*personal aggregation. Maybe (someone might say) we can make some sense of the idea of an individual person's deciding which of various possible actions he would most like to do, on the grounds that it would give him more pleasure or happiness than the alternatives. But is it equally easy to make sense of the idea of deciding between whole groups of actions that are going to affect

whole groups of people? As we might put it, each of us can know in his
own case how much a given pleasure means to him; but he cannot be
so sure how much that same pleasure will mean to someone else. So
even if we can aggregate happiness within one life, does it follow that
we can aggregate happiness across lives? We might think that there was
something faintly totalitarian about even trying. Surely, we might say,
it is up to each individual to decide *for himself* what makes his own life
go best. It is, after all, *his life.*

That it is harder to aggregate across lives than within them is widely
acknowledged among utilitarians. That it is impossible to aggregate
interpersonally is a much stronger claim, and a much more controversial one. As with the last question, there are two ways a utilitarian can
go to explain how interpersonal aggregation might be possible. One is
to imagine us all voting together on what arrangement we think will
make most of us most happy, and say that it is the verdict of the majority
that settles how best to aggregate interpersonally. This explanation of
interpersonal aggregation tends towards a subjectivist and preference-
based view. The other is to imagine an expert whose role it is to *work
out* what arrangement best captures the most happiness for the most of
us. This time, Bentham seems to be on the side of the expert (indeed he
writes in a way that suggests that the utilitarian is himself the expert):

> Sum up all the values of all the pleasures on the one side, and
> those of all the pains on the other. The balance, if it be on the side
> of pleasure, will give the *good* tendency of the act [or practice] on
> the whole ... if on the side of pain, the *bad* tendency of it on the
> whole.   ([1789] 1962: 40)

This latter explanation tends towards an objectivist (and more elitist)
view of interpersonal aggregation. Both options have their adherents
in contemporary philosophy.

A third option that is also interesting is to allow *intrapersonal*
aggregation while rejecting *interpersonal* aggregation: to say that we
can measure and compare amounts of happiness within lives, but not
between them. If we take this line, we might end up with a theory that
is utilitarian within lives, but non-utilitarian between lives. That is an
interesting possibility, but it is not really a form of utilitarianism at all.
(You could take this route and end up with a theory that was [roughly]

Kantian or contractarian overall, but had a utilitarian-looking frag-ment within it, namely the bit of the theory that deals with individuals' choices within their own lives.) Since our topic here is utilitarianism, I shall say no more about this possibility here.

One final question about aggregationism is this: why should I *care* about the interpersonal aggregate of happiness? Utilitarianism tells me (as we shall see) that what I have reason to do is bring about the great-est possible amount of happiness in general. But *why* do I have reason to do that? Why do I have reason to do more than bring about *my own* happiness?

This question is the utilitarian version of the well-known problem of egoism, a problem closely related to Chapter 3's "Why be moral?" prob-lem. In another way, the question brings us back to the issue of internal and external reasons raised in Chapter 6. One way of responding to it is to look for an argument – as I did in §6.7 – for thinking that every-one has the same internal reasons, and that these include reasons to bring about the general happiness. Another way of responding to it is to accept that we do not necessarily have internal reasons to bring about the general happiness, but argue that we do have *external* reason to do this, and that it would be nice if our internal motivations were to line up to match this external reason. This seems to be the strategy of argu-ment that is pursued by, for instance, Peter Singer (1995), who takes "the moral point of view", defined in the utilitarian way in which he understands it, to be something that we may or may not want to adopt.

I have no space here to do more than note these possibilities for a utilitarian theorist who is developing his aggregationism. The main point for the moment is simply that, in one of these ways or another, the utilitarian does need to be able to make aggregationism workable. For unless he can measure the good, he will not be able to deploy the third component of his view: his maximalism. I turn to maximalism in the next section.

9.5 Maximalism

Maximalism, recall, is the thesis that it is always obligatory to take the best option available. I said in §9.2 that some intuitions tell in favour of this thesis: if you can go for the best, why go for anything less? On the other hand, some other intuitions tell against it. It is natural to think that there are some actions that are "above and beyond the call of duty": it is good if we do them, but we are not wrong not to do them. Heroic or superhuman virtue cannot reasonably be *demanded* of people, as maximalism suggests it should be. (But perhaps the maximalist can separate his commitment to the view that "It is always wrong not to bring about the best" from his views about blame. Perhaps he can say that blame too is only justified if it brings about the best, and that blaming people for not bringing about the best is not, itself, a practice of blaming that brings about the best. So, at any rate, many utilitarians have suggested.)

The maximalist thesis that it is always obligatory to take the best option available presupposes that there always *is* a best option. This presupposition, however, can be challenged. One sort of challenge arises from the sort of difficulties for aggregationism noted in §9.4. If the goodness of alternative options is always a matter of the happiness or pleasure that they produce, but there is no good way of ranking instances of happiness or pleasure, then there will be no best option either.

The maximalist can point out, in reply, that no one would deny that we can meaningfully compare *some* options for goodness or badness, and that very often their goodness or badness has something to do with happiness or unhappiness, pleasure or pain. It is better to hand out chocolate bars than hand grenades in the playground, and at least part of the reason why is clearly that chocolate bars cause children pleasure, whereas hand grenades cause them pain. The maximalist can say that his position is simply a generalization of these moves.

This generalization faces another kind of problem, about the difficulty of knowing that any option you identify *is* the best one. There seem to be indefinitely many ways of doing anything, and all of them can be counted as different options. Since they are different options, the question arises which of them is the best. This commits the agent who takes maximalism seriously to working out which of them is the best. But that looks like a task of indefinite length.

Of course, when faced with this task a maximalist can respond "Enough deliberating: we've surely fixed on the best option by now". But that you have found the best option is a substantial assumption. Unless you are quite sure that it is correct, maximalism gives you no permission to act on it. It always seems possible that a little more thought would have enabled you to see a better option than the one you have so far identified as best; if so, you should have deliberated further, and taken that option. There again, it always seems possible that a little more thought would have been a waste of time. The trouble is that it is very hard to tell which of these alternatives is true. And if we cannot tell, then we cannot answer the question "Should I act on this option, or deliberate further about what to do?": not, at least, if we are determined to take *literally* the best option available.

Here a maximalist might remind us of the distinction between *deliberative procedure* and *criterion of rightness* that I made in §8.5. Surely, he will say, we need not suppose that agents must actually, in deliberation, think through all the options in order to determine which of them is best. Certainly agents could not function if they even tried to do that. But so what? Maximalism says that the agent acts rightly iff he takes the best option. It does not commit the agent to deliberating in such a way as to sort through all the options until he has spotted the best one. My criticism, he will say, confuses deliberative procedure and criterion of rightness. Keep them distinct, and we can accept the maximalist criterion of rightness without worrying too much whether anyone can follow that criterion of rightness in practice, or indeed whether anyone ever does, strictly speaking, act in a way that the maximalist will count as correct.

This response raises two further questions. First, if the maximalist agrees that we should not attempt to identify best options in real-time deliberation, then how, according to him, *should* we deliberate? His most promising answer seems to be: "By whatever means of deliberation maximizes good consequences". But this answer prompts another question: which method of deliberation maximizes good consequences? And that question, apparently, is merely a new variant of the original problem. Instead of choosing an action from an indefinitely large range of alternatives, we are now trying to choose a method of deliberation from an indefinitely large range of alternatives. Has the maximalist escaped the problem by modularizing his theory? Or just relocated it?

The second further question is this. If the maximalist's criterion of rightness is not to be used in actual deliberation, then when *is* it used? (Cf. a question I asked about virtue ethics in §8.5.) The difficulty about identifying the best option does not go away when we turn from deliberative processes to a criterion of rightness. If the best option is so hard to identify, then not only is it hard to identify in real time deliberation; it is equally hard to identify in calm reflection in a quiet hour.

"It is not to be expected", writes Bentham, "that this process [of evaluating consequences] should be strictly pursued previously to every moral judgement, or to every legislative or judicial operation. It may, however, be always kept in view" ([1789] 1962: 66). What, we might wonder, does "keeping in view" mean here?

Apparently Bentham's idea in distinguishing deliberative procedure from criterion of rightness like this is to suggest that there is some possible standpoint from which we can look over our deliberative practices and our choices in general, to try to make sure that they are optimal even when we assess them from a detached viewpoint. But if it is difficult to identify the best option, it must be equally difficult to identify, or know we are occupying, this detached viewpoint.

Here a point that I made in §9.1 comes back into focus, about the crucial importance, for ethical theory, of actual deliberative processes. The present difficulty for maximalism is that it proposes a criterion of rightness ("Do the best option") that, by definition, is likely to come adrift from any actual deliberative process. In practice, maximalists tend to get round this difficulty by identifying the best option *that there is* with the best option *from whatever small and manageable set of options they actually work with*. However, the best option *that maximalists can think of* might easily not coincide with the best option *that there is*. After all, the options that people actually come up with, when they try to generate a list, are likely to be shaped by their antecedent view of the world – their prejudices, their obsessions, their blind spots and so on – in just the kind of modularizing way that Table 2 (§8.3) describes, only without the prior, and separate, attempt to become virtuous. The danger here for maximalism is the danger of seeming to deliberate more rationally than they really do.

These difficulties about maximalism might prompt the question: can a utilitarian reject it? The answer is yes, in principle. There is obviously nothing incoherent about a moral theory that accepts welfarism, aggregationism and consequentialism, but denies maximalism. The main difficulty in rejecting maximalism is simply what will replace it.

Maximalism, remember, is an answer to the question "Which options should we take?". If a utilitarian accepts no other theory to fill the gap left by maximalism, then the utilitarian will have a hole at the heart of his moral theory. If he accepts some other theory, then there will be an interesting question about what theory this will be, and how stable its relation will be to the rest of his view.

It is easy enough to propose a *satisficing* version of utilitarianism, like this:

> *Satisficing utilitarianism:* An action is right iff it is any action that produces good enough consequences.

The difficulty with satisficing utilitarianism is to say what counts as "good enough", and why. The utilitarian has two options in answering this question: he can argue that there is some uniquely correct answer to this question, or he can just stipulate an answer. Either way, a maximalist utilitarian is likely to be his fiercest critic. As before, the intuitively gripping question is: why should we ever settle for less than the best we can do?

So much for maximalism, for now. I shall have more to say in §9.7 about the relation between moral theory and actual deliberative procedures. These comments will be relevant to the assessment of maximalism, although they will arise from the assessment of utilitarianism overall. In §9.6 I turn to the fourth and last component thesis of utilitarianism: consequentialism.

9.6 Consequentialism

Consequentialism, I said in §9.2, is the thesis that *the goodness of any option depends only on the goodness of its consequences*. Note that "only". Consequentialism goes much further than the obvious and intuitive view that the consequences of what you do are morally important. It goes further, even, than the plausible view that the consequences are *always* important. Consequentialism is the view that *only* the consequences are *ever* important.

One question for consequentialism is: how are we to identify the consequences of any action? Not all actions *have* consequences, not, at least, in the same way. Some actions are like pushing a button that operates an ejector-seat. They are straightforward cause-and-effect sequences, with a means–end structure. The point of the action of pushing the button is the consequence of pushing the button, the end to which pushing that button is a means: namely, the operation of the ejector-seat. But other actions do not have this sort of structure. Playing the violin may be a way of enjoying yourself, something you do "for pleasure". But that does not mean that violin-playing is to enjoyment as pressing the button is to the flight of the ejector-seat. Violin-playing is not a means to the end of enjoyment; rather, it is an instance of enjoyment. (Here again is the distinction between instrumental and constitutive relations that we saw in §5.1.)

Perhaps the consequentialist can accommodate this by a small technical wiggle. Can he not say, truly enough, that the consequence of my violin-playing is that it will then be true that I have played the violin? However, this does not seem quite right. My reason for playing the violin is not that I want to *have played* the violin, but that I want *to play* the violin. So perhaps what the consequentialist ought to say is that my violin-playing is, so to speak, *its own* consequence. And likewise with other actions that, like violin-playing and unlike pressing the ejector button, do not aim at anything beyond themselves.

Perhaps this idea can be made to work. Whether or not it can, the consequentialist still has another question to face up to. The normal notion of a consequence – before we stretch the notion in the theory-driven way I have just suggested – is the notion of a future effect of what I do now. So a consequence-based reason for action has to be a reason for action that comes from the future. But, someone might say, our reasons for action do not *have* to come from the future; they can come from the past or the present as well. For example, training now for a marathon next month is action on a reason that comes from the future. My reason for training is that, when the marathon comes, I want to be physically ready for it. But greeting you warmly as you arrive in my room is action on a reason that arises in the present: here you are, and I want to express my friendly feelings towards you. And punishing or thanking someone for what they did yesterday is action on a reason that comes from the past: you did whatever-it-was, and it is now time to respond appropriately to your deed. Consequentialism finds it natural to assume that all reasons for action come from the future. But there seem to be reasons that are best understood as coming from the past or the present. The question remains: how should consequentialism handle these reasons?

A related criticism is this: the consequentialist thinks not only that reasons come from the future, but also that they come from future *states of affairs*. But thinking again about the case of violin-playing, we might wonder whether it is any state of affairs at all that I am aiming at in playing the violin. Isn't my aim an *activity*, not a state of affairs? And similarly, if I greet you in a friendly fashion, might we not say that my aim is a *relationship* (with you), not a state of affairs? Or if I thank you or punish you, isn't my aim an *expression of my views*, not a state of affairs? When you think about it, consequentialism seems to invest quite a lot in the idea that value-bearing entities can only be states of affairs, not items from other categories such as, for instance, activities or relationships or expressions. But this idea has been questioned, for example by Williams: "We do not merely want the world to contain certain states of affairs ... it is a deep error of consequentialism to believe that this is all we want" (1985: 56).

A different sort of question about consequentialism is raised by the point that we need to decide *which* consequences we are going to look at. In the definition of consequentialism that I have given, there is no justification for doing anything but looking at literally the total consequences of any option that is taken. But if we do that, we will face two very difficult questions. One is the question we have already considered: what counts as a consequence of something? And the other is: when can we be sure that we have seen the *last* consequence of anything? Is my writing these words a consequence of the Norman Conquest, and if so, is it something that the Normans should have taken into account in deciding whether to invade England in 1066? (It is not exactly obvious that William the Conqueror and his army cared about any moral considerations, let alone those relating to 900 years in the future.) Again, a deed might have nothing but mildly good consequences for 1000 years, and then catastrophic consequences for 10,000: the discovery of petroleum, for instance. It is a very familiar complaint about consequentialism that it is hard to know how to assess future consequences.

To deal with this problem, consequentialists can distinguish between *subjective* and *objective* rightness. The subjectively right thing to do is the one based on the calculus of foreseen consequences; the objectively right thing is the one based on the calculus of all consequences, seen and unforeseen. We are always justified in doing the subjectively right thing, provided we do our best to ensure that "subjectively best" and "objectively best" coincide.

One question worth considering about this manoeuvre is this: how do we draw a stable line between foreseen and unforeseen consequences? Notice that the more I reflect and try to find out, the more I will foresee. So I will face a series of decisions about whether it will produce better consequences for me to deliberate further in order to get a clearer idea of the consequences of my various options, or to assess them as I understand them now. These decisions look as if they might be pretty tricky.

Another way of dealing with the problems of consequentialism brings us to consider an important subgroup of theories within the utilitarian group: namely the "indirect" or "rule" versions of utilitarianism.

9.7 Rule utilitarianism

The basic consequentialist thesis says that the rightness or wrongness of any action depends only on the goodness of its consequences. But consider the group of contemporary theorists whom we may call rule utilitarians. (This is my name for them, in line with my definitions. They usually call themselves "rule consequentialists", because they use "consequentialist" in the broad sense of "utilitarian-style but not actually utilitarian").

Instead of looking at individual actions, rule utilitarians look at *policies* of action. They propose that the rightness or wrongness of any general policy of action depends on the goodness of the consequences of generally implementing that policy. This revision helps the rule utilitarian to explain why we should keep various sorts of basic moral rule, such as "Do not steal", even in situations where a more act-oriented utilitarian would have to say that we ought to steal, because the one-off action of stealing will be better for overall utility.

If we adopt this sort of view, we can produce a version of utilitarianism on which the account of right action will read something like this:

Rule utilitarianism: An action is right iff it is an action in accordance with the set of rules that, if they were accepted as a general policy, would produce the best consequences.

This formulation suffers from the problem noted above: the problem of ever being sure that the consequences of anything are literally the best possible. Indeed rule utilitarianism suffers from a more severe form of that problem than "straight" utilitarianism (act utilitarianism). For it is bound to be harder, and more complicated, to compare the possible consequences of following a whole variety of alternative general policies or codes of ethics, than to compare the possible consequences of a variety of alternative single actions.

Rule utilitarians could deal with this problem by softening the maximalism inherent in their account of rightness to produce a satisficing theory parallel to the one displayed in §9.5:

Satisficing rule utilitarianism: An action is right iff it is an action in accordance with any set of rules that, if they were accepted as a general policy, would produce good enough consequences.

Satisficing rule utilitarianism still faces the same problems about knowing what consequences any action or policy will produce. There is also the problem that I noted with the previous satisficing theory, about knowing how good "good enough" is. Nonetheless, this theory might seem less threatened than ordinary rule utilitarianism by difficulties about identifying the best of all possible general policies.

Another way of raising problems for rule utilitarianism is to probe the phrase "general policy"; that is, to ask questions about the different possible degrees of compliance with any rule. Any set of rules is likely to produce one set of consequences if everyone complies with it, but quite another set of consequences if only 80 per cent of people comply with it, and different consequences again if the compliance rate is only 40 per cent. And our obligations under any rule apparently vary, depending on how many other people comply with it. The fact that it would be nice if everyone in my society voted, or paid their taxes in full, does not show that I am morally obliged to vote or pay my taxes even if everyone else is a non-voting tax-dodger.

There are structural similarities between this problem for rule utilitarianism and the "moral weightlifting" problem that I noted for virtue ethics in §8.5. In both cases we have an idealized account of right action that fails to apply to actual agents because a feature of reality has been idealized away: the fact that actual agents are never *fully* virtuous in the case of the "moral weightlifting" objection; the fact that 100 per cent compliance with any code of rules is almost unheard of in the case of the present objection. One possible response (the "variable-rate" response; see Ridge 2007) is to treat rule utilitarianism as a *disjunction* of codes. We can say, in effect: here is the code that it prescribes given 80 per cent compliance, here is the code it prescribes given 70 per cent compliance, and so on; together with a general injunction to promote conformity to the 100 per cent code, or at least the highest-compliance code possible.

There is an obvious analogy between this variable-rate rule utilitarianism and the version of the virtue ethical account of rightness at which we eventually arrived in Chapter 8, which specifies what to do if you are a minimally virtuous or approximately virtuous rather than a fully virtuous agent, but also tells you to aim to become more virtuous. However – and here the analogy with virtue ethics runs out – this "variable-rate" proposal also raises fairly daunting epistemic problems. To formulate the variable-rate version of rule utilitarianism, we do not just need to know the consequences of *one* level of compliance with *one* set of rules. That might be hard enough; but what we need to know is the consequences of *every* level of compliance with *as many different sets of rules as turn out to be needed to cover all levels of compliance,* from 0 per cent to 100 per cent. To go beyond formulating variable-rate rule utilitarianism and actually implement it, we need to know still more: not only what we need to know to formulate the position, but also what level of compliance we are actually dealing with in the real world now. This sets up the worry that variable-rate rule utilitarianism contains too many unknowns for us to have much idea what verdicts on real decisions that theory might offer.

I turn to a different question that we might raise about rule utilitarianism: why *rules* particularly? There is a possible indirect utilitarian position that we might call virtues utilitarianism, which says this:

Virtue utilitarianism: An action is right iff it is an action in accordance with the set of virtues that, if they were generally accepted in society, would produce the best consequences.

And there is another called motive utilitarianism, which says this:

Motive utilitarianism: An action is right iff it is an action in accordance with the set of emotions that, if they were generally felt by people in our society, would produce the best consequences (see Adams 1976).

The question "Why rules particularly?" can be read as a challenge to justify the indirect utilitarian's usual focus on optimific rules rather than, say, virtues or motives or emotions (or other entities such as responses or choices or deliberations or laws or institutions; cf. §9.1). It can also be read as a plea, not for any sort of indirect utilitarianism, but for a *global* utilitarianism: maybe the actions to look for are the ones that are based on *everything* that is optimific.

Contemporary debate about this problem connects with a different objection to rule utilitarianism, which usually comes from other utilitarians. This objection – the *collapse* objection to rule utilitarianism – focuses on its *indirectness*. The whole point of utilitarianism, this sort of critic will say, is to maximize the goodness of outcomes. So does rule utilitarianism's focus on general rules (such as "Do not steal"), rather than on particular decisions (such as whether or not to steal here and now), have that effect? Does accepting rule utilitarianism's account of rightness maximize the goodness of outcomes?

The question poses a dilemma for rule utilitarianism. Suppose the rule utilitarian's focus on general rules such as "Do not steal" *does* maximize the goodness of outcomes. But in that case, the rules that the rule utilitarian tells us to keep are rules that the act utilitarian tells us to keep too. For act utilitarianism tells us to do whatever maximizes the goodness of outcomes. If that includes acting as we would if we were obeying rules such as "Do not steal", then act utilitarianism tells us to act that way. And then rule utilitarianism turns out to be just a complicated and roundabout way of saying what act utilitarianism says more simply. As people say, rule utilitarianism *collapses* into act utilitarianism (see Lyons 1965).

Suppose, alternatively, that the rule utilitarian's focus on general rules such as "Do not steal" *does not* maximize the goodness of outcomes, because it leads us to lose utility that we could get by breaking the rule against stealing every now and then. If, by contrast, we accepted act utilitarianism, then we would break the rule against stealing whenever there was more utility to be gained by breaking that rule than by keeping it. So the only distinctive effect of rule utilitarianism on our choices will be to lose us utility. The only differences between the verdicts given by rule and by act utilitarianism, in practice, will come in those cases where rule utilitarianism tells us not to steal, even though there is more utility in stealing than in not stealing. Therefore rule utilitarianism is bound to be a theory the accepting of which produces less utility than the accepting of act utilitarianism does. So given the choice between the two theories, we have a good utilitarian reason to prefer act utilitarianism: namely, that accepting it produces better consequences than accepting rule utilitarianism.

The rule utilitarian has two possible responses to this objection. One is to abandon maximalism. The rule utilitarian who takes this line will accept that rule utilitarianism is sub-optimal: it does not produce as much utility as act utilitarianism. However, he will say, that loss of utility is worthwhile, because it means that rule utilitarianism can reflect our intuitions about situations where we ought not to do what promotes utility, for example undetectable theft or murder, better than act utilitarianism can. (This is one of the things that Hooker [2003] says about the objection; in this sense Hooker is not what I mean by a consequentialist, either.)

Alternatively, the rule utilitarian can say that his theory is not sub-optimal at all. He can argue that any serious attempt to advocate and practise an act utilitarian moral theory will lead to all sorts of unintended negative effects – loss of trust due to optimific stealing, for example – and that the best way to avoid these unintended negatives is to advocate or practise not act utilitarianism, but rule utilitarianism. In other words, rule utilitarianism is the best way, in practice, of aiming at the act utilitarian target. Or as we might also put it, the best reason for being a rule utilitarian is that act utilitarianism is true, but *unthinkably* true.

This point about unthinkability brings us back to the notion of modularity with which I began this chapter. In "two-level" utilitarian theories (as they are called), there is, typically, a set of rules, values or aspirations close to those found in common-sense morality, which is defended by appeal to a deeper theory that justifies these rules or values on utilitarian grounds. The various species of indirect utilitarianism are the results of this sort of thinking, rule utilitarianism being the best known of these theories. The whole point of such "two-level" theories is to introduce into utilitarianism something like the modularity that the virtues introduce into virtue ethics (see §8.3). It is easy to justify such modularity on utilitarian grounds in *general* terms. After all, as I argued in §9.5, there is a problem about how there can be any finite deliberation without such modularity. However, two problems then follow.

First, the utilitarian theory that does the justifying sinks into the background. The common-sense rules that have been justified become the main feature of the theory, and it becomes unclear how exactly the resulting theory counts as a *utilitarian* theory, especially when, as is often the case, that theory contains views or attitudes, for example about rule-keeping or the nature of friendship, with an explicitly anti-utilitarian content.

Secondly, the utilitarian faces a real difficulty in attempting to justify any specific form of the modularity that he wants. As we saw in §9.4, any distinctively *utilitarian* justification of this modularity would have, itself, to be a non-modular justification. That is, it would have to be a justification that showed that the preferred form of modularity was to be preferred *because it was literally the best version of modularity available*. But the whole reason we are looking for modularity in the first place is that (as I argued against the ethical rationalist in §8.3) non-modular justifications of this form are very difficult, if not impossible, to sustain.

This means that utilitarianism faces a difficulty about how to combine two of its central ambitions. One is to keep actual deliberative practice manageably finite and definite; the other is to give actual deliberative practice the sort of unique rational authority that could only come from knowing, of any verdict of actual deliberative practice, that it was a literally maximizing verdict.

I shall say more about this difficulty for utilitarianism (and other theories that face the same problem) in Chapter 11. In the meantime, these difficulties about utilitarianism might lead us to attempt to develop an ethical theory on a quite different basis: not on the basis of the promotion of well-being that utilitarianism starts from, but from an examination of the content of the notion of practical reason. This latter line is the one followed by the Kantian. I turn to it in Chapter 10.

10

Kantianism and contractarianism

In theory, there is no difference between theory and practice; but not in practice. (Anon.)

Those are my principles. If you don't like them, I have others.
(Groucho Marx)

10.1 Introducing Kantianism

In the two chapters I have devoted so far to normative ethics, I have said little or nothing about rules. This might seem surprising. When philosophy students first begin thinking about normative ethics, they usually assume that it is mainly about rules, or at least basically about rules. But this certainly is not true of either virtue ethics or utilitarianism. (This is not true, at least, if it is specific rules you have in mind. You could see these theories' accounts of rightness as rules in themselves, so that virtue ethics becomes identical with some rule such as "Always do the action that the virtuous agent would characteristically do in the circumstances", and utilitarianism becomes identical with some rule such as "Always do the action with the best consequences for happiness or pleasure". But this is not what people usually mean by talking about rules.)

It is not that either virtue ethics or utilitarianism is necessarily hostile to rules. Both theories can involve laying down moral rules, including, quite possibly, unbreakable rules. (Or at any rate, rules that a moral agent *should view* as unbreakable, which is not quite the same thing.) Rules are obviously an important part of *rule* utilitarianism, and of some other "two-level" utilitarian theories (see §9.7). However, the rules are not fundamental in any of these theories, not even rule utilitarianism. For virtue ethicists and utilitarians, the point of having a rule against, say, stealing is that the recognition and practice of such a rule is necessary if human beings are to live well. The rule is not basic or fundamental. In both moral theories, it is derived from the notion of well-being, which *is* fundamental.

When we turn to Kantianism in this chapter, we might perhaps expect this to change: we might expect to encounter a moral theory in which rules are fundamental. In fact we do not. As I shall explain, rules are not the fundamental thing in Kantianism either, rational agency is.

All the same, rules are probably the best place to start if we want to understand Kantianism. My initial characterization of Kantianism in §3.1 said this:

Kantianism: An action is right iff it is in accordance with a universalizable principle and not contrary to any universalizable principle.

This looks like a formulation that puts principles or rules (are they the same thing, or slightly different things?) at the very heart of our ethical thought. And this impression is only strengthened when we take our first look at the three most famous things in Kant's own moral writings, the three formulations of his "Categorical Imperative" in his *Groundwork of the Metaphysic of Morals* (or, rather, the three best-known formulations, and the ones that he focuses most on; he gives other formulations as well). The first of these three formulations tells us this:

Formula of universal law: "Act only on that maxim through which you can at the same time will that it should become a universal law" (Kant [1785] 1948: 84).

This is clearly an injunction to formulate rules, or principles, and live by them. So is the second formula, which gives us this instruction:

Formula of ends in themselves: "Act in such a way that you always treat humanity, whether in your own person or in the person of any other, never simply as a means, but always at the same time as an end in itself" (*ibid.*: 91).

The third formula too is obviously intended to enunciate a rule or principle:

Formula of the kingdom of ends: "All maxims as proceeding from our own making of law ought to harmonise with a possible kingdom of ends as a kingdom of nature" (*ibid.*: 98).

How do these three formulations relate to each other? Kant explains that they are all different ways of expressing the same idea: these "three ways of representing the principle of morality are at bottom merely [three] formulations of precisely the same law" (*ibid.*: 97). As the word "formula" itself suggests, his idea is that each of the three formulations is deducible from either of the other two. Each can be rewritten as either of the other two, rather as the algebraic equation $4x - 4 = 12$ can be rewritten as $4x = 12 + 4$, or as $4x = 16$, or as $x = 4$, and so on.

To understand the formulas and their interrelations, let us start with the first formulation, "Act only on that maxim through which you can at the same time will that it should become a universal law". What does this tell me to do?

It tells me, when I am considering performing any action, to ask myself what the "maxim" of that action is: what principle I am expressing by performing it, or as we might also put it, *what I am saying* by doing it. For example, suppose I grab all the cake for myself and leave you none. What am I saying by my action? Well, that depends on the context, of course. Perhaps there is something unusual about the context that we have not been told: maybe, for instance, I am grabbing all the cake for myself in order to distribute it to the starving. But if there is nothing unusual about the context, then what I am saying by this action is that I deserve to have as much cake as I like, that I do not care whether you want any cake, that you do not deserve any cake – something like that. Alternatively, suppose I slice the cake carefully in half and offer some to you before I take any. What am I saying by *this* action? Unusual contexts aside, I am saying that you have the same right to cake as I do, that you deserve cake too, that I respect you and care about you – something like that. As Kant would put it: the "maxim" of grabbing the cake for myself is (roughly) "I shall take what food I want without regard to others", and the "maxim" of sharing the cake with you is (roughly) "I shall share food with others, who may well want it just as much as I do".

Now I have the maxims of these two possible actions. The next step is for me to ask myself, about each of these two maxims, "Can I will that this maxim should become a universal law?" That is to say, could *everybody* consistently act in this way: either the cake-grabbing way or the cake-sharing way? Kant thinks that the answer is no for cake-grabbing, and yes for cake-sharing: as it is often put, cake-sharing is universalizable, but cake-grabbing is not. Hence cake-sharing is rationally and morally permissible, and cake-grabbing is not.

But *why* (we should ask here) is cake-sharing universalizable, and cake-grabbing not universalizable? It is not exactly difficult to imagine a world where everyone grabs cake and nobody shares it. We are only too close to living in one! Kant agrees that a cake-grabbing world is possible, maybe even actual. But that is not his point.

So does he, perhaps, mean that a cake-sharing world is *better* than a cake-grabbing world, as a rule utilitarian would want to remind us here? Or that a cake-sharing world is *more desirable to live in* than a cake-grabbing world, as a rule utilitarian would also want to observe? Kant does, of course, believe that a cake-sharing world is better, and more desirable to live in, than a cake-grabbing world. But Kant is not a rule utilitarian, and the comparison of the two worlds for betterness or desirability is not his point either. (Nor, as he himself stresses in an unfortunately neglected footnote, is he just saying "Do as you would be done by": "Let no one think here that the trivial '*quod tibi non vis fieri, etc.*' [what you do not want done to you, do not do to others] can serve as a standard or principle … it is merely derivative from our principle" [*ibid.*: 92].)

Rather, Kant's point is that we cannot *will* cake-grabbing as a universal *law*. The two words that I have italicized in this sentence are the keys to understanding it. Willing, for Kant, does not just mean any old desiring or wanting or preferring; it means *rationally choosing*. And law, for Kant, is not just any old way the world might be arranged; it is a *rational system*, an arrangement of the world *in line with reason*.

Why, then, can we not rationally choose cake-grabbing rather than cake-sharing as a universal rational system? Because such a system would not *be* rational. Why not? Because in a cake-grabbing world, everyone would, in the words of the second formulation of the categorical imperative, "treat everyone else merely as a means, and not also at the same time as ends in themselves". In such a world, other people would just be potential obstacles to my own cake-grabbing activities, and they would see me the same way. In other words, no one would have any *respect* for anyone else. Or in the words of the third formulation, our maxims would not harmonize into a single rationally coherent system of choices (a "kingdom of ends"); instead, they would constantly be in conflict as we fight with each other to grab as much of the cake as possible.

But why can I not be treating the world as a rational system, a "kingdom of ends", unless I respect other people as ends in themselves, and try to harmonize my maxims with theirs? Because they *are* ends in themselves. I am not the only person who deliberates (or can deliberate) in the way that Kant describes: as a "maker of universal law". *Every* person, according to Kant, is someone who deliberates (or can deliberate) in this universal way. This capacity to deliberate universally is what Kant means by the word "humanity" in the formula of ends in themselves. And wherever we find humanity in this sense, he tells us that we are rationally obliged to respect it. This rational obligation is most obvious in my own case: if I do not treat my own capacity to deliberate universally with at least some respect, then I will lose or endanger that capacity. But the same capacity for "making universal law" that I find in myself, and must respect in myself, I can find in all other human beings too, and must respect it in them too for just the same reason, because to fail to respect it would be to endanger or destroy it.

In sum: for Kant, the reason why I should choose to share the cake with you, not grab it all for myself, comes from a difference that he finds between the two worlds where cake-sharing and cake-grabbing are the general practice. The difference is not that the cake-sharing world is possible, and the cake-grabbing world impossible: clearly both worlds are possible. Nor is the difference that the cake-sharing world is nice, and the cake-grabbing world nasty: that is true, but it is not Kant's point. The difference is that the cake-sharing world is a (realized) "kingdom of ends", a world in which each person chooses to act in a way that respects other people's capacity to choose in ways that respect everybody's capacities to choose. If I am to choose rationally, then *any* world that I choose must be a "kingdom of ends" in this sense. For if it is not, I will not be choosing in a way that respects *my own* capacity to choose such worlds. Instead, I will be choosing in a way that undermines or perhaps even destroys my own capacity to choose. Such choices are irrational because they are self-defeating or self-frustrating.

This brief summary of Kant's ethics may make it clear why I started by saying that rules or principles are not the fundamental thing in Kantianism: rational agency is. Certainly, for Kant, agency or choice cannot be rational unless it is universalizable, unless it is the kind of choice that is not self-defeating or self-frustrating in the kind of way just described. And Kant does think that universalizable choices will usually have to be choices that obey rules or principles. However, first, there are many ways of obeying a rule; I am currently obeying the rule against murder, and so (I hope) are you, but for all that we are very likely to be doing quite different things. And secondly, Kant thinks it quite possible that what is usually accepted as a general rule of ethics can turn out to be no more than a guideline: it all depends whether or not the rule in question is really founded on the requirements of rational consistency as Kant describes them.

Another way of explaining why, and how, Kant makes rational agency his starting-point is to develop a comparison with Kant's theory of knowledge. I pursue this rather more difficult, but also more fundamental, line of thought in §10.2.

10.2 Kant, scepticism and the Copernican turn

The starting-point of all Kant's philosophy – not just his ethics, but his theory of knowledge too – is his novel response to Cartesian scepticism. Descartes worries that he can do nothing to prove that it is possible for him to have any knowledge of the world outside his own head. Descartes himself, of course, was no sceptic: he proposed a solution to the puzzle set by this worry. But his successors, including Kant, have usually found Descartes's puzzle more impressive than his solution to it.

Descartes asked "What can be known about the world?", and found himself facing a problem about how to justify any claim to know. According to Kant, the root of Descartes's difficulty is that he is asking the wrong question. Instead of asking "What can be known about the world?", Descartes should have asked – and we should ask – "What kind of knowers are we?". Instead of trying to develop a theory of knowledge by focusing on the *objects* of knowledge, the world "out there", Descartes should have tried to develop a theory of knowledge by focusing on the *subjects* of knowledge: the minds that do the knowing.

This turn from the object of knowledge to its subject is Kant's famous "Copernican turn":

> Hitherto it has been assumed that all our knowledge must conform to objects. But all attempts to extend our knowledge of objects ... have, on this assumption, ended in failure. We must therefore make trial whether we may not have more success in the tasks of metaphysics, if we suppose that objects must conform to our knowledge ... We should then be proceeding [in the manner of] Copernicus .... Failing of satisfactory progress in explaining the movements of the heavenly bodies on the assumption that they all revolved around the spectator, he tried [supposing] that it was the spectator who revolved while the stars remained at rest.
>
> (Kant [1787] 1989: 29, B xiv)

Kant wants us to give up the assumption that "All our knowledge must conform to objects", and replace it with the assumption that "All objects must conform to our knowledge". He thinks that, instead of vainly trying to get at the reality of what the world is really like, in and of itself, we should try thinking about what pictures of what the world is really like are possible for minds like ours. What kind of order and structure is implicit in *any* picture of the world that we might adopt? What conditions of coherence and consistency must be satisfied by *any* account of reality that we can find credible?

Kant proposes that there is a range of such conditions of coherence. He calls them "rules for the understanding". According to Kant, rationality is a matter of finding and implementing these rules for the understanding. Implementing them is shaping and interpreting the world. Perhaps it is even *making* the world:

> The understanding is something more than a power of formulating rules through the comparison of appearances; it is itself the

lawgiver of nature. Save through it, nature, that is, synthetic unity
of the manifold of appearances according to rules, would not exist
at all.   (*Ibid*.: 148, A 126–7)

We can know about the world, indeed there can *be* a world for us, only
in so far as we can bring the chaotic variety of our experience ("the
manifold of appearances") into an organized system put together by the
mind ("a synthetic unity"). Such a synthetic unity has to be "according
to rules": it is only possible as we apply our rules for the understanding with complete consistency and universal generality. By universally
applying these rules in the same way everywhere, we construct a picture
of the world or, perhaps, we construct the world itself.

The point of this lightning tour of Kant's theory of knowledge is
that his theory of ethics exhibits a closely parallel structure. His theory
of knowledge begins with scepticism about the possibility of knowing
anything much about the world out there. And it stands epistemology
on its head by replacing the familiar question "What can we know
about the world out there?" with the novel question "What kind of
knowers must we be to know anything?". Likewise, Kant's ethics begins
with scepticism about the possibility of knowing anything much about
what "human nature" characteristically needs or wants to fulfil it. So
we cannot know anything much, according to him, about the content
of a true theory of well-being or happiness or *eudaimonia* such as the
virtue ethicist and the utilitarian usually seek as the foundation of their
ethical theories. (And even if we could know enough to arrive at a true
theory of well-being, this theory would have no *moral* significance;
Kant is as convinced as Hume is that no "ought" can be derived from
an "is" [§6.2].) Kant stands naturalistic moral theory on its head by
replacing the familiar question "What should we pursue in the world
out there?" with the novel question "What kind of agents must we be
to pursue anything?".

Kant's Cartesian scepticism about the possibility of knowing how
things are in the external world leads him into the philosophical strategy that is called *formalism*: the strategy of deriving the *content* that
any theory of knowledge may have from the *form* that all theories of
knowledge must have. Likewise, Kant's Cartesian scepticism about the
possibility of knowing anything definite about human nature and its
demands leads him into an *ethical* formalism, which, in parallel with

his theory of knowledge, derives the content of moral theory from its form.

Kant's basic question about knowledge is "How can reason apply to what I experience?"; and Kant's basic question about ethics is "How can reason apply to what I choose?". In his theory of knowledge, Kant begins from the hurly-burly, the "blooming, buzzing confusion", of experience. This confusion can only be made sense of by the imposition on it of the universal principles of reason that govern the very possibility of any experience. It is only by understanding those principles that we can come to construct a whole picture of the world on the basis that they provide. Similarly, in his theory of ethics, Kant begins from the hurly-burly confusion and profusion of our desires and wants. The only way to make sense of this confusion, he tells us, is to subordinate it to the universal principles of reason that govern the very possibility of any action: it is only by understanding those principles that we can construct a rationally compelling understanding of ethics. (This is why Kant's position is often called *constructivism*. It is also why I suggested in §7.5 that Kant is a *rationalist*: that what Kant thinks we are talking about, in ethical discourse, is what we have reason to do.)

In epistemology, the theory of knowledge, these universal principles are what Kant calls *concepts*: rules for the understanding that can be applied in the same way in every possible case. In ethics, the theory of action, these universal principles are Kant's *universalizable maxims*: proposals about how to act that can coherently and consistently be applied anywhere and everywhere.

From this parallelism there now emerges Kant's answer to this book's central question: how should life be lived? To ask that question, Kant would say, is to ask what sorts of lives are rationally justifiable. And the only rationally justifiable life, according to Kant, is one lived in accordance with universal maxims.

Hence the concern with universalizability that appears in the Kantian account of rightness, in parallel to the concern with universalizability that appears in the Kantian account of understanding. A principle for thinking by (a concept) is only rationally acceptable if it can be deployed anywhere and everywhere without inconsistency. Likewise, the principle on which an action is done (a maxim) is only rationally acceptable if it can be *universalized*: if anyone anywhere can act on it without inconsistency.

10.3 Reason in action: from form to content

Since the time of Hegel, Kant's first great critic, philosophers have always been putting the following question to Kant and his followers: how does reason in itself determine anything specific about ethics? How does it follow, just from rationality alone, that any moral requirements apply to anyone?

There is a strong tradition in ethics that says that nothing of the sort can possibly follow. According to this tradition, reason in itself lays down no moral guidelines at all: "'Tis not contrary to reason to prefer the destruction of the whole world to the scratching of my little finger" (Hume [1739] 1985: 2.3.3; see §4.3). Kant's claim that the form of pure reason alone is sufficient to determine completely the content of ethics stands in stark contrast to this Humean tradition. Kant defends it, as we have seen, by appealing to *consistency*.

What sort of consistency? The obstacles in Kant's way will seem formidable, if we think that the appeal that he makes is an appeal to consistency in either of the most common senses of the word: (i) making sure that we always act in the same ways in the same circumstances, or (ii) making sure that two or more ethical positions that we hold do not contradict each other.

The first of these notions of consistency – (i) always acting the same way in the same circumstances – is simply not clear enough to be made sense of, as it stands. We need further explanations. We need to know what similarities between which actions count as consistent behaviour, and why. If I consistently randomize in my practical choices, am I acting consistently? We will probably want to say no. But in one way at least, yes I am, because I keep following the possible rule that tells me "Always randomize". If I give one biscuit to every child in the class, am I acting consistently? We will probably want to say yes. But in one way at least, no I am not, because I am ignoring the possible rule that tells me "Always deprive green-eyed children of biscuits". We naturally want to say that being part of a randomizing policy is not a relevant similarity between possible actions, and that being green-eyed is not a relevant difference between actual children. But the notion of "always acting in the same ways in the same circumstances", in itself, implies nothing about which differences or similarities between ways and circumstances are relevant. If a view about what differences and similarities are relevant comes into our moral thinking, it comes in from somewhere else than from the concept of rationality.

Another question about this notion of consistency is the following: does the rule enjoining consistency mean that I must do only actions that *everyone* could do without inconsistency, or only actions that *anyone* could do without inconsistency? Clearly the former is a far more demanding rule than the latter. It seems to rule out hillwalking, for instance. The point of hillwalking is the enjoyment of natural beauty. But if everyone hillwalks, then their activity will destroy that natural beauty. Hillwalking therefore "subverts itself", as Kant would say, if everyone does it: universalized hillwalking defeats its own purpose. So, we may reason, the rule must be weaker; it must be a rule about what *anyone* can do without inconsistency. But then the rule does not seem strong enough to rule out a false promise! For apparently any *one* person could make *one* false promise without that single false promise subverting the whole institution of promising; the institution only collapses if *everyone* makes false promises.

The fact that this first understanding of consistency leads us into these difficulties is a reason for rejecting it. The Kantian rule about universalizability is not a rule about consistency in this sense.

The second notion of consistency that I outlined above – (ii) consistency between ethical positions that we hold – is inadequate because it has nothing to say about the *content* of those ethical positions. For all that this notion of consistency can show, the consistently vicious person need be no less consistent than the consistently virtuous person. Someone who thinks that all Jews should be gassed is consistent if, when it turns out that he himself is a Jew, he duly trots off to the gas chamber. This sort of consistency may perhaps make him seem braver, but it does not make him seem any less despicable overall. This objection is a well-known difficulty for Hare's moral theory, precisely because Hare's notion of consistency is this second notion. But this notion of consistency is not Kant's either.

If it is not (i) or (ii), what is Kant's notion of consistency? As we saw in §§10.1–10.2, his basic idea is a notion of consistency *with the existence and flourishing of rational agency*. What our actions and choices and policies need to be consistent with, in order to be consistent in the sense that really concerns Kant, is not some arbitrarily chosen rule; nor is it each other. What they need to be consistent with – not to undermine or defeat – is the fact that we are acting at all.

To act is to aim at some objective; to aim at some objective is to treat that objective as *worth* aiming at. So any action whatsoever that you may perform implies two views about value. First, it implies that you think that the objective of that action, no matter what it may be, is worth achieving. (If it was not, why would you pursue it?) Secondly, it implies that you think that the fact that you are able to act is a good thing. (If you could not act, how could you pursue it?) No matter what else we may think valuable, there is one thing that we must always implicitly be treating as valuable in every single thing we do: namely, the capacity to will and perform actions itself.

This is why Kant opens the *Groundwork* with these famous words: "It is impossible to think of anything at all in the world, or indeed even beyond it, that is good without limitation, except a good will" ([1785] 1948: 59). The point is that, no matter what else you value, you must value your own good will, meaning your own capacity for valuing things. And no matter what else you take as your aim in action, you must take it as your aim to protect and promote the capacity for *having* aims in action. Any action that you can possibly do always presupposes that you think it is worthwhile to be an agent, a doer of actions. So however else you act, it is always good for you to seek ways to enhance and promote the capacity to be an agent. And whatever else you choose, you must never choose to act in any way that destroys or undermines the status of agency. This is the sense in which Kant thinks that all action, if it is to be rational, must be consistent. It *can* aim at all sorts of ends that it may or may not happen to have (these aims ground what Kant calls "hypothetical imperatives"). But there is one aim that all agency *must* have, necessarily and constitutively. This one necessary aim is expressed in Kant's famous categorical imperative, in the various formulations that we reviewed in §10.1: it is the aim to protect and promote agency – to be consistent, in all I do, with the existence and the flourishing of agency.

Kant's argument, in short, is what he himself would call a *transcendental* argument: it is one that answers our questions, not by producing further evidence to answer them, but by looking at the presuppositions of the questions themselves. The presupposition of our questions about ethics is our own ability to be agents, to choose and act. Accordingly,

Kant says, any action that destroys or undermines agency, whether in me or in other persons, will be inconsistent with agency, and so both irrational and wrong. And the distinction between those creatures in the world who display agency and everything else in the world is absolutely fundamental to Kant's moral thinking: he calls it the distinction between "ends in themselves" and "means", and insists that, while means can be treated as having no value in themselves, we must always treat "ends in themselves", persons, with the fundamentally different attitude that he calls *Achtung*, respect or reverence.

It is for this reason that Kant structures the *Groundwork*'s discussion of the practical consequences of the categorical imperative around four examples of types of action that he believes the categorical imperative rules out: suicide, laziness, lying and refusing to help others.

Suicide involves destroying my own agency (in the most literal sense). But it is inconsistent to be committed both to the value of agency, and also to the particular act that denies that value, namely suicide. So suicide is ruled out by pure practical rationality itself: "a nature whose law it would be to destroy life itself, by means of the same feeling whose destination it is to impel towards the furtherance of life, would contradict itself and would therefore not subsist as nature" ([1785] 1948: 32).

Laziness involves the failure to develop my own talents, which according to Kant is a way of undermining my own agency. For laziness frustrates and stifles the development of a wider scope of abilities in me: "As a rational being, [any person] necessarily wills that all the capacities in him be developed, since they serve him and are given to him for all sorts of possible purposes" (*ibid.*: 33).

Making lying promises, again, destroys the agency of others (still in a literal sense, even if the destruction is less radical than killing them might be). Language and communication are crucial to human agency, because human beings interact with each other all the time; even on his own, any human being does much of his thinking and reasoning in language. Lying promises attack language as a tool of communication, because the point of communication, much of the time, is that it should be communication of *the truth* (about the speaker's intentions or some other state of the world), and that it should be trusted as such. But if we know that others will make lying promises to us whenever it suits them, then we have no reason to trust them, and no reason to expect the truth from them about what they intend; conversely, they have no reason to trust us, or take our attempts to make promises seriously. This makes it impossible for us to act with them, and for them to act with us.

Finally, *refusing to help others* means undermining their agency; it means denying them an opportunity to become capable of wider and more fruitful sorts of choice and action. This is inconsistent with due respect for agency, because it means willing a situation where, typically, I would not get assistance myself when I needed it:

> [A] will that decided this would conflict with itself, since many cases could occur in which one would need the love and sympathy of others and in which, by such a law of nature arisen from his own will, he would rob himself of all hope of the assistance that he needs himself. (*Ibid.*).

Notice one interesting feature of these examples. This is that Kant distinguishes between two categories of reason to act that he calls "perfect" and "imperfect duties". Perfect duties are those, like not committing suicide or not lying, that we can *complete* (Latin *perficere*). Imperfect duties are those, like developing our own talents or helping other people, such that there is always more to do in respect of them, no matter how much we have already done. This distinction is what enables Kant to accommodate the intuition that while we have a duty not to commit suicide, we do not have to do everything we can to stay alive. The duty not to commit suicide is perfect, the duty to keep ourselves healthy and ensure that we live good lives is imperfect. And so it need not be a breach of that duty for a very old, very ill person to allow himself to die.

Kant's distinction between perfect and imperfect duties is intuitively very attractive, but hard for a utilitarian to imitate. Utilitarians are maximalists: they say that we should *promote* the good, and that is naturally understood as always pursuing it as hard as we can, that is, as *maximizing* the good. This naturally leads the utilitarian to the thought that, if life is good, then it must always be wrong not to keep oneself alive. Since that seems an overly strong conclusion, many contemporary utilitarians are led by this train of thought to the conclusion that life cannot be good in itself. But there is another premise in this *reductio* argument that we might dispute, besides the premise that life is good in itself. We might also dispute the utilitarian's assumption that the only thing to do with a value is promote it.

The catalogue of four types of wrong action that I discuss above is not a complete catalogue of all the kinds of wrong actions that there are. But it is, according to Kant, a complete catalogue of the *ways* in which actions can be wrong. Actions can be wrong by (a) undermining or (b) destroying (i) our own agency, or (ii) others' agency. By permutation, that gives us four kinds of wrong action (ai, aii, bi, bii); and all four of these kinds are, Kant thinks, represented among his examples.

This completes my sketch of Kant's moral theory. In the next section, I shall raise and consider five questions facing Kant's view.

10.4 Five questions for Kant's moral theory

Criterion of rightness and decision procedure

The first question that I want to raise about Kant's moral theory is a question that I have already raised about utilitarianism. The question is just: what are we supposed to do with the theory? Is it supposed to help us in real-time deliberation? Or is it supposed to give us a criterion of rightness for reflecting on how we act and deliberate? Or is it meant to do both?

Kant seems close to saying that his moral theory is meant to help us in real-time deliberation when he famously says that action has no moral worth unless it is done "from the motive of duty" ([1785] 1948: 63), where "duty" is apparently his name for moral thinking in line with his theory. If this much-discussed phrase means that Kant expects us to go right through the categorical imperative decision procedure – that is, the line of thinking that I sketched in §10.1 – *every time we act*, then it surely demands too much. No one can realistically be expected to do all this thinking every time they do anything, if only because it is too complicated for there to be time to do it. On any plausible view, action is going to have to be more modular (§8.3) than this.

There might be other claims that Kant has in mind here, though, and not all of these are as implausibly strong as this one. Kant might mean, for instance, that although there is *nothing wrong* with acting without running through the categorical imperative decision procedure, it is only when we use that procedure that our action has *positive* moral worth. Actions involving Kantian moral reasoning are especially good, and better than other actions. That does not mean that other actions are positively *bad*. (Of course a virtue ethicist will disagree with Kant even over this much. He will not be prepared to agree that actions on deliberation are always better than actions on no deliberation, because he thinks, as we saw in §8.2, that quite often it is actually better to act *without* deliberation.) Or again, by "action from the motive of duty" Kant might simply mean that all morally good action must express reverence for the moral law, in which case it can clearly have "the motive of duty" and have other motives as well at the same time. (This interpretation is attractive, but harder to reconcile with what Kant actually says.) There are other possibilities as well, as Kantian scholars have pointed out in a number of essays defending Kant's notion of "the motive of duty". Whichever way he goes on this question, Kant will need to do something to address the question, raised in connection with utilitarianism in Chapter 9, about how any moral theory is supposed to relate to actual deliberative practice. That is an interesting question, but I shall leave it alone for now; we shall come back to it in Chapter 11.

The examples

As we have just seen, Kant reaches the conclusions that we should always be ready to develop our talents or to help others when they are in need, and that we should never make lying promises or commit suicide. The first two duties are examples of imperfect duties: they are not things we have to do on every possible occasion, but merely things we should *always be ready* to do when occasion arises. The latter two duties, by contrast, are examples of perfect duties: not making lying promises and not committing suicide *are* things that, according to Kant, we have to do on every possible occasion.

We might not see at once how to argue against Kant's claims about imperfect duties. The claim that "we ought to be ready to develop our talents or help others as occasion arises" is quite vague, and it certainly would not be attractive to counter that we should *never* develop our talents or help others.

By contrast, it is very easy to see how to argue against Kant's perfect duties. One way to do this is to question the logic that leads Kant to his examples. Why, for example, does Kant think that suicide, actively killing oneself, is *always* destroying one's own agency, in a sense that passively allowing oneself to die is not? Kant's reasons for this claim seem to commit him to something like the distinctions between doing and allowing, and between intending and foreseeing.

Another and simpler way to argue against Kant's perfect duties is just to build counter-examples. The easiest way to do this is to think of a situation where a lying promise, or an act of suicide, seems to be the only way to prevent a disaster. Perhaps I am a leader of the German Resistance during the Second World War who has just been forced by press-ganging Nazis to join the SS, and am now faced with two alternatives: to make the oath of loyalty to Hitler, or to be shot. It is hard to see why it should weigh with me here that my reading the words of the oath will be a lying promise, and will therefore "destroy the capacity for agency" of the Nazis who have press-ganged me. It would not be such a bad thing if their "capacity for agency" *was* destroyed, bearing in mind the kinds of things that they do with this capacity. But even if this consideration does weigh with me, it is hard to see why it should outweigh the counter-balancing consideration that I am the key player in all sorts of crucial German Resistance operations, all of which will be greatly helped if I can act as a "mole" within the SS, but all of which will fail if I am shot.

Kant could make a number of responses to this sort of problem, which was put to him, in his lifetime, by opponents such as Benjamin Constant (who objected that, on Kant's principles, one would have to tell the truth to an axe-murderer who asked you where his intended victim was). Kant's response to Constant, in a famous appendix to his *Critique of Practical Reason*, was to insist on a wide-ranging scepticism about consequences (and about consequentialism; see §9.6). Because we cannot know "the world in itself", we cannot know, at any particular moment, what will happen next. Because we do not know that, we have no justification for making predictions about what will happen next the basis of any part of our ethics. So against Constant's example, Kant replies that, for all you can tell, trying to mislead the axe-murderer by lying to him will backfire and lead him straight to his victim, whereas telling the axe-murderer the truth will accidentally misdirect him *away* from his victim. Consequences cannot be the basis for the calculus of right and wrong; the future is inscrutable, and all sorts of unexpected consequences can result from anything we do. Even in cases where the consequences seem entirely obvious to us (as they do, of course, in Constant's axe-murderer case), consequences are *never* the right source for our ethical decisions, which can only be rational if they arise from something like the categorical imperative decision procedure.

It can be questioned whether Kant's own theory implies that this is the best way for him to meet an objection like Constant's. Kant's theory should certainly commit him to denying consequentialism (§9.6), the view that only consequences are ever relevant to the moral assessment of actions. But his response to Constant suggests that Kant not only denies consequentialism, but holds the view at the opposite extreme: the view that no consequences at all are ever relevant to the moral assessment of actions. This view is very hard to believe. It also seems inconsistent with things that Kant says himself. For instance, Kant apparently says that one reason why we should develop our talents is because doing so *will have the consequence* that the scope of our rational agency will be increased. That may not be the only reason that Kant thinks we have to develop our talents, but it does seem to be one of them. If Kant can appeal to consequences, why can Constant not do so?

Are all agents always "ends in themselves"?

Another response that Kant might have made (but did not) to Constant's axe-murderer example, or my Nazi oath example, brings us to a third question about his moral theory. This question is: do all human beings always really have the status of agency that Kant gives to all "humanity"?

Kant could have met counter-examples like mine and Constant's by saying that some people, in some circumstances, *do not deserve to have their capacity for agency respected.* This might be because they are mad, and thus not properly speaking agents at all (as with the axe-murderer). Or it might be because they are wicked, or acting wickedly at present, and thus themselves responsible for corrupting their agency in such a way that they have become serious threats to the agency of others including us, against which we urgently need to protect ourselves (as with the Nazis). *How* wicked or mad someone needs to be before we make an exception of them from the general rule that we have to respect others as ends in themselves is likely to be a matter of judgement (and another sign that we are dealing with "guidelines" here, not simply "rules").

However, Kant resists the temptation to ask "Does this agent, in these circumstances, *deserve* to be treated as an end in himself/herself?". He resists it even in the cases of war and capital punishment, where Kant's position is not that enemy soldiers, or condemned criminals, deserve to be treated merely as means, but rather that killing them is the way we show our respect for them as ends!

More generally, Kant never seems to allow that anything at all compromises the status of human agents as ends in themselves. No one is *more or less* genuinely an agent, as far as he is concerned. The fact that someone never *exercises* his capacity for rational choice as an agent does not prevent him from *having* the capacity for rational choice. It is simply because he has that capacity, whatever he may or may not do with it, that Kant counts him as an "end in himself".

Abstraction and egoism

This brings us to the fourth of my questions about Kant's moral theory. The question is: how can Kantianism take an interest in individuality?

On this issue, we should contrast virtue ethics and utilitarianism with Kantianism. In virtue ethics, the virtues that I have as a particular individual are crucial to determining how I should see the world and how I should act, especially since, as I suggested towards the end of Chapter 8, what actions are right for me depends in part on how virtuous a person I am. In utilitarianism, my particular character and individuality is important too, if not in quite the strong way that it matters in virtue ethics. In utilitarianism, my character and individuality matters because, along with everything else, it is a factor that I have to take into account in assessing consequences.

Kantianism is not interested in individual character in either of these senses. For the Kantian, determining what to do is a matter of determining what pure rationality directs me to do, and pure rationality is the same for everybody: if "Utilitarianism strikingly abstracts from the separateness of persons", Kantianism "abstracts in moral thought from the identity of persons" (Williams 1981: 3). Of course the individual is permitted by the Kantian account of moral rationality to make whatever choices appeal to him as an individual, provided they are not positively forbidden by Kantianism. But this (it might be said) makes individuality an afterthought in Kantian moral theory; the main and basic tendency of Kantianism is to *abstract away* from individuality.

Is this abstraction a defect of Kantian moral theory, or an advantage? A bit of both, you might think, because sometimes it is good to be impartial and impersonal, but sometimes it is not. Either way, this abstraction plays a key role in developing the last question about Kantianism that I will discuss here, concerning its route from self to others.

Self to others

As I have shown, Kant's strategy in ethics is to start not with the traditional question of naturalistic ethics that utilitarianism and virtue ethics start from – "What kind of objectives do we agents pursue?" – but with a transcendental question: what kind of agents must we be to pursue anything? And his answer to this question is: "No matter what *else* we are like, we must at least always be agents who value agency: the capacity to pursue anything." It is on this basis that Kant concludes that the basic principle of ethics is to promote and protect agency. But this might seem ambiguous: does it tell us *whose* agency to protect and promote?

The problem is that it is very easy to confuse the following four claims, all of which you might think Kant makes in the course of his argument:

(i)   Each person has reason to protect and promote *his own* rational agency.

(ii) Each person has reason to protect and promote *each person's* rational agency.

(iii) Each person has reason to protect and promote *everyone's* rational agency.

(iv) Everyone has reason to protect and promote *everyone's* rational agency.

All of these claims mean different things, except for (ii), which is ambiguous: it could mean the same as (i), or it could mean the same as (iii). Kant faces the charge that this ambiguity in (ii) leads to a slide from (i) to (iv). If this charge is right, then Kant does not succeed even in getting us away from egoism.

Kant might respond that I have an irresistible reason for treating your agency as having just the same value as mine. This is that agency is just the same thing, whether it is your agency or my agency. Since your agency and mine are *the same thing*, he can argue, they necessarily have *the same value*.

"The same value, perhaps", a determined critic can reply, "but *value* is one thing, and *value to me* is another. Your agency and mine may have the same *value*. But what I care about is *value to me*, and your agency and mine obviously don't have the same *value to me*. So why should I be interested in protecting or promoting your agency? Or in protecting or promoting anybody's agency, except my own?"

This choice between caring about *value* and caring about *value to me* ought to have a familiar ring to it. The question that the critic is posing the Kantian here is, in effect, a question about *external reasons* (§§6.5, 6.6). The challenge is to explain why someone who does not care about value, but only about value *to him*, can be moved by argument from this egoistic stance to a position where he does care about value, not just value to him, and so accepts that he has a reason to care not only about promoting and protecting his own agency, but likewise about promoting and protecting agency as such. It is an interesting question whether Kant, or a Kantian, has arguments to move such an egoist.

One possible line of argument would be to try to show that there is something irrational about caring about *value to me*, but not caring about *value*. Is that not (it might be asked) an arbitrary preference? Is it not a bit like claiming to be interested in art, but only on Tuesdays? "What magic is there", as the utilitarian William Godwin famously asked in a different context, "in the pronoun 'mine'?"

A second line would be to say that, while there is nothing irrational in the egoist's preference for *value for me*, there is nothing irrational, either, in the Kantian's preference for *value*, and the world will be a better place if the egoist adopts this latter preference. But this is an obviously consequentialist kind of argument, and even if Kant is not excluded from appealing to consequences, he might find it unattractive to try appealing to them in this crude fashion.

A third way for the Kantian to respond to this argument is for him to deny that it is any part of his purpose to meet it. I said above, provocatively, that if the argument works, then "Kant does not succeed even in getting us away from egoism". But the Kantian can retort that he is not trying to "get us away from egoism"; that we did not start with egoism in the first place. The Kantian project in ethics, he can say, is not to derive rules for practical rationality starting from an isolated individual (any more than the Kantian project in epistemology is to derive concepts for the understanding starting from an isolated individual).

Both are shared enterprises, in which *we* (not *I*) work together to find rules whereby to think, or to live together. O'Neill draws our attention to the motto, from Francis Bacon, that Kant placed at the beginning of the *Critique of Pure Reason:*

> Bacon refuses to speak of himself. His undertaking is not solitary: He invites his readers to join in a common task. The fist step is to discuss and plan together. The task ... should not be judged by unvindicated standards. Kant embraces and extends these Baconian themes. (O'Neill 1989: 7)

On this view, the answer to the challenge about how to get from *value to me* to *value* is that that is not where we started from anyway. Rather, we started from *value to us*. Kant's enterprise is not about *justifying* the universalistic stance, as against the egoistic one. It is about where the universalistic stance gets you, if you take it seriously.

It is still possible to wonder whether this universalistic stance is not leaving something out. Kant is inviting us to engage in what we might call Everyman thinking: thinking from the impartial perspective, as a way of doing ethics. But we might wonder whether the impartial perspective is really all we need:

> Practical deliberation is in every case first-personal, and the first person is not derivative or naturally replaced by *anyone* ... The *I* that stands back in rational reflection from my desires is still the *I* that has those desires and will, empirically and concretely, act; and it is not, simply by standing back in reflection, converted into a being whose fundamental interest lies in the harmony of all interests. It cannot, just by taking this step, acquire the motivations of justice. (Williams 1985: 69)

These thoughts bring us back to the issues about abstracting from the self that I raised earlier in the chapter; more about these issues in Chapter 11.

For now, I want to look in a different direction, one that is strongly suggested by the idea, just mooted, of ethics as a shared enterprise, rather than something in which the agent at least begins in the position of the egoist, and has to work his way out from there. This notion of ethics as a shared enterprise – in fact, as a negotiation – is central to the moral tradition of *contractarianism*. I turn to a brief survey of some varieties of contractarianism in the last section of this chapter.

10.5 Forms of contractarianism

Kant's own theory is itself a form of contractarianism. For (§3.1) contractarianism says this:

Contractarianism: An action is right iff it is required by the code that all rational persons would agree to in a free negotiation.

There are obvious resemblances between this account of rightness and a number of things that Kant says. Take, for instance, this restatement of the first formulation of the categorical imperative: "Act as if the maxim of your action were to become through your will a universal law of nature" (Kant [1785] 1948: 84). Or take this statement of the formula of the kingdom of ends: "A rational being must always regard himself as making laws in a kingdom of ends which is possible through freedom of the will" (*ibid.*: 95).

The central idea in contractarianism is the idea of "rational persons" engaging in a "free negotiation" to produce the moral code that will govern their own behaviour. Kant's talk about "rational beings" whose autonomy and freedom of will is their crucial feature, and who seek to act in ways that are not only compatible with "universal law", but actually *make* universal law, is just one form of (or variant on) this idea.

On one possible reading of Kant (one like O'Neill's as quoted in the previous section), Kant is not, in this respect, very different from other contractarians, such as Thomas Hobbes and Jean-Jacques Rousseau, the main contractarian thinkers who influenced him. In Hobbes and (most clearly of all) in Rousseau, human beings come together to agree their code, and there is no code until they have come together. In Kant too, on this reading, each rational person is constantly in consultation with other rational persons, throughout the process whereby the three formulas of the categorical imperative are derived.

True, the ordering of Kant's three formulations of the categorical imperative does seems to support a reading "from inside to out". In line with the *first* formulation, each rational person begins by learning to treat the world as his or her realm for the making of universal law. It is only once this has happened that each rational person can look like a fit object for the moral privilege expressed by the *second* formulation. As Kant explicitly tells us, it is *because* each rational person is a universal legislator that he is an end in himself for all rational persons. Then once we have a realm of such universal legislators – "a kingdom of ends" – the demand naturally arises that they should coordinate their legislating. Hence the demand made in the third formulation of the categorical imperative: that "All maxims as proceeding from our own making of law ought to harmonise with a possible kingdom of ends as a kingdom of nature" (*ibid.*: 98). It is most clearly at this third stage of Kant's argument that the idea of rational persons conferring with each other comes into view. But on a contractarian, "corporate" view of Kant's enterprise, it is nonetheless a shared enterprise, not a solitary one, from beginning to end.

In most other contractarian writers, it is clearer still that the conferring of rational persons does not happen *after* the ethical code has been made, as an afterthought whereby they are enabled to check that their private decisions about the content of that code have all been made in harmony. For most contractarians, indeed, the agreement of rational persons is what *constitutes* the ethical code. Without the agreement of rational persons on an ethical code that they are all to accept, there *is* no ethical code. This is true whether the agreement is supposed to be real, as in Locke, Hobbes and Rousseau, or hypothetical, as in the modern contractarians John Rawls, Robert Nozick and David Gauthier. And it is true whether the agreement is supposed to be past, as in Locke, Hobbes and Nozick, or future, as in Rousseau, or not indexed to any particular time, as in Rawls and Gauthier. For all of these writers the ethical code is a construct of the rational persons' deliberations.

(Notice, by the way, that saying that the ethical code is a "construct" is *not* the same as saying that it is "subjective". The question whether the deliberations of rational persons will lead to the construction of a merely subjective ethical code, or whether, on the contrary, the code that they construct will be objective precisely because they are *rational* persons, is a question that contractarians disagree about. Most contractarians, in fact, are ethical objectivists. The main exceptions are Hobbes and Gauthier.)

Objective or subjective, the ethical code cannot even exist, for most contractarians, without the co-deliberations of rational people; no more than a country's constitution can exist before a constitutional convention has been held. And the constitutional analogy is an apt one, because the relation of contractarianism to the history of democracy, and in particular of British, American and French democracy, is very close indeed. In Britain in 1690, and in America and France in the 1780s, when delegates convened to agree a new political settlement, they did so in a mood of high idealistic excitement. The ideals that inspired them were Locke's in 1690 and Rousseau's in the 1780s, and in all three cases were explicitly contractarian.

As my formulation of it shows, the basic ideas of contractarianism are simple and few. They are, however, open to strikingly diverse interpretations. The contractarian account of rightness says, as above, that "An action is right iff it is required by the code that all rational persons would agree to in a free negotiation". But there is a great deal of room for disagreement about what "rational persons" are, and likewise about what counts as a "free negotiation".

Kant's theory represents one extreme among contractarians about what rationality is like, and about what rational persons are like: how, for instance, they are motivated. According to Kant, as we have seen, practical rationality is simply pure reason in action, and what a rational person will do – including how he will treat other rational agents, and what sort of agreement he will make with them – unfolds in a purely *a priori* manner from the content of reason itself. Kantian motivation comes in two forms, "inclination" and "the motive of duty"; it is only when an agent acts on the latter motive that he counts as free and autonomous.

At the other extreme of the contractarian spectrum, Gauthier presupposes a maximizing account of practical rationality, and a Humean account of moral psychology: being rational means doing what you need to do to maximize your pay-off, and correspondingly all ingredients of an agent's deliberations will always be classifiable either as desires (which determine what counts as a high-scoring pay-off for you) or as beliefs (which determine your route to the satisfaction of your desires) (see §§4.3, 6.4).

The idea of a free negotiation is similarly contested among contractarians: indeed, both of the individual words "free" and "negotiation" are contested. To take "free" first: we are used to the thought that the word "freedom" is ambiguous between a legal/political notion ("democratic freedom") and a metaphysical one ("freedom of the will"). But for Kant, freedom in any worthwhile sense is only available to the *metaphysically* free. (There could be a state where there was political/legal freedom; but, Kant would say, this would be no *use* if everyone in the state was constantly dominated by their inclinations. It would be a nation of human beings who are wild beasts, not genuinely human beings at all.) And the only people who are metaphysically free are those who act on the motive of duty, not the motive of inclination: "morality is a law for us only as *rational beings*, [and] must be derived solely from the property of freedom" (Kant [1785] 1948: 108).

In this notion of Kant's that the only freedom is the freedom of the rational agent, there is an echo of Rousseau's famous (and notorious) words "forced to be free":

> In order then that the social compact may not be an empty formula, it tacitly includes the undertaking, which alone can give force to the rest, that whoever refuses to obey the general will shall be compelled to do so by the whole body. This means nothing less than that he will be forced to be free; for this is the condition which, by giving each citizen to his country, secures him against all personal dependence. (Rousseau, *Social Contract*, 1.7)

Rousseau's contractarianism is a strongly collectivist view. For him, it is only when human individuals unite their individual "particular wills" into the "general will" of a community that they become fully human. Rousseau takes to heart Aristotle's famous pronouncement that "man is a political animal" (*Politics* 1253a3). For Rousseau as for Aristotle (and perhaps Kant), it is a crucial part of the answer to our question "How should life be lived?" that human beings are made to live *together*, because only together, in a true political community, can they achieve the full political life of shared corporate agency for which they are fitted by nature. Hence the famous slogan about being "forced to be free" – a slogan the appropriation of which, in the French Revolution, led immediately to some drastically high-handed actions on the part of a state that took itself to be entitled to all sorts of coercion because it embodied "the general will".

Rousseau's collectivism is one way of understanding freedom. Like Kant's version of freedom, it involves the transformation of what individual persons want. Indeed in a sense – since as Rousseau says no one is truly or fully human outside civil society – it involves the *creation* of persons. Other contractarians do not see freedom as anything like this sort of transformation or creation. In Locke's and Nozick's theories, in particular, human beings come to the contractarian negotiation as fully formed persons already holding complete sets of "natural rights". The point of the contractarian negotiation is not to transform these persons, who in the right conditions might do perfectly well outside civil society as what Nozick calls "independents"; it is simply to ensure the enforcement of the rights that these persons have, in a way that is more advantageous for those persons than it would be for them to live outside society. If society cannot provide this sort of enforcement of rights, or if it becomes, in itself, an overweening source of rights *violations*, then individual persons – who (as Nozick stresses) have all along had a right to leave the society if they wish – will be perfectly justified in exercising that right.

Rousseau and Nozick thus represent opposite poles on the spectrum from "positive" to "negative" freedom (to use Isaiah Berlin's terms). The theorists of positive freedom see it as a matter of being liberated from external distortions so that you are able to express your true inner nature. Marx is a paradigm theorist of positive freedom: the name of the great distortion, in his theory, is of course "capitalism". By contrast the theorists of negative freedom, such as Locke and Nozick, and (on the whole) Berlin himself, see freedom simply as being a matter of *protection from being interfered with*. It is no one's business but your own to decide what your "true inner nature" is; above all, it is not the government's business. This account of freedom is about as far from the Rousseauian or Marxian authoritarian accounts as it is possible to be. Meanwhile Hobbes's version of contractarianism is a paradoxical mix of the worst of both extremes: it turns out on his view that the best way for an individual to protect himself from interference is to submit himself to a very strong form of authoritarian government. Life under Hobbes's Leviathan sounds bleak; but Hobbes thinks it is the best available alternative. Thus theories that deserve the name contractarianism have understood freedom "negatively", and "positively", and in intermediate ways, which helps to show how diverse contractarianisms can be.

This diversity carries over, too, into a diversity of conceptions of what counts as a negotiation. As we have seen already, the negotiation that contractarians envisage can be a full-blown constitutional convention, as it is in Rousseau or (differently) in Locke or Hobbes; or it can be a merely hypothetical event – a "potential explanation", as Nozick calls it. There are versions of contractarianism, like Gauthier's and T. M. Scanlon's, where the idea of any negotiation at all is relatively marginal. (Gauthier and Scanlon are perhaps reflecting this by calling their positions "contractualism" rather than "contractarianism"; but the verbal difference is not very important.)

Or, again, the negotiation can become a thought experiment, as it does in Rawls's work. Rawls (1971) famously argues that the way to understand principles of justice is to see them as the principles which would be chosen by rational deliberators from behind a veil of ignorance. "Rational" for Rawls means something like what it means for Gauthier: you are rational, on his account, if you maximize your expected benefit. But Rawls's point is not that this account of rationality ("economic rationality") is an accurate description of how real people in fact behave. Rather, Rawls is interested in advancing the claim that *even if* individuals are rationally self-interested (as Gauthier perhaps believes they are), they will still end up with something like principles of justice when they come together in society.

More specifically, Rawls's concern is to ask this question: "*If a rationally self-interested agent didn't know where in society he himself was going to end up*, how would he choose to order his life together with other people in a society?". The assumption that the rationally self-interested agent does not know where he will end up in society is the assumption that Rawls calls "the veil of ignorance". Agents choose a society, not knowing whether they themselves will be rich or poor in it, or black or white, or male or female, and so on. It is Rawls's contention that when rational agents choose a society under these conditions, a just society is the one that they will end up choosing. The question of choosing a society, for them, is a sophisticated version of the familiar question that we are all often confronted by, "How would you like it if somebody did that to you?".

Thus Rawls's deliberators are Everyman figures in something like the way Kantian deliberators are. They too are abstractions from actual choice, agents who have been whittled down by this theory to the bare essential part of them: their rationality. On the other hand, the rationality of Rawls's agents is not Kantian. Rationality for them is maximizing what is in their own self-interest, and Rawls makes no division, as Kant does, between inclination and duty, rational and irrational willing or desiring, or anything like that. Nothing in Rawls's basic theory prevents him from signing up for a basically Humean moral psychology.

Finally in this catalogue of varieties of negotiation we should note Scanlon's account of wrongness as *reasonable rejectability*. In Scanlon's own words:

> *Scanlon's contractualism*: "An action is wrong iff its performance under the circumstances would be disallowed by any system of rules for the general regulation of behaviour which no one could reasonably reject as a basis for informed, unforced general agreement" (Scanlon 1998: 227).

In Scanlon's variation on the original contractarian theme, the notion of a negotiation has become the notion of an "informed, unforced general agreement" about what the society's rules are to be; about the shape, as Kant might have put it, of the kingdom of ends. It is to this consensus about the best rules for a society that I appeal when I engage in the activity – much more central to Scanlon's theory – of *justifying my reasonable rejections*.

Scanlon's thesis that it is central to the definition of wrongness that wrong actions should be *reasonably* rejectable has prompted a perhaps predictable objection. Everything, it is charged, depends on what we count as "reasonable". Hence (the objection runs) Scanlon's theory is, in a certain sense, vacuous; it just presupposes a substantive account of reasonable rejectability. Without such an account (the objection continues), we have no idea what Scanlon's view comes to. But given such an account, it is that account that really defines the shape of Scanlon's commitments in moral theory, not the formulas about reasonable rejectability by which he claims to define wrongness (and hence rightness).

This charge is misguided, for at least two reasons. First, what is reasonably rejectable full stop is one thing; what "system of rules for the general regulation of behaviour" is reasonably rejectable "as a basis for informed, unforced general agreement" in a society is another. It may be a fair criticism to say that talk about "the reasonably rejectable", all on its own, gets us no further towards understanding how a moral theory might be designed. But that is not in fact how Scanlon talks. He talks in the latter, more complicated way, and the two ways of talking are clearly not equivalent.

Of course, there is still work to be done to show what makes any rejection of a system of rules, devised on a basis for free and well-informed agreement, a reasonable one. But this brings us to the second reason why the charge of vacuity against Scanlon is misplaced. Scanlon is not hiding a moral theory up his sleeve that will explain the meaning of "reasonable" in "reasonable rejection", so that we are then able to go on and formulate a second moral theory (the official Scanlonian view) in terms of this notion. Rather, "reasonableness" in "reasonable rejection" is not a matter of *moral* reasonableness at all (on this see Ridge 2001). The possible public enactments or rules that Scanlon wants to say individuals can reasonably reject are not those that override their moral convictions. Rather, they are those that override individuals' own private interests; their projects and commitments, as Williams would say. *It is when a possible rule would violate my private rights and my personal interests that I may be able to frame a reasonable rejection of it.* Reasonable rejection is thus not a covertly moral notion as Scanlon uses it: it is not a fully moral notion at all. Rather, it is the notion that bridges the gap between the private spaces of particular lives, and the public space of society at large. This makes it admirably suited to play the role that Scanlon in fact assigns the notion. It also reveals Scanlon as very much closer to the "negative" conception of freedom, freedom as non-interference, than other liberal contractarians such as Rawls.

This has only been a survey of contractarianisms. Not much more than that is possible here, given the range and variety of contractarianisms that have been offered. The contractarian position presents no uniformity of broad philosophical outlook in the way that the Kantian or utilitarian or virtue-ethical positions do, which is why I have not given it more extended treatment in its own right. Indeed, contractarianism is consistent with all three positions, and not only because it tends to be a political account, an account of how we are to live together. Someone who is a contractarian can also be a utilitarian; especially if he is a rule utilitarian, since then he already thinks that the best way for us to maximize our utility is for us to think about what rules we should agree on in society, and this is virtually a form of contractarianism. But someone who is a contractarian can be a virtue ethicist as well; there is nothing in virtue ethics to say that we should not formulate a code to live by in a free negotiation with other rational persons. And that someone who is a Kantian can also be a contractarian has already been demonstrated, since Kantianism is, as I said at the start of this section, simply one form of contractarianism.

This survey of contractarianisms completes my account of four major moral theories. To conclude this book, I now turn to a question about moral theory in general. I shall ask: is systematizing moral theory the best way to represent, or to think and argue about, our deepest moral concerns? I believe not. I shall explain why not in Chapter 11.

11

Theory and insight in ethics

I will not stir a finger to compress the world into a system, and it does not at present seem as if it was going to harmonise itself without compression.   (Sidgwick, *Letters*, quoted in Williams 1995a: 159)

A smart set of concepts may be a most efficient instrument of corruption.   (Murdoch 1970: 33)

The will to system is a lack of integrity.
                              (Nietzsche, *Twilight of the Idols*:
                              "Maxims and Arrows", [1889] 1968: 25)

11.1 The very idea of a moral theory

At the beginning of this book I defined ethics as the use of reason to determine an answer to Socrates' question how life should be lived. That definition immediately raised the question: what *sort* of use of reason? If reason applies to the question "How should life be lived?", *how* does reason apply to it?

Part of what is involved in applying reason to Socrates' question is a matter of working out what kind of justification, and what kind of truth or falsehood, any answer to that question could have. This was my concern in Chapters 5–7, where we looked at arguments for and against ethical subjectivism and objectivism. Another part of what is involved is the description and assessment of the various possible moral theories that might guide us in our choices about how to live. This has been my focus in Chapters 8–10.

Having examined these moral theories in previous chapters, it might seem natural to think, at the beginning of this last chapter, that the main question left is which of them to pick. Which of the theories is right, according to me, and why are all the others wrong? But that will not be my question here. Or if it is my question, my answer will be (depending on how you look at it) either that *all* of these moral theories are right, and we should pick all of them (or rather, pick *something* from all of them); or alternatively, that *none* of these moral theories is right, and we should not pick any of them.

This is not because I have some other moral theory to offer, which I prefer to all of the alternative moral theories I have considered so far. It is because I want to take seriously the suggestion that the kind of use of reason that we need to do ethics well – what we need to make best sense in answering Socrates' question – is not the sort of use of reason characteristically involved in moral theory at all. It is something rather different, to which I shall give the name of an *ethical outlook*, and which I shall say more about in §11.3.

But first, the problems with moral theory.

Most moral philosophers have thought that "using reason" can only mean *systematizing* reason, and that systematizing reason can only mean the kind of structure that philosophers call "moral theories": explanatory theories of right and wrong with, so far as they can achieve it, maximal applicability and minimal complexity, like the four systems that I assessed in Chapters 8–10 – virtue ethics, utilitarianism, Kantianism and contractarianism. The trouble I see in such explanatory theories is what Nietzsche, in my third epigraph, calls "the will to a system". In one way, what I mean is captured by the "iff"s in the definitions of these four theories that I gave in §3.1 and §8.1. It is the moral theorist's aspiration to provide an explanation of rightness and wrongness that is both *general* and *exclusive*. In each case the claim is that the moral theory explains *every* instance of rightness or wrongness, and explains them *on its own*.

It is systems of this sort that I am opposing in opposing moral theory. (Note well that many other activities that go on under the *name* "moral theory" are not my target here; for instance, nothing in meta-ethics or moral psychology is, unless it feeds into a reductive theory of right and wrong.)

Total generality and exclusivity is the aspiration, but a moral theorist will often settle for less than this (while retaining the aspiration). He may concede that his particular moral theory achieves a bit less than everything. Perhaps it explains *nearly* every instance of rightness or wrongness, and explains them *almost* on its own. But then moral theorists tend to lose interest in the cases or the factors that are not adequately represented by their moral theory, often with unfortunate consequences for those cases. The problem is a bit like what notoriously goes wrong in cost-benefit analysis, when it fails to include "unquantifiable" elements such as beauty, heritage value and environmental integrity in its calculations. What cannot be represented in the sum ends up being represented as *zero* in the sum. Rather similarly, utilitarians have often been justly accused of not taking enough interest in forms of well-being that cannot be ranked, merely *because* they cannot be ranked, and so are not easily handled by the utilitarian machinery. Contractarians and Kantians have been likewise accused of leaving out of their theory those beings – animals and small children, for instance – that cannot easily sign up to a contract, or engage in universalizing reasoning. Nor can everything be neatly included – without what Sidgwick, in my first epigraph, calls "compression" – under the criterion of rightness that virtue ethics supplies. Even if it is true that what is right is what the virtuous person does, and vice versa, it is easy to feel that this formula sometimes gives not enough explanation (as when we are told that everything depends on the virtuous person's judgement); sometimes gives the wrong sort of explanation (as when we are told that something is right *because* the virtuous person judges it right); and sometimes gives no explanation that we could not give anyway, whether or not we were virtue ethicists (as when we are told that the virtuous person will not engage in cruelty, because cruelty is a vice).

Two other ways in which moral theories necessarily cannot attain complete determinacy or generality have to do with two particularly important issues that are not themselves settled by any moral theory: the nature of persons, and the scope of responsibility. It is possible for philosophers to argue that every human being, from conception on, counts as a person; it is equally possible for them to argue that nothing counts as a person unless it is capable of agreeing to a contract between

rational agents, or feeling pleasure and pain, or valuing things, or seeing itself as a person and so on. Similarly, there are philosophers who
argue that there is no significant moral difference between acting and
omitting, or between foreseeing a consequence and intending it; and
there are philosophers who argue equally forcefully for the opposite
conclusion. It is true that philosophers tend to follow the "party lines"
laid down by their moral theories on these issues. The denial of the
action–omission and intention–foresight distinctions are both particularly common among utilitarians, perhaps understandably given utilitarianism's interest in consequences. And the view that persons have to
be capable of feeling pain and pleasure, or experiencing or choosing or
valuing well-being, is also common among utilitarians, which again is
understandable given utilitarianism's concern with welfare. Nonetheless, there is no sense in which any moral theory *forces* a decision either
way on these questions; there is nothing *in utilitarianism* to oblige its
adherents to deny the difference between intention and foresight, or
reject the idea that the welfare that matters is every human being's
welfare, from conception or some other early point on. That means
that the major moral issues that are most affected by these distinctions
– end-of-life decisions, for instance, and abortion and infanticide – are
not settled, and cannot be settled, by the moral theories themselves.
In this way too, those theories are a good deal less than completely
general.

A moral theory can be seen as an explanatory theory of rightness
and wrongness, appealing constantly to a master factor such as universalizability or utility. Or it can be seen as a "decision machine": a way of
arriving at verdicts about what to do in real time, appealing constantly
to a master question. Or it can be seen as both (although there is a
suspicion of incoherence about that, to which we shall come in §11.4).
In all three cases, the moral theory can all too easily be a bad influence
on the agent.

To spell out why moral theory can be a bad influence, consider a
character whom most moral theorists are unlikely to welcome being
compared with: the kind of Christian fundamentalist who seeks to
resolve every practical issue by appeal to the single stark question
"What does the Bible say?". About this widely mocked, possibly even
existent, character, I imagine most moral theorists will tell us pretty
smartly that his decision procedure is narrow, diminishing, unim-

aginative, lacking in creative depth or space, humanly impoverished, fanatically monocular. Someone who runs or tries to run all his practical deliberation exclusively in line with the fundamentalist's simplistic model is, they will tell us, living within the constraints of a deeply *boring* mode of deliberation. And, they will add, someone who comes into this model of deliberation from outside it – as it might be, at conversion – has been *corrupted*. He has become a worse person, because – a little like Mr Bast in *Howards End* – he has replaced the polymorphic and polyvalent richness and diversity of real life for the grey uniformity of a theory:

> The three hurried downstairs, to find, not the gay dog they expected, but a young man, colourless, toneless, who had already the mournful eyes above a drooping moustache that are so common in London … One guessed him as the third generation, grandson to the shepherd or ploughboy whom civilisation had sucked into the town; as one of the thousands who have lost the life of the body and failed to reach the life of the spirit. Hints of robustness survived in him, more than a hint of primitive good looks, and Margaret, noting the spine that might have been straight, and the chest that might have broadened, wondered whether it paid to give up the glory of the animal for a tail coat and a couple of ideas. (E. M. Forster, *Howards End*, ch. 14)

Here the very complaint that moral theorists might make against the fundamentalist can seem to apply to them as well. Suppose we agree that it is boring to make your decisions solely by reference to the question "What does the Bible say?", and that it is humanly diminishing to move from richer and more natural modes of deliberation, to the mode that uses that question and nothing else. Well, do the moral theories do much better on this score? The master questions "What would promote utility?" or "What is universalizable?" have, when you get down to it, not that much to recommend them over the master question "What does the Bible say?". To resolve every practical issue by means (basically) of a single master question is a diminishing way to conduct our deliberative lives even where it seems adequate; and most of the time, it obviously does not. To get going the pretence that such a life is a real option for us, it is necessary to convince ourselves that other questions besides the master question really do not get to the heart of things (at least, not ultimately), and that nothing except the master factor is really of any importance (at least, not ultimately). This pretence must either involve self-deception; or it must involve us in making ourselves less sensitive, narrower-minded and more monocular, than we were when we started out; or both. And that just reveals the strong tendency of moral theory to pull us in the wrong direction.

Why does moral theory have this narrowing and "over-moralizing" tendency? At least partly it is because of moral theory's predilection for three crucial, and crucially misleading, mistakes. The first is that *there is no question of context*; the second is that *ethics should be like science*; the third is that *moral theory can capture everything*. I have already said something about the third mistake. I say a fair bit more about the first two, and just a little more about the third, in §11.2.

11.2 Three of moral theory's favourite mistakes

I speak of moral theory's *predilection* for these mistakes to cover the fact that I am not claiming that every version of moral theory is committed to all three, not at least in the strong forms in which I am about to present them. The point is rather that the very enterprise of moral theory necessarily involves *pressure towards* these mistaken commitments. Where moral theorists succeed in resisting these pressures, as of course they sometimes do (see, for instance, the quotation from Hursthouse in §4.2), it is quite often at the cost of ceasing to offer a systematic moral theory at all.

The first mistake of moral theory is *to ignore context*. In real life, where a method of settling a problem or a dispute is offered, there is always a question about whether that method is the right or the best one *in this context*. If I am in dispute with my neighbours and arbitration is offered, the first question for me is whether I think arbitration is the right way or a good way to resolve our dispute. If we have to award a gardening prize, we might award it by popular vote, or by the vote of the judges only, or by finding that garden that all the judges least object to, or by some other method; and again, before we can make any decision, we have to agree that the method we have chosen to decide is the best method, or at least a method that we are all happy with.

Likewise in ethics, we might suggest that before we settle some particular case by a Kantian appeal to universalizability, or a utilitarian appeal to utility, or by an appeal to what the virtuous agent would do or what the virtues demand, we had better have settled already what seems far from automatic: that this criterion is a good one to apply to this case. In actual practice, this is always a good question. In moral theory, the question tends too easily to become invisible. Either it cannot be asked at all, or the answer to it is, most unrealistically, that the same criterion is equally applicable everywhere. After all, part of the point of a moral theory is to pre-empt the question of context by giving us a way of assessing rightness and wrongness that will apply in any and every context. To raise again the question whether the favoured theory's master factor really is the one to deploy in this context is a kind of heresy against the theory.

Here we come to the sense in which my answer to the question "Which moral theory should we pick?" is "All of them". For all of the major theories are some help somewhere: they would hardly have become *major* theories if they were not. Certainly each of the major moral theories provides materials that can be put to use, provided that they are put to use in the right contexts. *Some* moral questions are well resolved by thinking about the criterion of utility; *some* are well resolved by thinking about the criterion of universalizability; others again by the virtue ethicist's criterion; and so on. (Maybe there are even some that are well resolved by asking "What does the Bible say?") Some issues, too, are well resolved by a combination of these questions. All of these approaches can bring something to the party. The trouble only starts when any one of them tries to take over the party.

It will take *judgement* to know which of these criteria to use and when: judgement, and not a further criterion – for on pain of regress, there can be no rule about how to apply a rule.

Seeing how the moral theories characteristically tend to underestimate the importance of context leads us very quickly in the direction of something like intuitionism or particularism:

Intuitionism: In ethics everything depends on "seeing things" right – on good judgement or accurate moral perception.

Particularism: In ethics there are no general principles; there are only particular cases.

We are led "in the direction of" intuitionism or particularism, but not all the way. Not *everything* in ethics depends upon seeing things right: it is possible to see that criterion A is the right one to apply in case B, and then misapply it; or to see case C with accurate moral perception, and then do nothing to respond to this perception. (Talk about moral perception, at least as I intend such talk [cf. §7.4], is not another form of moral theory, but an alternative to moral theory.) Nor is it obviously right that "in ethics there are no general principles". A cursory look around the ethical landscape suggests that there are plenty of general principles; but no general principle can itself furnish us with a rule about its own application to particular cases.

The second of moral theory's most important mistakes is the idea that *ethics should be like science.* As it is usually developed (explicitly or otherwise), this misconception embodies a familiar sort of misplaced cultural deference to the sciences. It also embodies important misunderstandings of what science is actually like. One of these misunderstandings is simply another form of the point about context just made. Typical scientific principles are models or idealizations. The ideal gas law, for instance, or the principle of the conservation of matter, do not tell us what actually happens, but only what happens *under ideal conditions* or *within a closed system.* It is a misunderstanding of science to take these principles as true without these qualifications. And it is a second misunderstanding, of ethics, to think that ethics should aspire to the same sort of unqualified truth as scientific principles are supposed to have according to the first misunderstanding.

Besides this illusion of unqualified truth, the main features of science that moral theorists want to emulate are, usually, its systematicity and its reductiveness. A scientific theory is a good one if it explains a maximal number of complex phenomena or observations by way of a minimal number of simple principles. Newton's three laws of motion, for example, can be stated in a sentence each. But those three sentences give us the makings of an extremely (although not perfectly) accurate explanation of most (although not all) of the behaviour of physical bodies throughout the known universe. Similarly, systematic moral theories typically aim to explain as much as possible by means of as little as possible. Just like the Newtonian physicist's, the moral theorist's ambition is to systematize, unify and reduce everything we say about ethics by translating it into the home vocabulary of the theory and showing that, in that vocabulary, what we want to say can either be vindicated as true, in so far as it is synonymous with something that the theory itself says, or rejected as false, in so far as it is synonymous with something that the theory denies.

I have already pointed out that this reductive ambition is an odd one for moral theorists to have, because it seems to take us in just the direction that we do not need to go in in ethics: the direction of getting narrower-minded, not broader in our moral vision: "Theory typically uses the assumption that we probably have too many ethical ideas, some of which may well turn out to be mere prejudices. Our major problem now is actually that we have not too many but too few, and we need to cherish as many as we can" (Williams 1985: 117). Another curiosity about the science-imitating ambition in moral theory is its selectiveness. Scientists do not aim only to streamline the phenomena and to be as reductive as possible. They also aim to maintain a deep respect for the data. Why do moral theorists who aspire to imitate science typically put so little stress on *this* aim of science?

Observational data in experimental science are, of course, fallible. After all, what scientists have counted as observational data have often included contradictions. Scientists can misunderstand what they actually see, or get false readings through carelessness, inattention or equipment glitches; or they can home in inadvertently on a misleading subset of all the observations that they might have made. In all these ways and others, scientists' reports of their observational data are fallible. Nonetheless, it is a fundamental part of a working scientist's integrity to respect the rule not to falsify, ignore or downplay those data when they are inconveniently out of line with what the scientist is looking to prove or confirm.

The reason for giving scientific observations a priority in our thinking is their certainty. Some scientific phenomena are better known to us than any scientific theory that explains them. For example, we are more certain that things drop – that unsupported large bodies near the earth's surface tend to move towards the earth's centre – than we are that there is such a thing as gravity. Ask an ordinary person *whether* things drop, and he will happily agree that things do drop. Ask an ordinary person *why* things drop, and he may be less sure. He may have nothing to say except "They just *do*". Or he may offer you the rudimentary explanation "Because of gravity," and then prove quite unable to say what gravity

192

is. Or again, if he has some scientific training, he may be able to say something illuminating about what gravity is, although he will not be able to give you a complete theory of it, because in our current state of knowledge nobody can do that. None of this haziness about or ignorance of the scientific theory about gravity undermines our right to say that things drop. That they do is an obvious and undeniable matter of everyday experience.

Likewise – to pick up a notion that I introduced in §7.4 – we should give moral perceptions a priority in our ethical thinking because of their high degree of certainty. Some moral phenomena are better known to us than any moral theory that explains them. For example, we are more certain that it is wrong to cause pain – that in normal circumstances, and where there is no special reason or excuse for doing so, it is morally impermissible to hurt creatures that are capable of being hurt – than we are of any moral theory that offers to give an explanation of this fact. Ask an ordinary person *whether* it is wrong to cause pain, and he will of course agree. Ask him *why* it is wrong to cause pain, and he may well be at a loss: even if he is a philosopher, he may find little to say beyond "Because pain is bad". None of this haziness about or ignorance of the reasons *why* it is wrong to cause pain undermines our right to say that it *is* wrong. For, once more, the fact that causing pain is wrong is an obvious and undeniable matter of moral experience. The idea that we need a theoretical explanation of this datum in order to be justified in believing it seems back to front. There is no theoretical claim about which we are *more* certain than we are about this datum of experience; so there is no obvious way for a theoretical deduction of the datum to add to our certainty about it. If anything it is the moral theory that stands in need of justification, not the experiential datum.

I am not saying that moral perceptions are infallible, any more than I would claim that scientific observation data are infallible. They cannot be infallible, because the moral perceptions that people have claimed to have have often included contradictions. But I do want to suggest that such moral perceptions, like the observation data of science, are rationally sacrosanct. When a scientific observation is repeatedly made, under the most reliable and stable observation conditions that we can devise, we have no rational right to ignore it. Even if the observation is in fact, objectively speaking, wrong, we would be irrational, subjectively speaking, to reject or deny it. For *according to the best evidence that we can possibly have*, namely that we have observed it, it is true.

Similarly in ethics, when a moral perception repeatedly occurs, under the most reliable and stable observation conditions that we can imagine, we have no right to ignore it. Even if the perception is in fact, objectively speaking, wrong, we would be irrational, subjectively speaking, to reject or deny it. For *according to the best evidence that we can possibly have*, namely that we have observed it, it is true. So the analogy between scientific observations and moral perceptions is at least this strong: where either comes about in epistemically favourable conditions, it is rationally sacrosanct.

The rational sacrosanctity of scientific observations runs deep; so deep that when reliable and clear scientific observations conflict decisively with a scientific theory, it is the theory that has to give way. The theorist is not allowed to say that those observations count against his theory, and therefore must be regarded as mistakes. If the observational evidence is good enough, he is rationally required to give up his theory. When faced with clear and unambiguous contrary evidence, the *most* the scientific theorist is allowed to do is to wait and see whether or not further data confirms this evidence. After a certain time, he is not even allowed to do that: he has no intellectually respectable option but to admit that his theory must be wrong. And he must do this even if the data suggest no alternative theory. Even if the new observations lead us from a nice neat theory to a complete theoretical mess, the scientist is still rationally obliged to respect them.

If we want to take seriously the analogy between ethics and science, then the rational sacrosanctity of moral perceptions should go equally deep. I suggest that in practice, it often does not. Typical moral theorists, who are capable of finding it puzzling what is wrong with murdering small children, putting charitable donation ahead of buying my daughter a birthday present, or breaking promises to dying grandmothers, have something to learn about respecting the rational sacrosanctity of the data from scientists. In this respect at least, it would be good if moral theory were *more* like science, not less.

However, there is an important difference too. To put it very simply, it is a matter of common experience that the data of ethics are much *messier* than the data of science. This is a further reason why the moral theorists' second mistake, that *ethics should be like science*, is indeed a mistake: because faithfulness to the data of moral experience suggests the conclusion that ethics cannot really be systematized or streamlined in the way that science sometimes is. It is also part of the explanation of the third mistake: it is because ethics is so messy that no *moral theory can capture everything.*

Opposition to moral theory should not be confused with opposition to careful and detailed moral thinking. The trouble with systematic moral theory is not that it makes us think too much; it is that it tends to encourage narrow-minded and over-simplified ethical thinking. It tends to teach us to suppress or ignore the vital question of the context of ethical reasoning. It tends to encourage us to do ethics as if ethics were science – but not in a good way: and it takes over the streamlining and reductive impulse from science, while bypassing the scientist's almost reverent respect for the data, and the scientist's willingness to admit that his theories are approximations, models, that we need to be careful to contextualize before using, and cannot always treat as straightforwardly universally true.

If moral theory has these flaws, what is the alternative? The alternative I propose goes under the name of an *ethical outlook*; the notion of moral perceptions that I have just described is central to this alternative. I develop it in §11.3.

11.3 The idea of an ethical outlook

Anybody who is going to live a genuinely worthwhile and a fully human life will have to live out a set of views and commitments about the central questions concerning value: what is worth living for and what is worth dying for; what is really admirable and what is really contemptible; what we must do at all costs and what we must not do no matter what; and so on. This set of views and commitments need not be very explicit; but it must run deep – must be sincerely and indeed passionately held. And it need not be very systematic; but it must be as considered, rationally defensible and coherent as possible. Any such set of views about value is what I shall call an *ethical outlook*.

What must a set of views and commitments be like to constitute a credible and liveable ethical outlook? One difficulty in answering this

question is that no universally quantified generalizing answer to it, of
the kind usually preferred by systematizing philosophers, is available.
In fact it is a key part of what I shall argue in this section that credible
ethical outlooks are known by recognition, not definition.

A second difficulty is that what counts as a credible and liveable
ethical outlook is dependent on how the world is. If there is no God,
for instance, or if the God that there is is the Christian God rather
than, say, the Odin of Norse myth, or if determinism or evolutionary
reductionism or classical Marxism or Freudianism is true, whatever
the truth about these big questions may be, it is bound to constrain
what counts as a genuinely credible and liveable ethical outlook. This is
hardly the place to decide between these alternatives. But if we do not,
how can we say what ethical outlooks are credible or liveable?

These two difficulties do not stop us from identifying some examples
of what are surely at least *prima facie* credible ethical outlooks, and
some features that all such ethical outlooks must surely have in common. Here is one example.

> He was but three and twenty, and had only just learned what
> it is to be in love – to love with that adoration which a young
> man gives to a woman who he feels to be greater and better than
> himself. Love of this sort is hardly distinguishable from religious
> feeling. What deep and worthy love is so, whether of woman or
> child, or art or music? Our caresses, our tender words, our still
> rapture under the influence of autumn sunsets, or pillared vistas,
> or calm majestic statues, or Beethoven symphonies all bring with
> them the consciousness that they are mere waves and ripples in
> an unfathomable ocean of love and beauty; our emotion in its
> keenest moment passes from expression into silence, our love at
> its highest flood rushes beyond its object and loses itself in the
> sense of divine mystery. And this blessed gift of venerating love
> has been given to too many humble craftsmen since the world
> began for us to feel any surprise that it should have existed in the
> soul of a Methodist carpenter half a century ago.
>
> (George Eliot, *Adam Bede*, ch. 3)

Dinah Morris and Seth Bede are uneducated and undistinguished
people, adherents of the unsophisticated and undistinguished creed

Primitive Methodism. But as the highly intellectual agnostic George Eliot shows us, it is their deeply felt faith in that creed that gives their ethical outlook its profundity. At this point in the novel, Seth is in anguish because Dinah has just rejected his proposal of marriage. The simplicity and inarticulacy of Seth's mind, religion and character do not mean that there is anything shallow or crude about his emotion and his attachment to Dinah, or about the overall ethical outlook of which his attachment is a part. After all, the "unfathomable ocean of love and beauty" that Seth is brought to touch on by his love for Dinah is there in Plato's *Symposium* too (210d). Seth and Dinah have a *prima facie* credible ethical outlook, even though, as good Primitive Methodists, they believe "in present miracles, in instantaneous conversions, in revelations by dreams and visions". Indeed it is the beliefs of their faith, and what those beliefs mean to them, that gives their ethical outlook its shape and tone.

Something more like Eliot's own ethical outlook is famously expressed by Matthew Arnold in the closing lines of "Dover Beach":

Ah, love, let us be true
To one another! for the world, which seems
To lie before us like a land of dreams,
So various, so beautiful, so new,
Hath really neither joy, nor love, nor light,
Nor certitude, nor peace, nor help for pain;
And we are here as on a darkling plain
Swept with confused alarms of struggle and flight,
Where ignorant armies clash by night.
(Matthew Arnold, "Dover Beach")

Here too is a *prima facie* credible ethical outlook, albeit at the opposite extreme of pessimism from the rapturous and ecstatic Platonism that Eliot sees underlying the simple faith of Seth and Dinah. The most disturbing part of it is, of course, the implicit tension between the plea "Let us be true to one another!" and the universal darkness that Arnold finds around him. If the world contains *no* "certitude, nor peace, nor help for pain", then it inexorably follows that no lovers can be sure of being true to each other, or hope to help each other's pain even if they are.

No credible theistic ethical outlook can deny that the world very often at least seems to fit Arnold's tragic vision of it, as a place of unheeded routine agony and brutal chaos; whatever a theist may go on to say about that "seems". Certainly Gerard Manley Hopkins's Christian outlook, for example, does not lead him to deny it in "God's Grandeur":

The world is charged with the grandeur of God.
   It will flame out, like shining from shook foil;
   It gathers to a greatness, like the ooze of oil
Crushed. Why do men then now not reck his rod?
Generations have trod, have trod, have trod;
   And all is seared with trade; bleared, smeared with toil;
   And wears man's smudge and shares man's smell: the soil
Is bare now, nor can foot feel, being shod.

And for all this, nature is never spent;
   There lives the dearest freshness deep down things;
And though the last lights off the black West went
   Oh, morning, at the brown brink eastward, springs —
Because the Holy Ghost over the bent
   World broods with warm breast and with ah! bright wings.
             (Gerard Manley Hopkins, "God's Grandeur")

A very different kind of theist from Hopkins has no trouble with the obvious clash between divine benevolence and the malignity of the world, because he does not see the divine as benevolent in the first place. At the close of Sophocles' *Women of Trachis*, Hyllus watches the removal from the scene of his father, Zeus's stricken son Heracles; Heracles is dying in agony because he put on the shirt of Nessus that was sent to him as a present by Hyllus's mother, Deianeira; Hyllus has just provoked Deianeira to suicide by accusing her of deliberately killing Heracles. Hyllus says this:

Attendants, take him up. And pity on me,
Pity and compassion for my fault,
All while the unpitying gods indifferently
Watch these things unfold and call no halt.
They make us and they claim the name of fathers

Then stand afar and watch our suffering.
No one knows what the future time will offer;
The present time, for us, means suffering,
And for the gods means shame;
It means worse than any human suffering
For him on whom this doom of anguish came.
Girl, come away, and leave this house behind.
New shapes of enormous death now fill your mind,
Novelties of agony, pain beyond all use;
And nothing in all this that is not Zeus.
                    (Sophocles, *Trachinae* 1264–78; my translation)

Hyllus's ethical outlook is as bleak as Arnold's. That does not, unfortunately, make it any less credible.

Even if we cannot capture the idea of a credible and liveable ethical outlook in a definition, we can use examples like these four to draw out some features that credible ethical outlooks will normally have. Here are six such features.

First, despite the clear religious content of at least three of my four examples, an ethical outlook does not need to have any explicitly theological or even philosophical content to count as *prima facie* credible. Its import is, as they say, existential, and it is an open question whether existential concerns are best expressed by theological conceptions, or by philosophical ones, or indeed by neither.

Secondly, and connectedly, an ethical outlook needs to match and to encapsulate lived human experience. It needs to be true to experience, or at least to have a *prima facie* chance of being true. And it needs to be *generally* true, not just partially or occasionally true. That is, it needs to match and encapsulate a wide and generous range of human experience, not just a small and gerrymandered selection from, or a distortion of, human experience such as we all too often find in moral theory.

Thirdly, a credible ethical outlook needs to contain two sorts of elements that I shall call *commitments* and *perceptions*. By "commitments" I mean the things we care about: our life-shaping relationships and our life-shaping projects. Who (or what) I love, and how I love them, is a crucial ingredient in making my ethical outlook what it is; indeed, it is perhaps *the* crucial ingredient. Furthermore, it is hard to imagine a credible or liveable ethical outlook that does not have love for someone or at least something at its heart. (It is not at all hard to imagine a moral theory that does not have love at its heart: more about that in the next section.) It is equally hard to imagine a credible or liveable ethical outlook that does not include at least some things like ambitions, interests, vocations – "ground projects" as Williams calls them – and these too are commitments.

I have already said something about the idea of moral perceptions in §7.4 and §11.2. At the foundations of any normal person's first-order morality stand a variety of basic moral convictions, learned in experience, by reference to which her other views are justified, and from which her other convictions are inferences or extrapolations. For instance, for most of us today the claims that, at least in nearly all conceivable cases, it is very seriously wrong to torture, steal, murder or rape will be basic moral convictions in this sense. We will regard these basic claims as *obviously* true, and our access to them will at least seem to be direct and quasi-sensory, which is why I call them perceptions. We will regard these perceptions as more certain than any argument or theory that we can imagine being brought forward either to support them or to undermine them. They will strike us with such evidential force that it would be at least subjectively irrational for us to abandon them under the influence of some argument or perception that is itself much less persuasive or vivid than they are. New or doubtful moral claims will be tested against these basic convictions; if the new claims contradict the basic convictions, the new claims will normally be rejected. Although our perceptions obviously have cognitive content, they are also a third sort of commitment alongside our relationships and our projects. We care deeply about respecting our strongest moral intuitions, and feel as personally violated by having to go against them as we do by having to abandon or betray our relationships or our projects.

Fourthly, and as a corollary of the second feature, about truthfulness, a credible ethical outlook needs to be *open-edged*: an ethical outlook must be sensitive to the possibility of new experiences, and of resulting new perceptions, new projects and new relationships. It must also be open to the converse possibility: that new experience might show up old perceptions, projects or relationships as no longer worth their while, or never worthwhile in the first place.

Fifthly, a credible and liveable ethical outlook needs (as I put it above) to be "as considered, rationally defensible and coherent as possible". Put this together with the points I have just made about truthfulness, and this much should be clear: a credible and liveable ethical outlook, unlike a moral theory, displays no more system or coherence than is true to life itself. It does not automatically seek to reduce the obvious diversity of the projects, relationships, perceptions and other commitments that are its elements to any sort of neat theoretical uniformity, for example by representing novel and hitherto "unprocessed" experiences as mere variants on previous experience. It is always open to the thought "Perhaps this is not the same thing again, but something new". In real ethical life, it is crucial to keep thinking this thought, to keep our minds and our eyes open. It would be too much to say that moral theory prevents us from having the differentiating thought; but it would not be wrong to say that moral theory tends to suppress it, and to work in the other direction – to assimilate, not differentiate.

Lastly, the willingness of a healthy ethical outlook to live with diversity is also a willingness to live with complexity and even conflict. In sharp contrast to what is expected of moral theories, we may say that a credible ethical outlook does not have to include a way of resolving every possible value conflict, or even every actual value conflict, that occurs within it. Only a few of the indefinitely many value conflicts that are possible even could come up within any actual life, and there is no particular reason to think that those that do come up are all sure to be resolved.

I do not mean to deny by this that *often* such conflicts can be resolved within a credible ethical outlook; and their resolutions can involve reasoning, rather than just being a matter of a sheer change of perspective. (As one humble example, take the reasonings that Dinah and Seth have just been engaging in with each other about whether to marry, immediately before the quotation from *Adam Bede* given above.) However, value-conflict resolution within an adequate ethical outlook, where the values in conflict are ones that the agent actually has a genuine stake in, is typically an experiential and narrative business: "The choice between one potential love and another can feel, and be, like a choice of a way of life, a decision to dedicate oneself to these values rather than these" (Nussbaum 1992b: 328).

Such choices are not about weighing and measuring different quantities of some arcane theoretical entity that only trained philosophers know how to detect accurately, called "value". They are about asking "What do I want to do about the place in my life-story of these two values, given that I cannot go on giving both of them the place that they have had up to now?". (I am using the vague place-holding term "values"; it may help to sharpen the focus if the reader thinks of these values as *persons*, which they often are when this sort of question comes up. They certainly are in Chapter 3 of *Adam Bede*, for instance.) The process of working out an answer to such a question is costly, and personal. It is not abstract, deductive and weightlessly theoretical, as the rankings of values within the axiological schedules beloved of some philosophers typically are. If that sounds messy, we may reply, with David Ross, that it is no messier than real life:

> If the objection be made, that this catalogue [of perceptions] is an unsystematic one resting on no logical principle, it may be replied … [that the first principles of any moral theory are] reached by exactly the same method – the only sound one in the circumstances – viz. that of direct reflection on what we really think. Loyalty to the facts is worth more than a symmetrical architectonic or a hastily reached simplicity.   (Ross 1930: 339)

Or, as Aristotle puts it, in about the clearest statement he ever gives us of his own method in ethics:

> Just as we did in our other inquiries, we must take hold of what looks to be true, and start with the problems about that. This is the best way to prove perhaps all of our intuitive beliefs (*endoxa*) about these experiences – or if not all, then the majority of them, and the most authoritative. For if the difficulties raised by our intuitive beliefs can be resolved in a way that leaves those intuitive beliefs standing, that should be all we need to prove their truth.
> (*Nicomachean Ethics* 1145b3–8, my translation)

So this is what an ethical outlook is. Can any moral theory be a credible or liveable ethical outlook? In §11.4 I argue for the answer no.

11.4 "Ethical outlook" and "moral theory": some contrasts

Every systematic moral theory aspires, or at least starts out with the aspiration, to be an ethical outlook. It is not clear what point there would be to a moral theory, or what use we could put it to, if it did not have this aspiration. But there are problems about supposing that any moral theory could adequately play the role that we want, and need, our ethical outlook to play.

Some of the reasons why this is so should be clear already from §11.3. Others begin to appear when we note the intimate connections that an adequate ethical outlook will inevitably have with motivation and deliberation on the one hand, and explanation and prediction on the other. We want our ethical outlook to be something that can be the source of our reasons to act (*motivation*), and that can structure our real-time thinking and deciding about how to act (*deliberation*). We also want our ethical outlook to be something that, offline, can articulate and deepen our understanding of what counts as good or bad and right or wrong action, and why (*explanation*). And we want it to be something that can explain what will or would be good or bad and right or wrong action, in future or hypothetical situations that we ourselves have not actually met, but which we or others might conceivably meet (*prediction*).

Systematic moral theory is ill fitted for any of these four roles. Let us take them one by one.

Motivation

I have just said that "we want our ethical outlook to be something that can itself be the source of our reasons to act." At first sight, it seems that utilitarianism identifies the overall good as the thing for good people to be motivated by; that Kantianism's motivational goal is rational action, in a special sense of "rational", or duty, in a special sense of "duty"; that virtue ethics tells us to act out of the virtues; and so on. Perhaps some moral theorists in these schools do think about motivation in this direct way. Singer, for example, seems more than once to suggest that we really should aim to be motivated by "the overall good"; that there is nothing better to be motivated by, because (roughly) there is nothing bigger ("If we take the point of view of the universe we can recognise the urgency of doing something about the pain and suffering of others, before we even consider promoting other possible values"; 1995: 276).

But this is not the commonest line among moral theorists about what should motivate us. The reason why not is obvious: the sheer implausibility of the moral theories' adopting any such direct account of motivation. This is Stocker's point in the story of Smith the hospital visitor that I quoted in §4.2. And others have made the same point, for example Susan Wolf:

> There is something odd about the idea of morality itself, or moral goodness, serving as the object of a dominant passion in the way that a more concrete and specific vision of a goal (even a concrete *moral* goal) might be imagined to serve ... when one reflects, for example, on the ... Saint ... giving up his fishing trip or his stereo or his hot fudge sundae at the drop of the moral hat, one is apt to wonder not at how much he loves morality, but at how little he loves these other things. (1997: 43)

Nobody sane normally or standardly acts so as to realize utility, or "on the motive of duty" (Kant's own phrase), or "for the sake of virtue itself" (Aristotle's own phrase). What really motivates most of us, most of the time, at least if we are moderately good people or better and are not being distracted by false motives such as concern about "what others will think", is *love*: love for spouses, love for children and parents, love for friends, love for God, love for ideals, love for valued places or artworks or possessions, love for pet projects, love for pets and so on (depending on the individualities of the individual). The centrality of love is a striking feature of any typical credible ethical outlook. The marginality of love in the moral theories that typically dominate contemporary ethical research is equally striking. (Of course there is *some* recent research on love, and some of it really excellent; Nussbaum [1992b], Velleman [2005] and Frankfurt [1998] come to mind at once. Still, even the fine online resource the *Stanford Encyclopedia of Philosophy* contrives to supply thirty-eight articles on logic, but only one on love.) Love is at the heart of our ethical outlooks. It is love, and not concern with what is right and wrong, that mostly drives us into action. In that sense love puts us "beyond good and evil", and beyond morality. While morality is a constraint on what motivates us (*a* constraint – there are others), love is the very engine of motivation.

Their disregard of love is one major reason why none of the moral theories can itself furnish us with the central and most important source of our motivations. Hence cautious and sophisticated moral theorists, perhaps picking up on the important and correct point that love always needs to be subject to the constraints of justice and the other virtues, quickly retreat to a "filter view" of the role of moral theory in motivation. That is, they suggest only that our maxims must pass the tests of rationality (if they are Kantians or contractarians); or that our motivations should be whatever motivations it is in fact best for us to have (if they are utilitarians); or that we should act, not on thoughts about virtue, but on the thoughts that the virtuous person will have (if they are virtue ethicists); and so on.

Before we ask the question whether this retreat leaves the moral theories in a plausible position, the first thing to notice is that it is a retreat. This retreat is made necessary by the apparent fact that the moral theories do not themselves provide us with any realistic set of motivations; for it is hard to see how any of them could, in itself, plausibly become the main source of our deepest and most pervasive aims in life. By contrast, a credible and liveable ethical outlook *will* provide us with our deepest and most pervasive motivations. In so far as all moral theories fail to give themselves any chance of playing this role, they fail to meet the first criterion for being an adequate ethical outlook.

Deliberation

"We want our ethical outlook to be one that can structure our thinking and deciding about how to act as it actually happens." It is difficult to imagine a really clean separation between questions about motivation, what moves us to act, and about deliberation, our reasoning about how to act. For any well-constituted agent, reasoning about how to act will be an integral part of being moved to act, and *vice versa*. So doubts about the place of moral theory in motivation carry over into doubts about the place of moral theory in deliberation. If utility or duty or virtue cannot be the mainspring of our motivation, then it cannot be central to our deliberation either. It is no more plausible to say that a psychologically healthy moral agent's deliberations are typically guided by the question "What would maximize utility?" than it is to say that she typically acts on the motive of maximizing utility.

It is unsurprising, therefore, that cautious and sophisticated moral theorists retreat at this point too, although they have found some divertingly elegant ways of covering their retreat. One is another application of the "filter view". Moral theorists will talk about moral theory as providing a *constraint* on deliberation, or the form of deliberation, rather than the subject matter or content of deliberation. Deliberation, they will say, may take as its subject matter whatever desires or pro-attitudes in fact motivate us, but it must always pass the universalizability test, or must always be maximizing deliberation, or must never be contrary to the rules laid down by the virtues, and so on. But this is a retreat from our expectations of an ethical outlook, which, we might have hoped, would provide both the content and the form of our deliberation. We would be disappointed in an ethical outlook that was topic-neutral in the familiar instrumentalist way that Humean moral theories are (§4.3): one that had nothing to say about *what* we desired, and told us only how to pursue it.

But anyway, it is unrealistic to hope that moral theory will give us even the form of deliberation, never mind both the form and the content. Given the messiness of the moral (§11.2), there is little reason to think that *all* good deliberation must, in any non-trivial sense, be universalizable or in accord with the virtues, or that it must satisfy such supposed rules of rationality as a maximizing rule. Our earlier thoughts about context come back here. Of course good deliberation *sometimes* calls on considerations that look very like thoughts about universalizability or utility or maximization, but not always, and even when good deliberation does deploy one of these thoughts in one context, that is no guarantee that it must deploy that same thought in every other context. As soon as we look in detail at actual good agents actually deliberating, the idea that any moral theory even gives the form of their deliberations becomes quite implausible. Good deliberation does not seem to be that programmed.

Other aspects of good agents' deliberations, as actually seen in real life, are simply missing in typical moral-theoretical accounts of what deliberation should be like. One notable absentee is the moral imagination. To understand properly what is involved morally speaking in, for example, choosing to torture someone cannot merely involve making theory-based calculations about the general value or disvalue of the abstract action-type *torturing*. It must involve the imagination in thinking out what it would be like for me, concretely and actually, to torture someone. This is not just because reflection on the concrete and actual detail of torture is likely to be a powerful emetic. It is also – and perhaps more importantly – because it is only as we reflect on those concrete details that we will understand in full what the structure and orientation of our planning and intending is going to have to be like, if we are to be torturers: what choosing torture really requires us to will and choose, and to go on willing and choosing. By contrast, the abstraction from the hard (or gory) detail of particular cases that is so evident in and typical of so much moral theory is another feature of moral theorists' practice that is perhaps modelled on the practice of science. But abstraction in moral theory is not what it is in science, a virtuous dispassionateness; it is a self-blinding refusal to consider in anything but the most schematic and vague way the detail of what we are actually proposing to do.

Once it becomes implausible to think that good agents who are deliberating must be *explicitly and consciously* using some moral theory as a constraint on that deliberation, it seems natural to ask: might not moral theory serve everywhere as an implicit constraint on their deliberation, even if it is only occasionally an explicit one? That is to say: can their deliberations not *in fact* be always responsive to a theoretical constraint (a "criterion of rightness", as it is often called; §§8.5, 9.4), even if that constraint is not always a conscious part of their *actual thoughts* in real-time moral reasoning – part of their "decision procedure"?

Once more, my main point about the moral theorist who proposes this is not to query the feasibility of his proposal, although we can query that too, of course. My main point about this proposal is that the moral theorist who offers it is retreating. It is a crucial part of what we hope for from an ethical outlook that it should guide our deliberations explicitly; that it should be consciously present in our decision procedures. We want our ethical outlook to serve a bigger role than the merely implicit one that this proposal gives to moral theory, as a pattern that some detached observer can pick out in our deliberations and critically assess us for adhering to or not, irrespective of whether we realize the pattern is there. The central concepts of an adequate ethical outlook must be, as we might put it, *psychologically real*: our most normal and natural forms of deliberation must, actually and consciously, be about them, and must present themselves to us as being about them. If the central concepts of a moral theory cannot – either by the theory's own admission, or just as a matter of common sense – be psychologically real in this way, that reveals another sense in which that moral theory must struggle to pass muster as an ethical outlook.

In any case, as I say, we might wonder whether a moral theory that is only implicitly applicable to our deliberations, and not explicitly, can have any grip on the psychological reality of deliberative life as it actually happens. Wondering about this brings us to consider the two "off-line" roles that we want an ethical outlook to play: explanation and prediction.

Explanation

"We want our ethical outlook to be something that can articulate and deepen our understanding of what counts as good or bad and right or wrong action, and why." We might have expected moral theories to be on home ground here. After all, explanation (and prediction, which I treat separately below) are supposed to be the main strength of sophisticated moral theories. Those moral theorists who admit that moral theory cannot plausibly be directly involved in motivation and deliberation see its main role, instead, in explaining why it is good for agents to be motivated, and to deliberate, in whatever way it is that their theory recommends.

But this is already a puzzling claim. What these theories are telling us is that it is good, or best, that people should deliberate and be motivated in ways that do not directly involve the terms of the moral theory itself. But if the moral theory is true, why would that be so? Surely a good deliberative or motivational process will involve the best possible materials for deliberating over or being motivated by. And surely the *best possible* materials will include *the truth* and, in particular, the real explanations of goodness and badness, rightness and wrongness.

Not so, if the moral theorists are correct. On their account, the best possible materials for deliberation and motivation about what it is good and right to do, and why, do not include the truth about what it is good and right to do, and why. But then we have to ask: who is supposed to know that this moral theory is true? And how does their knowledge of its truth relate to *their* practices of deliberation and justification? If you do not find this question puzzling, you cannot be taking it seriously.

However, this is not a question that we would expect to arise for any plausible ethical outlook. Plausible ethical outlooks typically take the pursuit of the truth as one of the most non-negotiable and fundamental aims, for everybody. Even if the truth turns out to be hard to live with, to create deep conflicts with our other aims, it is not an aim that we naturally think we can just *ignore*. The idea of bypassing our commitment to the truth is not at all easy to swallow. Here, too, notice what we lose when we try to systematize the ethical into a moral theory.

Typical moral theories do not seem to be very good at explanation in this sense anyway. Very often they do not succeed in "articulating and deepening our understanding" of good/bad or right/wrong. In many cases moral theory creates problems that did not exist at all before it came along. In other cases the explanation it offers either fails to add anything much to our understanding, or actually darkens counsel.

One case where moral theory creates gratuitous problems is a supposed difficulty about punishment. When someone is punished for a crime, the crime (which is one bad thing) has already happened, and now the punishment (which is another bad thing) is proposed as a way of dealing with it. But, the objection runs (it is an old one, going back at least as far as Plato's *Protagoras*), how can it be good to make two bad things happen instead of just one? The heart of this "problem" about punishment is the theory-driven assumption that all reasons must be future-directed: that wherever there is a reason to act, it is because there is some future state of affairs that can be brought about by so acting (cf. §9.6). It is not difficult to find this assumption rather implausible, especially given the difficulties it makes for our understanding of punishment, and of desert in general.

Another case where moral theory seems (at best) to add nothing is the explanation of the wrongness of murder: the deliberate killing of an innocent human being. To any sane ethical outlook, including the ethical outlooks of many off-duty moral theorists, the wrongness of murder is a *paradigm* of wrongness. It is a perfect example of the kind of action that strikes us immediately and perceptually as wrong; we do not know about its wrongness merely by inference from other and more basic sorts of wrongness, but directly. Yet moral theorists have tied themselves in the most remarkable knots about this fundamental question.

Utilitarian-influenced moral theorists, for instance, have tended, in line with their general and characteristic preoccupation with the future, to suggest that the wrongness of murder lies in something like its depriving its victim of a "future like ours" or a "future life of value" (Marquis 1997). Such suggestions seem off-target. Knowing that some person's future will be radically unlike "ours", or drastically deprived of positive value, seems well short of what we need to know in order to know not only that it is not wrong for that person to die; not only that it is not wrong for someone to kill that person; but also that it is not wrong for us to kill that person.

Virtue ethicists, by contrast, will typically speak of murder as an act of injustice. That does not seem too hard to believe, but (at least on its own) it does fail to tell us *why* murder might be unjust. More difficulties appear when we look at the explanation more closely. As many have commented, justice is a very difficult virtue to give an account of, and it would be nice to have an explanation of the wrongness of murder that does not need to drag us through these dense and thorny philosophical thickets.

Kantians and contractarians, meanwhile, are likely to speak of murder either as a non-universalizable choice, or as a failure to respect someone as an "end in himself", or as a proposal that anyone threatened by it could reasonably reject. These descriptions too seem right, as far as they go. But the idea that they *uniquely* capture *everything* that is wrong with murder is not plausible. Also, the appeal to universalizability or "the reasonably rejectable", or to the notion of a failure to respect an end in himself, all involve us in appealing to notions that we are far less sure of than we are of the wrongness of murder. It seems nearer the truth to say that we understand these notions by reference to the wrongness of murder than to say what the moral theorist must say: that these notions give us an *explanation* of the wrongness of murder. A similar point applies to Finnis-style natural law theories of the wrongness of murder (see Finnis 1980). These tell us, in their proprietary vocabulary, that the wrongness of murder consists in a violation of the good of life, thereby raising a host of difficult questions about what violation is, and what the good of life is, that were not in any very obvious way prompted by the original question about what is wrong with murder.

Moreover, there is one very basic and obvious point about murder that all of these moral theories seem to miss. This is that murder is not just a matter of treating someone badly, unjustly, unfairly or in a way that deprives them of goods (although it is that, of course). In murder you do not so much take something away from someone as take away the someone; you deprive him, not of this or that good, but *of himself*, by destroying him. This seems to be the most central wrong involved in murder, and most moral theories, remarkably enough, do not even get around to mentioning it.

One moral theory that does mention it – whatever its other faults may be – is the version of natural law theory that I have defended in some of my previous publications (1998, 2002), which takes the wrong of murder to be the violation of the individual good that the human person is: that individual good is violated in the most obvious and radical way – by being destroyed. The problem with this, too, it now seems to me, is not that it is wrong, but simply that the specifically moral-theoretical aspects of such a claim do not add anything to its explanatory value. It is undoubtedly explanatory to be told that the wrongness of murder consists in the badness of destroying a person; but there is nothing specifically of the nature of *moral theory* about this explanation. It is unclear that we are told anything more, or anything that sheds any interesting or useful light on matters, by the bit of this story that is specifically a piece of moral theory: the addition that persons are individual goods, and that murder violates such goods.

On this evidence, all these theories' explanations of our normal moral verdicts are redundant at best, and often worse than useless. Of course, I do not pretend that my wafer-thin selection of evidence – I have looked at just two cases, the rightness of punishment and the wrongness of murder, and four or five moral theories – is sure to be representative of all the evidence there is. Perhaps there are cases where a systematic moral theory's explanation of why something is wrong or right, good or bad, is genuinely illuminating and richly explanatory, in a way that no non-theoretical explanation could possibly be. The suspicion remains that where moral theory does well in explaining, it does so in spite of its systematic character, not because of it.

Prediction

We want our ethical outlook "to explain what will or would be good or bad and right or wrong action, in future or hypothetical situations that we ourselves have not actually met, but which we or others might conceivably meet". Prediction is, of course, just the future or hypothetical correlate of explanation. Still, it is worth considering separately, because thinking about prediction brings out more clearly some difficulties for moral theory that are already latent in the notion of explanation.

Moral theory's difficulty about prediction is basically the same problem about context as I discussed in §11.2. To put it another way, it is a problem of over-ambition. What the moral theorist wants to say is that

211

hypothetical case *A would inevitably be* a case of right action (or wrong action, or good or bad action, or whatever) because case *A* is just like real case *B*, which is right action: or again, that cases *A* and *B* both fall under moral type *T*, and every instance of type *T* is a case of right action.

The problem here is not restricted to the cases, common though they are, where moral theorists expect us to produce clear and definite intuitions about hypothetical cases that are very complicated (like many of the trolley cases in the literature; Kamm 2007), or very unlikely (like Warren's [1997] encountering-aliens scenario), or both. The trouble is completely general, and it begins with the "inevitably". As moral theorists frequently point out, it is a requirement of rationality that the same moral verdict must be returned on two qualitatively indiscernible cases. Of course. The only problem is that there *are* no qualitatively indiscernible cases, not even in everyday life, never mind in trolley or reduplicated human-shield problems. There are only cases that are more or less roughly similar. Judgements about which similarities and which differences matter, and how much, and why, and which exceptions override which similarities, and how often, and why, can certainly be made (although they cannot always be articulated). But the idea that there is any set of similarity judgements that is *rationally required* of us is simply a myth. Picking up a similarity judgement between two cases as the one that matters morally is not a matter of pure reason or value-neutral logic; it is itself an exercise of moral perception.

My point is not exactly that non-theoretical ethical outlooks do better at prediction than moral theories do. Rather, it is that moral theories have an over-ambitious explanatory pretension that they cannot realistically hope to sustain, because it rests on the false assumption that some pattern or other of similarity judgements is rationally required, and that anyone who fails to judge in line with this pattern is cognitively deficient.

In sum, typical moral theories fail to fill the deliberative and motivational roles that we want our ethical outlook to play, as the most sophisticated moral theorists themselves agree. And the explanations that moral theory offers of goodness and badness, rightness and wrongness, besides being typically disconnected from what moral theory has to tell us about motivation, face another objection too. They typically do not articulate or deepen our understanding of right and wrong and goodness and badness, as a good ethical outlook does (often by increasing the vividness with which we perceive, or feel, goodness and badness). Where moral theory's explanations are not clearly false or frustratingly incomplete, they are generally just unhelpfully obscure. In the final role that we want our ethical outlook to play – prediction of what will be right/wrong and good/bad in hypothetical cases – moral theory typically proves over-ambitious. It tries to enforce a uniformity of similarity judgements that cannot be rationally required, but must depend, where uniformity is present at all, on the deliverances of moral perception or judgement. In all these respects, typical moral theories fail the tests that they need to pass to count as credible or liveable ethical outlooks.

All this is more evidence for my main claims in this chapter: that "the use of reason to decide how life should be lived" does not have to involve the conception of reason that is typically found in systematic moral theory, and that we do much better if we do not invoke that conception, but are guided instead by the more flexible, deeper, and more humane conception of reason that is found in credible and liveable ethical outlooks such as the ones I described in §11.3. The project of moral theory is, in a sense, an attempt to simplify and "operationalize" the working of these ethical outlooks. As I have argued here, the attempt cannot succeed, and in any case leaves out or marginalizes many of the most crucial things of all that are captured by fully adequate ethical outlooks: in particular, the central place that is bound to be taken in good human lives by our moral perceptions, and by love.

It is perhaps only as we take these thoughts on board that ethics in the fullest sense – the living out of an ethical outlook, not of a moral theory – becomes a possibility for us. If we are to begin to be able to apply reason properly to the question how we should live, what we need is not moral theory, but moral insight.

Further reading

Chapter 1. The turn to reason: how human beings got ethical

The five books in Douglas Adams's well-known *Hitchhiker's Guide to the Galaxy* series are all packed with interesting philosophical questions. No serious student of philosophy should be without them.

Socrates' claim that the most important question in philosophy is "How should life be lived?" comes at the beginning of *Republic* Book 2, where he is asking whether the virtue of justice is an important part of the answer to that question. The passage deserves careful study. Many English translations of the whole of Plato's *Republic* are available. Perhaps the best is still Benjamin Jowett's 1871 version, which is also available on the internet (e.g. http://classics.mit.edu/Plato/republic.3.ii.html [accessed April 2009]).

Chapter 2. Demarcation: what does "ethical" mean?

Aristotle begins his famous work the *Nicomachean Ethics* by raising the question of what roles we occupy in life, and what it is to do well in each of those roles. This gives him a way of working towards his main concern, which is the more fundamental question: what is living well? It is worth finding a good modern translation, such as Sarah Broadie and Christopher Rowe's, and reading slowly and carefully the first five chapters of Book 1 of the *Nicomachean Ethics* (2002: 95–8), to see how Aristotle's argument develops.

Chapter 3. Motivation: why be moral?

For a forceful argument that living morally has nothing whatever to do with living well, see the opening sections of Kant's *Groundwork of the Metaphysics of Morals* ([1785] 1948).

For the tension between living well and living morally, see Henry Sidgwick, *The Methods of Ethics* (1874) on "the dualism of practical reason".

Prichard's famous question "Does moral philosophy rest on a mistake?", and his answer (yes), are in his *Moral Obligation* (1949: 1–20). And compare John McDowell, "Are Moral Requirements Hypothetical Imperatives?" (1998: 90).

For a compromise between living well and living morally, see Linda Zagzebski's "The Admirable Life and the Desirable Life" (2006).

For egoism, see Callicles' and Polus' arguments in Plato's *Gorgias*.

Chapter 4. Deliberation: the question of reason

John Keats's philosophical poem "Lamia" is in effect an expansion of his remark to Bailey, "O for a life of sensations rather than of thoughts". That remark comes in the famous letter to Benjamin Bailey of 22 November 1817.

Aristotle's *Protrepticus* can be found online at: www.chass.utoronto.ca/~phl102y/Protrepticus.pdf (accessed April 2009).

A. J. Ayer's best known work is still *Language, Truth and Logic* (1937). Few philosophers today accept its argument. Nearly all philosophers find it interesting.

Two book-length defences of expressivism are Allan Gibbard's *Wise Choices, Apt Feelings* (1990) and Simon Blackburn's *Ruling Passions* (1998).

Bernard Williams's doubts about moral theory are most fully presented in *Ethics and the Limits of Philosophy* (1985). The central paper for the Internal Reasons Thesis (arguably for the whole of Williams's ethics) is "Internal and External Reasons", in his *Moral Luck* (1981).

Chapter 5. Introducing subjectivism and objectivism

Three readings that nicely move the debate about ethical objectivity and subjectivity from the "informal" and "non-philosophical" stage to a deeper level are the first chapters of Gilbert Harman, *The Nature of Morality* (1977), J. L. Mackie, *Ethics* (1977) and Francis Snare, *The Nature of Moral Thinking* (1992); the first four sections of Bernard Williams's *Morality* (1971) is also recommended. All four of these readings, especially the first two, are also useful preparatory reading for Chapter 6.

Chapter 6. Five arguments for ethical subjectivism

On relativity and relativism, see Bernard Williams's *Morality* (1971: 34–40); J. L. Mackie's *Ethics* (1977: ch. 1); Gilbert Harman, *The Nature of Morality* (1977: ch. 1).

On the is–ought gap, see *Theories of Ethics*, edited by Philippa Foot (1967), Readings IV–VIII (by Geach, Hare, Foot, Searle and Hare).

For naturalism, try David Papineau's "Naturalism" (2007), and Michael Rea's *World Without Design* (2002).

Questions about moral motivation are discussed in depth in Michael Smith's *The Moral Problem* (1994).

For the Internal Reasons Thesis begin with Williams's *Moral Luck* (1981), as for Chapter 4, and compare John McDowell's "Might There be External Reasons?" (1995) and Williams's "Replies" (1995).

Chapter 7. The content of ethics: expressivism, error theory, objectivism again

For different versions of expressivism, see Simon Blackburn's *Spreading the Word* (1984), *Ruling Passions* (1998) and "Liberalism, Religion, and the Sources of Value" (2004), and Allan Gibbard's *Wise Choices, Apt Feelings* (1990).

On error theory see J. L. Mackie, *Ethics* (1977), and Richard Joyce, *The Myth of Morality* (2001); for the fictionalist version of the theory see Mark Kalderon's *Moral Fictionalism* (2005).

On the thesis that moral properties are patterns, see, for example, John McDowell's "Virtue and Reason" (1979), David McNaughton's *Moral Vision* (1988) or Jonathan Dancy's *Moral Reasons* (1993). On the thesis that the general ontology of patterns makes the specific case of moral properties quite unproblematic, see my "Moral Perception" (2008). For more on patterns and pattern-detection in general, see Daniel Dennett's "Real Patterns" (1991).

Chapter 8. Virtue ethics

G. E. M. Anscombe's "Modern Moral Philosophy" (1958) is the foundation charter of modern virtue ethics. Its influence is particularly obvious in Alasdair MacIntyre's *After Virtue* (1981), where his project is to argue at book length the thesis that Anscombe argued at article length: that there is something gravely wrong with the state of modern moral theory, and that what we need to address the problem is a return to thinking about the virtues. In *Ethics and the Limits of Philosophy* (1985), Bernard Williams more or less agrees with Anscombe and MacIntyre on the negative part of the thesis, but offers a different positive proposal.

Philippa Foot's "zoological" virtue ethics is argued for in some of the essays in her *Virtues and Vices* (1977), and more systematically and at greater length in her *Natural Goodness* (2001). Rosalind Hursthouse's *On Virtue Ethics* (1999) offers a less "zoological" and more "particularist" version of virtue ethics.

A variety of recent perspectives on the idea of an ethics of the virtues is offered in my collection *Values and Virtues* (2006).

Chapter 9. Utilitarianism

The foundation texts of utilitarianism are John Stuart Mill, *Utilitarianism*, and Jeremy Bentham, *Introduction to the Principles of Morals and Legislation*. These, and other useful materials including Mill's famous "Essay on Bentham", are collected together in one volume by Mary Warnock (1962).

There is a lively debate between utilitarianism and anti-utilitarianism in J. J. C. Smart and B. A. O. Williams's *Utilitarianism* (1973).

Two useful recent introductions to utilitarianism are Roger Crisp's *Mill on Utilitarianism* (1997) and Tim Mulgan's *Understanding Utilitarianism* (2007).

A broader sketch of what a modern theory in the act utilitarian style might look like is Philip Pettit's "Consequentialism" (1993). The classic modern exposition of rule utilitarianism (rule consequentialism, in his terminology) is Brad Hooker's *Ideal Code, Real World* (2003).

An application of something like a utilitarian aggregationist strategy to some difficult practical questions is John Broome's *Weighing Lives* (2004).

Chapter 10. Kantianism and contractarianism

Kant's moral theory is most clearly stated in his *Groundwork of the Metaphysics of Morals* ([1785] 1948), although "most clearly" here is a decidedly relative matter. For much clearer statements of Kant's views than his own, see Onora O'Neill's "Abstraction, Idealisation, and Ideology in Ethics" (1989), Christine Korsgaard's *Creating the Kingdom of Ends* (1996) and Marcia Baron's *Kantian Ethics almost without Apology* (1999).

For a first look at contractarianism, see Jean-Jacques Rousseau's *Social Contract* ([1762] 1968), John Rawls's *A Theory of Justice* (1971: ch. 1), and the Introduction in T. M. Scanlon's *What We Owe to Each Other* (1998).

Chapter 11. Theory and insight in ethics

For more about the anti-theoretical direction in ethics, begin with G. E. M. Anscombe's "Modern Moral Philosophy" (1958) and Bernard Williams's *Ethics and the Limits of Philosophy* (1985); also relevant is Alasdair MacIntyre's *After Virtue* (1981).

For more about particularism and intuitionism see, for example, Jonathan Dancy's *Moral Reasons* (1993) and *Ethics without Principles* (2004) and John McDowell's "Virtue and Reason" (1979).

Bibliography

Ackrill, J. L. (ed.) 1987. *A New Aristotle Reader*. Oxford: Oxford University Press.

Adams, D. 1979. *The Hitchhiker's Guide to the Galaxy*. London: Pan.

Adams, R. 1976. "Motive Utilitarianism". *Journal of Philosophy* 73: 467–81.

Annas, J. 1993. *The Morality of Happiness*. Oxford: Oxford University Press.

Anscombe, G. E. M. 1958. "Modern Moral Philosophy". *Philosophy* 33(124): 1–19. Re-printed in *Human Life, Action and Ethics: Essays by G. E. M. Anscombe*, M. Geach & L. Gormally (eds), 169–94 (Exeter: Imprint Academic, 2005).

Aquinas, T. 1961. *Summa Theologiae*. Madrid: Bibliotéca de Autores Cristianos.

Aristotle 1992. *Eudemian Ethics*, M. Woods (ed. & trans.). Oxford: Clarendon Press.

Aristotle 2002. *Nicomachean Ethics*, S. Broadie & C. Rowe (eds & trans.). Oxford: Oxford University Press.

Ayer, A. J. 1937. *Language, Truth and Logic*. Harmondsworth: Penguin.

Baron, M. 1999. *Kantian Ethics almost without Apology*. Ithaca, NY: Cornell University Press.

Bennett, J. 1966. "Whatever the Consequences". *Analysis* 26: 83–102.

Bennett, J. 1995. *The Act Itself*. Oxford: Oxford University Press.

Bentham, J. 1825. *The Rationale of Reward*. London: J. & H. L. Hunt.

Bentham, J. [1789] 1962. *An Introduction to the Principles of Morals and Legislation*. In *"Utilitarianism" and "On Liberty": Including Mill's "Essays on Bentham" and Selections from the Writings of Jeremy Bentham and John Austin*, M. Warnock (ed.), 33–77. Harmondsworth: Penguin.

Berlin, I. 1969. "Two Concepts of Liberty". In his *Four Essays on Liberty*, 118–72. Oxford: Oxford University Press.

Blackburn, S. 1984. *Spreading the Word*. Oxford: Oxford University Press.

Blackburn, S. 1993. *Essays in Quasi-Realism*. Oxford: Oxford University Press.

Blackburn, S. 1998. *Ruling Passions*. Oxford: Oxford University Press.

Blackburn, S. 2004. "Liberalism, Religion, and the Sources of Value". The Lindley Lecture, Department of Philosophy, University of Kansas.

Boonin, D. 2003. *A Defense of Abortion*. Cambridge: Cambridge University Press.

Bostock, D. 2000. *Aristotle's Ethics*. Oxford: Oxford University Press.

Braine, D. 1992. *The Human Person*. Indianapolis, IN: University of Notre Dame Press.

Broome, J. 2004. *Weighing Lives*. Oxford: Oxford University Press.

Bryson, B. 2004. *A Short History of Nearly Everything*. London: Black Swan.

Burke, E. 1931. *Reflections on the French Revolution*. In *Edmund Burke: Selections*, A. M. D. Hughes (ed.), 128–59. Oxford: Oxford University Press.

Burnyeat, M. 1987. "Wittgenstein and Augustine *De Magistro*". *Proceedings of the Aristotelian Society*, supplementary volume **61**: 1–12.

Carruthers, P. 1992. *The Animals Issue: Moral Theory in Practice*. Cambridge: Cambridge University Press.

Chappell, T. 1996. *The Plato Reader*. Edinburgh: Edinburgh University Press.

Chappell, T. 1998. *Understanding Human Goods*. Edinburgh: Edinburgh University Press.

Chappell, T. 2001. "Option Ranges". *Journal of Applied Philosophy* **18**(2): 107–18.

Chappell, T. 2002. "Absolutes and Particulars". In *Modern Moral Philosophy*, A. O'Hear (ed.), 95–117. Cambridge: Cambridge University Press.

Chappell, T. 2005. *The Inescapable Self*. London: Orion.

Chappell, T. (ed.) 2006. *Values and Virtues: Aristotelianism in Contemporary Ethics*. Oxford: Oxford University Press.

Chappell, T. 2008. "Moral Perception", *Philosophy* **83**: 421–37.

Cicero 1998. *de Finibus*, L. D. Reynolds (ed.). Oxford: Clarendon Press.

Clarke, S. & E. Simpson (eds) 1989. *Anti-Theory in Ethics and Moral Conservatism*. Albany, NY: SUNY Press.

Coope, C. 2006a. "Modern Virtue Ethics". See Chappell (2006), 20–52.

Coope, C. M. 2006b. *Worth and Welfare in the Controversy over Abortion*. London: Palgrave Macmillan.

Crisp, R. 1997. *Mill on Utilitarianism*. London: Routledge.

Dancy , J. 1993. *Moral Reasons*. Oxford: Blackwell.

Dancy, J. 2004. *Ethics without Principles*. Oxford: Oxford University Press.

Darwall, S. 2006. *The Second-Person Standpoint*. Cambridge, MA: Harvard University Press.

Davidson, D. 1980. *Essays on Actions and Events*. Oxford: Clarendon Press.

Dennett, D. 1987. *The Intentional Stance*. Boston, MA: MIT Press.

Dennett, D. 1991. "Real Patterns". *Journal of Philosophy* **88**(1): 27–51.

Diels, H. & W. Kranz 1974–5. *Die Fragmente der Vorsokratiker*, 7th edn. Berlin: Weidmann.

Diamond, C. 1991. "The Importance of Being Human". In *Human Beings*, D. Cockburn (ed.), 35–59. Cambridge: Cambridge University Press.

Dworkin, R. 1993. *Life's Dominion: An Argument about Abortion and Euthanasia*. Harmondsworth: Penguin.

Duff, A. 1982. "Intention, Responsibility, and Double Effect". *Philosophical Quarterly* **32**(126): 1–16.

Eliot, G. 1982. *Adam Bede*. Harmondsworth: Penguin.

Engelhardt, T. 1989. "Ethical Issues in Aiding the Death of Young Children". In *Euthanasia: The Moral Issues*, R. M. Baird & S. E. Rosenbaum (eds), 653–8. Buffalo, NY: Prometheus.

Evans, J. D. G. (ed.) 1988. *Moral Philosophy and Contemporary Problems*. Cambridge: Cambridge University Press.

Finnis, J. 1980. *Natural Law and Natural Rights*. Oxford: Clarendon Press.

Foot, P. (ed.) 1967. *Theories of Ethics*. Oxford: Oxford University Press.

Foot, P. 1977. *Virtues and Vices*. Oxford: Blackwell.

Foot, P. 2001. *Natural Goodness*. Oxford: Oxford University Press.

Forster, E. M. 2000. *Howards End*. Harmondsworth: Penguin.

Frankfurt, H. 1998. *Necessity, Volition and Love*. Cambridge: Cambridge University Press.

Geach, P. 1977. *The Virtues*. Cambridge: Cambridge University Press.

Geach, M. & L. Gormally (eds) 2005. *Human Life, Action and Ethics: Essays by G. E. M. Anscombe*. Exeter: Imprint Academic.

Gibbard, A. 1990. *Wise Choices, Apt Feelings*. Oxford: Oxford University Press.

Glover, J. 1977. *Causing Death and Saving Lives*. Harmondsworth: Penguin.

Grice, H. P. 1957. "Meaning". *The Philosophical Review* **66**: 377–88.

Griffin, J. 1985. *Well Being*. Oxford: Oxford University Press.

Guenin, L. 2006. "The Nonindividuation Argument against Zygotic Personhood". *Philosophy* **81**: 463–503.

Haldane, J. B. S. 1927. *Possible Worlds and Other Essays*. London: Chatto & Windus.

Hare, R. 1963. *Freedom and Reason*. Oxford: Oxford University Press.

Harman, G. 1977. *The Nature of Morality*. Oxford: Oxford University Press.

Harman, G. 1999. "Moral Philosophy Meets Social Psychology". *Proceedings of the Aristotelian Society* **99**(3): 315–31.

Harris, J. 1985. *The Value of Life*. London: Routledge.

Hobbes, T. [1668] 1994. *Leviathan*, E. Curley (ed.). Indianapolis, IN: Hackett.

Hooker, B. 2003. *Ideal Code, Real World*. Oxford: Oxford University Press.

Hornby, N. 2006. *A Long Way Down*. Harmondsworth: Penguin.

Howard-Snyder, F. 2002. "Doing vs. Allowing Harm". *Stanford Encyclopedia of Philosophy* http://plato.stanford.edu/entries/doing-allowing/ (accessed April 2009).

Hume, D. [1776] 1977. *Enquiry Concerning the Principles of Morals*, P. H. Nidditch (ed.). Oxford: Oxford University Press.

Hume, D. [1739] 1985. *Treatise concerning Human Nature*, E. C. Mossner (ed.). Harmondsworth: Penguin.

Hursthouse, R. 1999. *On Virtue Ethics*. Oxford: Oxford University Press.

Jardine, L. 1999. *Ingenious Pursuits*. London: Little, Brown.

Joyce, R. 2001. *The Myth of Morality*. Cambridge: Cambridge University Press.

Kalderon, M. E. 2005. *Moral Fictionalism*. Oxford: Oxford University Press.

Kamm, F. M. 2007. *Intricate Ethics: Rights, Responsibilities, and Permissible Harm*. Oxford: Oxford University Press.

Kant, I. [1787] 1989. *Critique of Pure Reason*, N. Kemp Smith (trans.). London: Macmillan.

Kant, I. [1785] 1948. *Groundwork of the Metaphysic of Morals*, H. J .Paton (trans.), in *The Moral Law*. London: Hutchinson.

Korsgaard, C. 1996. *Creating the Kingdom of Ends*. Cambridge: Cambridge University Press.

Kripke, S. 1973. *Naming and Necessity*. Oxford: Blackwell.

Lipton, P. 2003. *Inference to the Best Explanation*. Cambridge: Cambridge University Press.

Locke, J. [1690] 1924. *Two Treatises of Government*, W. S. Carpenter (ed.). London: Everyman.

Locke, J. 1690. *Of the Conduct of the Understanding*. www.ilt.columbia.edu/publications/CESdigital/locke/conduct/toc.html (accessed April 2009).

Louden, R. 1992. *Morality and Moral Theory*. New York: Oxford University Press.

Lyons, D. 1965. *Forms and Limits of Utilitarianism*. Oxford: Oxford University Press.

MacIntyre, A. 1981. *After Virtue*. London: Duckworth.

MacIntyre, A. 2001. *Dependent Rational Animals*. La Salle, IL: Open Court.

Mackie, J. L. 1977. *Ethics: Inventing Right and Wrong*. Harmondsworth: Penguin.

Maddy, P. 1997. *Naturalism about Mathematics*. Oxford: Clarendon Press.

Marquis, D. 1997. "An Argument that Abortion is Wrong". In *Ethics in Practice*, H. LaFollette (ed.). Oxford: Blackwell.

McDowell, J. 1979. "Virtue and Reason". *The Monist* **62**: 331–50.

McDowell, J. 1995. "Might There be External Reasons?". In *World Mind and Ethics: Essays on the Ethical Philosophy of Bernard Williams*, J. E. J. Altham & R. Harrison (eds), 68–85. Cambridge: Cambridge University Press.

McDowell, J. 1998. "Are Moral Requirements Hypothetical Imperatives?". In his *Mind, Value, and Reality*, 77–94. Cambridge, MA: Harvard University Press. [Originally published in *Proceedings of the Aristotelian Society (Supplementary Volume)* **52** (1978), 13–29.]

McMahan, J. 2002. *The Ethics of Killing*. Oxford: Oxford University Press.

McNaughton, D. 1988. *Moral Vision*. Oxford: Blackwell.

Mill, J. S. [1863] 1962. *Utilitarianism*. In *"Utilitarianism" and "On Liberty": Including Mill's "Essays on Bentham" and Selections from the Writings of Jeremy Bentham and John Austin*, M. Warnock (ed.), 251–321. Harmondsworth: Penguin.

Miller, A. 2003. *An Introduction to Contemporary Metaethics*. Cambridge: Polity.

Moore, G. E. [1903] 2002. *Principia Ethica*, rev. edn with "Preface to the second edition" and other papers, T. Baldwin (ed.). Cambridge: Cambridge University Press.

Mulgan, T. 2007. *Understanding Utilitarianism*. Stocksfield: Acumen.

Mulhall, S. 2002. "Review of Jeff Macmahan, *The Ethics of Killing*". *London Review of Books* (22 August): 16–18.

Murdoch, I. 1970. *The Sovereignty of Good*. London: Routledge.

Nietzsche, F. [1889] 1968. *Twilight of the Idols*, R. F. Hollingdale (ed.). Harmondsworth: Penguin.

Nietzsche, F. [1887] 1956. *The Genealogy of Morals.* In *The Birth of Tragedy* and *The Genealogy of Morals*, F. Golffing (trans.). London: Doubleday.

Nozick, R. 1974. *Anarchy, State, and Utopia.* Oxford: Blackwell.

Nussbaum, M. 1992a. "Aristotelian Social Democracy". In *Liberalism and the Good*, B. Douglass, G. Mara & H. Richardson (eds), 219–24. New York: Routledge.

Nussbaum, M. 1992b. *Love's Knowledge.* Oxford: Oxford University Press.

Oderberg, D. 2000a. *Moral Theory: A Non-consequentialist Approach.* London: Routledge.

Oderberg, D. 2000b. *Applied Ethics: A Non-consequentialist Approach.* London: Routledge.

'Neill, O. [1987] 1988. "Abstraction, Idealisation, and Ideology in Ethics". In *Moral Philosophy and Contemporary Problems*, J. D. G. Evans (ed.), 55–70. Cambridge: Cambridge University Press.

Papineau, D. 2007. "Naturalism". In the *Stanford Encyclopedia of Philosophy*, http://plato.stanford.edu/entries/naturalism/ (accessed April 2009).

Parfit, D. 1984. *Reasons and Persons.* Oxford: Oxford University Press.

Pettit, P. 1993. "Consequentialism". In *A Companion to Ethics*, P. Singer (ed.), 230–40. Oxford: Blackwell.

Pettit, P. & F. Jackson 1998. "A Problem for Expressivism". *Analysis* 58: 239–51.

Plato 1871. *The Dialogues of Plato*, B. Jowett (ed. & trans.), 4 vols. Oxford: Clarendon Press.

Prichard, H. H. 1949. *Moral Obligation.* Oxford: Clarendon Press.

Prinz, J. 2007. *The Emotional Construction of Morals.* Oxford: Oxford University Press.

Rachels, J. 1975. "Active and Passive Euthanasia". *New England Journal of Medicine* 292(2): 78–80.

Rachels, J. 1986. *The End of Life.* Oxford: Oxford University Press.

Rawls, J. 1971. *A Theory of Justice.* Oxford: Oxford University Press.

Rea, M. 2002. *World Without Design: The Ontological Consequences of Naturalism.* Oxford: Clarendon Press.

Reid, T. [1783] 1967. *Essay upon the Intellectual Powers of Man*, B. Brody (ed.). Cambridge, MA: MIT Press.

Ridge, M. 2001. "Saving Scanlon: Contractualism and Agent-Relativity". *Journal of Political Philosophy* 9: 472–81.

Ridge, M. 2007. "Introducing Variable-Rate Rule Utilitarianism". *Philosophical Quarterly* 56 (223): 242–53.

Ross, W. D. 1930. *The Right and the Good.* Oxford: Clarendon Press.

Ross, S. 1982. "Abortion and the Death of the Foetus". *Philosophy and Public Affairs* 11(3): 232–55.

Rousseau, J.-J. [1762] 1968. *The Social Contract*, M. Cranston (trans.). Harmondsworth: Penguin.

Russell, B. 1944. "Reply to Criticisms". In *The Philosophy of Bertrand Russell*, P. Schilpp (ed.), 679–742. Evanston, IL: Northwestern University Press.

Scanlon, T. M. 1998. *What We Owe to Each Other.* Cambridge, MA: Belknap Press.

Schapiro, T. 1999. "What is a Child?". *Ethics* **109**(4): 715–38.

Sidgwick, H. 1874. *The Methods of Ethics*. Cambridge: Cambridge University Press.

Singer, P. 1982. *The Expanding Circle*. London: Plume.

Singer, P. 1993. *Applied Ethics*. Cambridge: Cambridge University Press.

Singer, P. 1995: *How are We to Live?* Amherst, NY: Prometheus.

Smart, J. J. C. & B. A. O. Williams 1973. *Utilitarianism: For and Against*. Cambridge: Cambridge University Press.

Smith, M. 1994. *The Moral Problem*. Oxford: Blackwell.

Snare, F. 1992. *The Nature of Moral Thinking*. London: Routledge.

Sober, E. 1994. *From a Biological Point of* View. Cambridge: Cambridge University Press.

Stocker, M. 1976. "The Schizophrenia of Modern Ethical Theories". *Journal of Philosophy* **73**(14) (12 August): 453–66.

Strawson, P. F. [1962] 2003. "Freedom and Resentment". Reprinted in *Free Will*, G. Watson (ed.), 72–93. Oxford: Oxford University Press.

Tait, K. 1970. *My Father Bertrand Russell*. New York: Harcourt Brace.

Teichman, J. 1996. *Social Ethics*. Oxford: Blackwell.

Thomas, A. 2006. *Value and Context*. Oxford: Oxford University Press.

Thomson, J. J. 1971. "A Defense of Abortion". *Philosophy and Public Affairs* **1**: 47–66.

Tollefsen, C. & R. George 2008. *Embryo: A Secular Defense of Life*. New York: Doubleday.

Tooley, M. [1972] 1987. "Abortion and Infanticide". In *Applied Ethics*, P. Singer (ed.), 57–86. Oxford: Oxford University Press.

Toulmin, S. 1986. *The Place of Reason in Ethics*. Chicago, IL: University of Chicago Press.

Trinkaus, E. & P. Shipman 1993. *The Neandertals: Changing the Image of Mankind*. New York: Knopf.

Velleman, D. 2005. *Self to Self*. Cambridge: Cambridge University Press.

Warren, M. A. 1997. "On the Moral and Legal Status of Abortion". In *Ethics in Practice* H. LaFollette (ed.), 72–82. Oxford: Blackwell.

Williams, B. 1968. *Descartes: The Project of Pure Enquiry*. Harmondsworth: Penguin.

Williams, B. 1971. *Morality: An Introduction to Ethics*. Cambridge: Cambridge University Press.

Williams, B. 1981. *Moral Luck*. Cambridge: Cambridge University Press.

Williams, B. 1985. *Ethics and the Limits of Philosophy*. Harmondsworth: Penguin.

Williams, B. 1995a. "Replies". In *World, Mind, and Ethics*, J. Altham & R. Harrison, 185–224. Cambridge: Cambridge University Press.

Williams, B. 1995b. *Making Sense of Humanity and Other Philosophical Papers*. Cambridge: Cambridge University Press.

Williams, B. 2006. *Philosophy as a Humanistic Discipline*. Cambridge: Cambridge University Press.

Wittgenstein, L. 1951. *Philosophical Investigations*. Oxford: Blackwell.

Wolf, S. 1997. "Moral Saints". In *Virtue Ethics*, R. Crisp (ed.), 79–98. Oxford: Oxford University Press.

Woodward, P. A. (ed.) 2001. *The Doctrine of Double Effect: Philosophers Debate a Controversial Distinction*. Indianapolis, IN: Indiana University Press.

Wordsworth, W. 1959. *Selected Poems*, H. H. Margoliouth (ed.). London: Collins.

Wright, C. 1992. *Truth and Objectivity*. Cambridge, MA: Harvard University Press.

Wright, C. 1995. "Truth in Ethics". *Ratio* (new series) **8**: 209–26.

Zagzebski, L. 2006. "The Admirable Life and the Desirable Life". In *Values and Virtues: Aristotelianism in Contemporary Ethics*, T. Chappell (ed.), 53–66. Oxford: Oxford University Press.

Zangwill, N. 1996. "Moral Supervenience". In *Midwest Studies in Philosophy: Volume 20: Moral Concepts*, P. French, T. Uehling & H. Wettstein (eds), 240–62. Notre Dame, IN: University of Notre Dame Press.

Index